Kevin Barry

Kevin Barry

And His Time

By the same author
Dreamers of Dreams: Portraits of the Irish in America,
Dublin, 1984

Kevin Barry

And His Time

Donal O'Donovan

GLENDALE

First published in Ireland by
THE GLENDALE PRESS LTD.
1 Summerhill Parade,
Sandycove
Co. Dublin

British Library Cataloguing in Publication Data

Kevin Barry and his time.
1. Ireland. revolutionary movements. Role of Barry,
   Kevin, 1902-1920
I. Title
322.4'2'0924

ISBN 0-907606-67-9
ISBN 0-907606-68-7 pbk

Origination by Wendy A. Commins, The Curragh
Make-up by Paul Bray Studio
Printed and bound in Great Britain at
The Camelot Press plc, Southampton

For my daughter Síofra
who thought of this book

And in memory of my father Jim
who laid the foundations

Contents

Acknowledgements

Much of the joy that writing this book has given me came from the many people – well over one hundred – who took the trouble to talk to me, write to me or telephone me. To Kevin Barry's family, I owe a special debt of gratitude – to my aunt Elgin, his sister; Rita, his sister-in-law; my brother Gerry and all the cousins who were so generous with time, material, suggestions and encouragement.

Posthumously, I thank my father Jim, who laboured so long to produce a book and found that publishers were not interested. I thank Kevin's sisters and his brother, all of whom readily agreed to help Jim when he asked.

My heartfelt gratitude goes to the following people whose names I give in the order in which I was in touch with them: Seán MacBride, Brother Jim Nolan, Michael Kelleher, Eunan O'Halpin, Oliver Snoddy, Peg Scully, Pat Gorman, May Deering, Bride Butler, Evanna Kennedy, Seán Flood, Gerry McAleer, Uinseann MacEoin, John F. Carroll, Jim Brennan, Seán Cronin, Bridget Doyle, Joe Doyle, Alfie Flood, Jimmy O'Toole, Máirín Johnston, Honoria Aughney, Seán Lowry, Seán O'Mahony, John Comerford, Mag Leonard, Moira Lysaght, Bruce Bradley SJ, Pádraig Ó Cuíll OFM Cap., Philip Kelly OSA, the Very Rev. John Meagher, Elaine Williams, Marcus Bourke, Kyra Donnelly, John Foley, Francis Devine, Thomas P. O'Neill, Jim Lamon, Jim Petherbridge, Michael O'Brien, John Doyle, Cecil van Cauwelaert, Tom Turley, Brian Spain, John O'Gorman, Michael Baynes, Karen King, David Davin-Power, Des Cooney, Maura Lunt, Charles Horton, Seamus Murphy, Johnny Morrissey, Paddy Boyle and Anna MacBride White.

9

My thanks go too to Diarmuid Breathnach, first and most
helpful reader of the manuscript; Paula Howard, ever-careful
curator of the Gilbert Library; the staff of the Public Record
Office in Kew; the trustees of the Imperial War Museum for
allowing me access to Sir John French's diaries; the staff of the
National Library of Ireland; my wife Jenny for her patience,
understanding and the gift of a garden shed, and my daughter
Síofra who made me shorten my sentences.

ABBREVIATIONS

CAB	British Cabinet Papers
GOD	Gerard O Donovan's private papers
IWM	Imperial War Museum
KB	Papers and information from Kevin Barry of Tombeagh, nephew of Kevin Gerard Barry
LOB	León Ó Broin Papers
NLI	National Library of Ireland
NMI	National Museum of Ireland
PRO	Public Record Office, London
PROD	Public Record Office, Dublin
CSI	Situation in Ireland Committee of the British Cabinet
UCD	University College, Dublin

Foreword

Kevin Barry's face appears on the obverse side of the physical force coin, the capacity to endure as well as to inflict. It was this factor that made his death, along with that of Terence MacSwiney, one of the great moral turning points in the phase of the Anglo-Irish struggle which culminated in the Treaty and the setting up of the two Irish states we see today.

He was a lad who saw the same sort of faces and places that Dubliners see today. He walked their streets and talked their talk. I went to his school for a time, Belvedere, and I was friendly with a man who used to criticise him bitterly — because he won a berth as an out-half from him!

In other words a normal lad who would have had normal pre-occupations had he lived in a normal society. Dublin, however, was not a 'normal' society in his day. It is not a 'normal' society today either. When 'lads of eighteen summers' sing the ballad which bears his name in Belfast, they generally do so in the spirit of the other side of the physical force coin and they present many people not with a moral turning point, but with a moral stumbling block.

The same moral stumbling block is created in another form by the presence in English jails at the moment of three other young Irish students, very much the same sort of student that one might come across in the Kevin Barry political society in UCD. They were found in the precincts of a farm owned by Mr. Tom King, the Secretary of State for Northern Ireland, with maps and money; and for this dangerous activity they received twenty-five years each in a Winchester Court after what many Irish people feel was a trial by tabloid during which

11

Mr. King himself joined in the press conference without apparently coming to any harm from the legal guardians entrusted
with the administration of the laws of contempt of court.

At the same time there is in a North of Ireland jail a gentleman called Stone, of loyalist persuasion, who received a telephone number sentence which effectively comes down to the
'not less than thirty years' which the presiding judge laid down
should be translated from the telephone number. Mr. Stone
had been found guilty of the murder of six Catholics. In real
terms, therefore, Mr. Stone must serve five years for each paddy
killed and the three Winchester paddies must serve twenty-five
years for whatever threat they may have posed to an English
politician.

It has not been clearly established just what they were doing
on Mr. King's property. What is clear is that the moral stumbling block in the Winchester Three's case was very clearly
fashioned out of very similar materials to those from which
the morality of the Kevin Barry situation was hewn.

In his day Kevin Barry's fate aroused such attention that
the Pope was amongst those moved by it to a point where
British diplomacy in the Vatican lost a significant percentage
of its persuasiveness. When Lloyd George said he had 'murder
by the throat', the effectiveness of his phrase was diminished
by the reflection that the type of life he was throttling was
that of figures like Barry.

And even though the torture 'just before he faced the hangman' in the propaganda version of the ballad of Kevin Barry
is not borne out by Donal O'Donovan's admirably low-keyed
and meticulously researched work, the actual hanging was
horrific enough to be one of the forces that moved public
opinion and Lloyd George to the conference table.

Michael Collins, influenced by his reading of Fenian executions, had decreed that there would be 'no more lonely scaffolds', and there weren't. Kevin Barry died calmly and proudly,
but his death was a media event. An event which the Ireland
of 1989, that slunk rather guiltily past the anniversary of the
First Dáil and the commemoration of the Easter Rising, may
not feel altogether comfortable at recalling. It's easier to focus
one's attention on pictures of Mr. Tom King 'reviewing the pro-

gress of the Anglo-Irish Agreement at a top level conference'.

But the focus is still blurred by moral ambiguity and they're still singing Kevin Barry in Belfast, Boston and Crossmaglen no matter what Section 31 says. Yesterday's heroes cast uncomfortable shadows over today's problems. But the illumination of history's complexities is good work. Not to do so condemns succeeding generations to blindly make the same mistakes.

Donal O'Donovan has shown moral courage in holding his lamp aloft. We may not condone the deeds of the singers of Belfast and Boston but at least we cannot pretend now not to understand why they sing about Kevin Barry.

Tim Pat Coogan
April, 1989

1 Beginnings

Begin at the beginning', the King said, gravely, 'and go on till you come to the end; then stop'. Lewis Carroll's is good advice, and generally in this book it will be followed. Not faithfully, just generally. You cannot begin by saying: 'Kevin Gerard Barry was born at No. 8 Fleet Street, Dublin, on 20 January, 1902', without then going back in time and place to the Wicklow neck of Carlow where truly it all began. However. . . .

Kevin Gerard Barry was born at No. 8 Fleet Street, Dublin, on 20 January, 1902. His mother Mary was assisted at his birth by the family friend and retainer Kate Kinsella in the old house the Barrys had lived in for ten years. He was the fourth child in a family of seven, which we are told means that he would have to fight to keep his end up or be swamped by the older and younger factions.

The Barrys, Tom and Mary and Tom's sister Judith, ran a prosperous dairy business in a city which had well over 500 of them. It was larger than most, a sophisticated enterprise which involved the eighty-six-acre family holding at Tombeagh, Hacketstown, Co. Carlow; grazing cows on conacre* on the outskirts of Dublin city; a dairy yard at Pimlico in the heart of old Dublin, and a retail dairy below the house in Fleet Street.

In time we shall meet the whole family, but now, because it was the custom of the time, Kevin has to be christened quickly. The baptism took place in the parish church of St. Andrew in Westland Row, the day after the birth. His godfather was his

---

*The Irish custom of letting land in small portions for a single crop or for pasture, not for more than eleven months.

maternal uncle, Jimmy Dowling of Drumguin, across the road from Tombeagh. The other sponsor was Elizabeth Browne of Knocklishen, a neighbouring townland to the north.

Having children baptised within a few days of birth was the norm for Catholic families, but there may have been another reason why Mary and Tom Barry wanted Kevin formally registered as a Catholic so soon. Mary Barry had had a number of miscarriages. She was twenty-eight years younger than Tom, whom she married in 1895, and she already had three children when Kevin was born. The parents may have felt that they wanted to take no risks with Kevin's chances of getting to Heaven.

By July, 1904, Kevin had become a sturdy fair-haired young fellow with his two feet planted firmly on the ground at the ten-to-two position and his eyes belying his age with their steady gaze. A contemporary photograph taken by Stanley in the nearby studio in 22 Westmoreland Street shows him at two-and-a-half years of age dressed in the fashion of the day: boots, stockings, a dark half-sleeved petticoat covered by a white broderie anglaise pinafore, and a broad round straw hat with upturned brim, perched well back on his fringed head.

*

The Barrys of Tombeagh and the Dowlings of Drumguin were by the standards of the nineteenth century what is known as 'strong farmers'. They had survived the Great Famine and in time, as successive Land Acts were passed, they became the owners of their holdings on the rolling uplands of north Carlow where it borders Wicklow.

The Barrys could trace their ancestry back to Black Tom,[1] who married a widow in 1750. Family tradition has it that the Barrys, a Norman family, had a property in Cork from which they were forced to flee when Oliver Cromwell invaded the country, trampling Ireland with his generals.

Tombeagh became the family's settling place and by the early 1800s almost the whole townland was farmed by Barrys. One of Black Tom's sons, also Tom, married a Finn from Ladystown and had four children. It was then that the name Kevin first entered the family records. The eldest of Black Tom's grandsons was Kevin. He went to America and, having died on the ship taking him home again, nevertheless returned to Tombeagh as a ghost seen several times by members of the present generation in the dusk of a summer's evening. Kevin's brother Michael had two children, Judith and Tom. Tom became Kevin Barry's father.

Tombeagh lies on the Douglas River, just north of the Derreen, and the Barry farm contains medium-sized sloping fields covering about eighty-six acres of pasture. The Duke of Ormonde once owned the land which he sold to the Howards – the family name of the Earls of Wicklow. It was part of the Clonmore estate which is almost coterminous with that part of Carlow that juts up into Wicklow. Sir Ralph Howard sold Clonmore to John Henry Parnell, who needed the 12,000 acres to give as his patrimony to his youngest son Henry Tudor, brother of Charles Stewart Parnell of Avondale.

Henry Tudor Parnell thus became the Barrys' landlord for about fifteen years, and we know that on 21 April, 1874, he signed the receipt for half a year's rent, £19 8s. 8d., received of Michael Barry in cash.[2]

Parnell, who was quite a clever land speculator, sold the Tombeagh holding and a number of others with it to William Fitzm. Dick, MP, of Humewood, Kiltegan. To Dick's agent, Mr. Fenton, Michael Barry made his penultimate payment on 22 December, 1875. He made his will in July, 1876, and died soon afterwards.[3]

In his will he followed custom by first bequeathing his soul to God. Then he left £20 yearly to his sister Ellen together with a two-storey, two-roomed house with an outside staircase of stone, which still stands in the yard at Tombeagh.

He went on: 'I also will and bequeath to my daughter Julia Barry [Aunt Judith] £100 provided she takes it for choice to go into the convent. And in case she may not go there I will and bequeath her £150'. Judith settled for the bigger sum and the secular life.

The most important bequest was obviously taken for granted and left to the end. Michael's son Thomas was to get the house and farm of land.

On Kevin Barry's mother's side were the Dowlings. Among

the insurgents at the Battle of Hacketstown in 1798 was John Hutchinson of Dualla, near Cashel, Co. Tipperary. He was a god-son of Sir John Lentaigne, whose people came from Caen in Normandy. Hutchinson, who had been a yeoman officer before he espoused the United cause, was Kevin Barry's maternal great-great-grandfather. He survived the battle in which 350 rebels lost their lives.

John Hutchinson married Kate Meagher, and was promptly cut off by his family, presumably because Kate was a Roman Catholic. His godfather rescued him from penury by buying him a farm at Ballyhacket, Co. Carlow, north of the market town of Tullow. There Kate bore him two sons and a daughter, Margaret.

Margaret married a Catholic neighbour, Lawrence Dowling of Ballyhacket House. They had seven children. One of them, James Dowling was born in 1821 and was forty-eight when he married Ellen McArdle, the daughter of Patrick McArdle of Drumguin. Thus the Dowlings came to Drumguin, the next holding to Tombeagh.

James and Ellen Dowling had five children. James died in 1907 at the age of eighty-six, and his wife Ellen (Granny Dowling to the Barry family) followed him in 1920. Both lie in the next grave to Kevin's parents in Tinneclash, Kiltegan, on the Wicklow border.

The eldest of their children was Michael (Uncle Mike) who farmed the home place, was noted for his skill with horses' ailments, and had nine children. His brother Patrick (Uncle Pat) left for Dublin and prospered as a grocer and wine merchant in Terenure and South Circular Road. Unmarried, he died aged sixty-four in 1941. Margaret became a Bon Secours nun and as Sister Cecilia was matron of the Bon Secours Hospital in Cork for many years. Her younger brother James (Uncle Jimmy), who died in 1929 at forty-eight, was the subject of a special condition in his father's assignment of Drumguin to Michael in 1907.[4]

Mike was charged with giving Jimmy £10 at once and £140 either in one payment or spread over four years. Mike was to clothe and maintain Jimmy and 'allow him to keep and feed from the produce of said farm two head of cattle, under three years old . . .' In return, Jimmy was to work at Drumguin 'as far as he reasonably can'. In this manner Jimmy's future was provided for until the age of thirty years. He later married and settled in a house behind Tombeagh.

Mary Dowling, who pronounced her name Doolan from the Irish (Ó) Dúlaing, married Thomas Barry of Tombeagh and Dublin in 1895 and became Kevin Barry's mother.

By the time he could call the land his own under the Land Acts, Tom Barry was already well established in business in Dublin. But he did not neglect Tombeagh. In February, 1897, he bought an additional sixteen acres there, for £100 from Mr. James Neill. He was advised by Patrick Murphy, his Dublin solicitor, to travel with him to Carlow, bringing the money for the sale. 'In the event of Neill signing,' wrote the solicitor, 'it will be of great advantage to have you down to take up formal possession'.[5]

Long before these events, Thomas Barry had begun to look beyond the horizons of his Carlow acres. The attraction was the burgeoning city of Dublin, and his strategy was the modern one of concentric diversification. He was a progressive farmer: Dublin needed ever-growing supplies of milk. In 1879, he sent his only sibling Judith to reconnoitre.

2 Fleet Street

Judith Barry was a woman of courage, determination and sagacity, with a capacity for affection that was later returned a hundred-fold by her nieces and nephews. She was in her late thirties when she set out alone from Tombeagh for Dublin to find a new livelihood for herself and her younger brother Thomas.

Judith's search for premises suitable for use as a dairy yard and dwelling house led her to Fleet Street, a narrow thoroughfare parallel to the south quays and running from D'Olier Street across Westmoreland Street and west to Temple Bar.

Mrs. Case already ran a dairy at No. 56 and she was willing to sell. Judith duly sent for her brother and in the same year Thomas Barry, at the age of thirty-six, became the owner of a centre-city premises. At No. 56 the brother and sister team prospered for thirteen years, building up a herd of dairy cows which were grazed in summer wherever grass could be rented cheaply and conveniently. The city proper still lay within the two canals, the Royal and the Grand. Sandymount, Ballsbridge, Rathmines and Rathgar on the South side were rapidly developing as middle-class suburbs served by an extensive horse-drawn tramway system. But conacre grazing was still available anywhere from Bushy Park in Terenure to Tallaght, and as far west as the Long Mile Road beyond Inchicore.

The next move for the stocky and popular entrepreneur, whose hair was already thinning, was to take a lease on Nos. 58 and 59 Pimlico in the old heart of the Liberties of Dublin. These premises were owned by the Ducketts of Duckett's Grove near Tullow. Having secured the lease, Thomas proceeded to establish an extensive dairy enterprise in Pimlico, with a yard and stalls for one hundred and twenty cows.

In her book, *Around the Banks of Pimlico*, the author Máirín Johnston writes:

> Pimlico is a very long, narrow street which stretches from the top of the Coombe at Ardee Street up to the corners of Thomas Court Bawn and Marrowbone Lane. . . . It is one of the oldest streets in the Earl of Meath's Liberties and in medieval times it was called Donoure Street. When the French Huguenots and the English woollen workers settled in the Liberties in the late 1660s, the Earl of Meath leased out parts of his land to them, on which they built their own very distinctive style of housing. The English immigrants gave some of the streets in the area names like Pimlico, Tripoli, Marrowbone (Marylebone) Lane and Spitalfields.

Máirín Johnston's grandparents, Bridget and James Coyne, lived as did their neighbours in appalling housing. Illness and death, including miscarriages, were an integral part of their poverty. Unemployment was the common lot. Four doors down from Thomas Barry's premises James Connolly, the labour leader, came to live in 1897 with his wife Lillie and their children. It was from there, No. 54, that Connolly founded *The Worker's Republic*. Six other families, a total of thirty people, lived in No. 54 at that time.

As well as numerous dairies there were twenty-four farmsteads and outbuildings, including eight piggeries, eight fowlhouses and two stables in Pimlico in 1901.

As Tom Barry's business grew, he travelled down frequently to Tombeagh, leaving Judith to manage the dairy in Fleet Street. Since his Dublin interests involved the supply of milk only, like other Dublin dairymen he bought the cows freshcalved and milked them until they went dry. There was no facility for putting the cows back in calf again, nor would he have wanted to. That would have interrupted the flow of milk

Milch cows were usually bought in the Dublin Market, but Thomas Barry was not above driving a herd of cows in front of him. He sometimes bought at Baltinglass Fair and drove the cows up the road through Blessington and Tallaght to wherever his summer grazing might be, a two or three day walk of forty miles. Neither cattle nor milk were sent by rail from Tombeagh to Dublin in his time.

The impact of technology came with unexpected force when the Corporation of Dublin decided to site the city's first power plant in Fleet Street, taking in Nos. 49 to 56 for its 'electric light station'. It opened in 1892 and supplied about a dozen of the principal streets.

So the Barrys had to move. In fact they merely crossed the street to No. 8, and it was here in 1895 that Thomas Barry at fifty-two years of age brought his country bride of twenty-four. No. 8 remained the family home until after the Second World War. The seven children were born there, the first in 1896.

Kathleen Agnes was Aunt Judith's favourite. She was the eldest and soon fell into a position of leadership that she never relinquished. All the Barrys were known by names other than their given names, Kathleen's undergoing the greatest number of changes. She was known as Katherine, Kathy (what Kevin called her), and in later years Kitby. We shall stick to Kathy.

Sheila, who from now on becomes Shel, was the second-born. Her daughter Triona Maher gives us an insight into some of the family relationships as they developed:

> Very early on, Kitby was put in a position where she was taking the decisions. Mammy was always overshadowed by Kitby. She was just that kind of person. She didn't mind responsibility and she took it. The others didn't stand up to her, and Nana [Mrs Barry] thought a great deal of her. Kitby had been Auntie's favourite and Judith probably dominated Nana anyway.[1]

Michael, who was two years younger than Shel, became the tallest of the family. He was gentle and quiet-spoken, was expected as the elder boy to take over the farm at Tombeagh when he was old enough, and therefore had to be content with a limited formal education. He was born with a caul, an omen of good fortune.

About the time the infant photograph of Kevin was taken, another girl was in the cot in Fleet Street. Ellen, known as Eileen and later as Elgin, is the only survivor. She was a blonde child of striking looks, and, as we shall see, considerable courage.

The youngest two were Mary Christina (Maureen and for most of her life Monty), a vivacious child, and Margaret Dolores, born in 1906 and invariably known as Peggy.

The Barrys all went to the Convent of the Holy Faith in Clarendon Street, where the directress was Sister Mary Justine. There were four large schools in the complex, one for girls, two for boys and an infant school, with 700 pupils overall.

The Barrys were fee-paying children, as was Noel Purcell, the celebrated Dublin actor, who was in class with Kevin. Elgin, who was miserable at school, recalled that when the children in Clarendon Street invariably giggled at something, the nun would sigh despairingly: 'Girls, girls, Our Lady never laughed.' The best thing about the school, according to Elgin, was that it had a marvellous playground – on the roof. The asphalted play area extended across the public and private school roofs, stretching from the Carmelite church almost as far as Chatham Street.

One unchanging aspect of Fleet Street was Kate. Catherine Kinsella, who was born in 1853, became the cook in the Barry household in 1879. It was she who taught the children many of the rebel songs they sang, and it was her sharp mind and unending cheerfulness that helped the family through its many crises.

Although she came to live and work in Fleet Street from Cork Street in the Liberties, Kate originally sprang from a large family in Ringsend. She was the youngest and could recall the story of her mother carrying an infant in her arms outside the jail when Daniel O'Connell, the Liberator, was released, sick in mind and body after his trial and conviction for conspiracy in 1844.

Kate herself was a friend of Tim Kelly, one of the Invincibles who killed Lord Frederick Cavendish, Chief Secretary for Ireland, and Thomas Henry Burke, Under Secretary, in what became known as 'the Phoenix Park Murders' of 1882. Kelly and four others were hanged in Kilmainham Jail on the evidence of James Carey the informer.

Kate's father was very friendly with 'Skin-the-Goat', James

FitzHarris, who drove the cab carrying the Invincibles to the Park. FitzHarris was sentenced at Green Street court to sixteen years in Maryborough Jail (now Portlaoise). Kate disliked the advocates of physical force until 1916, her reason being that 'they let Skin-the-Goat die in the Union' (the workhouse). Kate was illiterate. She was present at Kevin's birth and as informant her mark, X, appears on the birth certificate issued five days before Kevin's execution.

Kate was in O'Connell (then Sackville) Street on Easter Monday, 1916, looking for news of the Rising. She lit two candles on a little altar 'for the boys that took the Castle'. They did not, as it happened, succeed in capturing Dublin Castle, but on that day the city was as full of rumour as it was of gunfire.

One of her more remarkable traits came from her lack of a formal education. 'She was', recalls Elgin, 'a wizard at mental arithmetic. We would read out sums for her from our books and she would do our sums in her head'.[2]

During the Civil War, when the Hammam Hotel was in flames, Frank Henderson, brother of Leo, gave Kathy Barry the Dublin Brigade funds, which amounted to £800. She was carrying the money under her clothes when she was arrested. She was marched unsearched down to Amiens Street, where she and Mary MacSwiney were released after an hour. Once home, she gave the money to Kate, who kept it hidden in her bosom until 26 November, 1922, four months later, when it was all gone. She had a receipt from Dublin Brigade for every penny of it. Kate, in effect, was the brigade's treasurer all that time, while Kathy was away in the South. Her ample bosom also contained GHQ and brigade despatches. She kept them wrapped in separate pieces of newspaper, never once confusing one with another.

Kate was eighty-four when she died in 1937. She is buried in Glasnevin Cemetery alongside Aunt Judith Barry.

For the older children in Fleet Street, the greatest treat was a Sunday drive in the pony and trap out into the country to see how the cows were doing. Shel recalls drives to the Long Mile Road and distinctly remembers passing the Halfway House public house. For Tom Barry it was a pleasure to take his

24

family for an outing that for him was also a duty.

The dairy enterprise totally vindicated Tom's original decision to open up in Dublin. Tombeagh was a fairly profitable farm and useful also as a holiday home where the growing family could keep in touch with their roots. But it was in Fleet Street that the future seemed to lie.

He was a deeply religious man and gave generously to the Church. To the Augustinian Church in John's Lane, he contributed a stained glass window. To the Franciscans in Adam and Eve's Church, he gave a mosaic floor for a side chapel. To the church at Ticknock, the nearest to Tombeagh, he presented plaster statues of the Sacred Heart and the Virgin Mary, and to Jervis Street Hospital, the records show that he made an annual subscription of 10s.

He had problems too. His heart was beginning to give him trouble and he consulted Sir Christopher Nixon, physician to the Lord Lieutenant and Professor of Medicine at the Catholic University School in Cecilia Street, just down the road from Fleet Street.

Nixon was eminent enough to charge a hefty fee, paid on the nail, for a visit to Fleet Street, an occurrence which became more frequent as Tom Barry's health declined. Mrs. Barry later blamed Sir Christopher for diagnosing her husband's condition wrongly. Whatever were the rights and wrongs of it, Thomas Barry died of fatty degeneration of the heart on 8 February, 1908, leaving a widow and seven children, and his beloved sister Judith. He was sixty-five. Nobody thought of burying him anywhere but in Tinneclash. Dublin was for making money. Tombeagh was home.

Kevin had just turned six.

3 Thwarted

Tom Barry's funeral was impressive. He had died on Saturday in Fleet Street and his remains were taken by train from Kingsbridge Station to Baltinglass on the following Tuesday. There they arrived at ten o'clock and a vast funeral cortège 'one of the largest ever seen in the district', according to a local newspaper, followed the coffin to Tinneclash, where Mrs. Barry had ordered a grave nine feet long by twelve feet wide, at a cost of £1 10s. She also paid £3 to the railway company for their services that day. Funerals were male rituals, so the women stayed at home preparing the food and ensuring that there was enough whiskey.

If the measure of a man's worth is the number of barrels of whiskey consumed at his funeral and the rank and quality of the priests attending, the occasion gave ample testimony to the universal esteem in which Tom Barry was held. Refreshments in Fleet Street cost the widow £3; she spent another £2 in Tombeagh, and Fanagan's the undertakers charged her £17 18s.

A month after Tom Barry's death, probate was taken out by his executors and trustees: Mary Barry, his widow; Michael Dowling, farmer; and Patrick Dowling, gentleman. His estate was worth £2,714 9s., which at today's prices would approximate to £150,000.

In his will he appointed 'my dear wife Mary Barry' guardian of his children and, in an attempt to govern from the grave, instructed the trustees to sell 8 Fleet Street and the dairy yard in Pimlico, as well as his cattle in the county and city.

To his widow he left £300; to his sister Judith £250; to the Rev. William Farrell, curate of St. Andrew's, Westland Row,

£10 'for the purpose of having Masses celebrated in Ireland in a place open for public worship for the repose of my soul and the souls of my deceased parents.' The Franciscans in Merchants' Quay were given £20 for a like purpose.

He directed that his farm at Tombeagh should be held for the benefit of all his children in equal shares, the sons to get their shares at twenty-one and the daughters at twenty-one or when they married, 'whichever should first happen'.

I desire that my wife and children during their minorities or until marriage as the case may be shall reside on my said farm at Tombeagh and that the farm shall be worked for the maintenance, education and benefit of the said children and for the maintenance of my said wife unless and until she shall remarry.

The will was dated 15 January, 1908, when he knew that he was dying and that his widow, nearly thirty years his junior, might well contract a new marriage.

The strange thing is that his widow did not pay a blind bit of heed to his principal wish.

After an abortive auction conducted in May by Patrick Coyle of 16 Stoneybatter, the dairy yard at Pimlico was sold by private treaty to John Grennan of 54 Meath Street for £90.

Between February and May, Mr. Coyle carried out another of Tom Barry's wishes. He sold all the cattle that were out on grass for the very handsome sum of £1,470 17s. 10d.

But Fleet Street was another matter. Since Mrs. Barry was, by common consent, a gentle person slightly bewildered by all that was going on around her, it must be assumed that the basic decision to run counter to Tom Barry's instructions was Aunt Judith's. Mrs. Barry was overshadowed by Judith. She, after all, had built up the dairy business with her brother before Mary Dowling came on the scene at all.

On 19 March, 1907, the family solicitor made 6s. 8d. out of a dramatic visit: 'Attending Mrs. Barry when she stated that, having considered the matter, she thought it best in the children's interest to remain in Fleet Street.' Mr. Murphy pointed out that the only way of achieving this was by Miss Judith Barry buying the house in the open market, 'having regard to the terms of Mr. Barry's will.' He promised to consider the matter between then and May.

On 31 March, Aunt Judith, who had no intention of waiting until May, called on Mr. Murphy: 'Attending Miss Barry when she stated that she wished to retain Fleet Street for the benefit of the children (but did not desire to put more than £200 into the business) and to continue the trading for say twelve months as an experiment'. He advised her that strict economy was necessary, and she agreed that if the place were worked at a loss trading would be discontinued.

There were few limits to Aunt Judith's power and determination in this matter. She was prepared to go to any lengths to help the widow — or at least the widow's young family.

Fleet Street was valued in April by Mr. Coyle. He pointed out that it was held on lease for thirty-one years from 1881 from Dublin Corporation at a rent of £40 a year, so there were in 1908 only four years to run. There was a possibility of renewing the lease 'on not unfavourable terms'. He considered, therefore, that the house and premises were worth £50. The household furniture, including the child's cot and two clocks, he put at £38 2s. 6d. and the shop fittings and milk vessels at £11 17s. 6d. Value of the whole lot: £100.

Tombeagh, including 42 heifers, 2 cows and a bullock, 21 sheep, 2 old horses and an old donkey, 3 calves and 2 traps, as well as hay and 2 pits of turnips, had already been valued in February by Mr. E.P. O'Kelly of Baltinglass at £734 5s.

In an inspector's report made in 1905 under the Land Law Act, Thomas Wheatley had said: 'This holding is in two divisions and inconvenient to work properly. It is mostly light and sandy and the lower portion wet and sedgy'. The house he described as comfortable and slated and the buildings were in excellent condition. In fact the rear wing of the house had been built as recently as 1903 of stones removed from a ruined house on the Upperland. (On the first floor of this wing is 'the New Room', which was used by Eamon de Valera on his flying visits to Tombeagh during the Civil War.)

In Dublin the scene had changed. Mrs. Barry and her brother Michael called on Mr. Murphy for thirteen shillings and fourpence worth of advice. They told him firmly that the executors desired to sell the Fleet Street house and furniture to Mrs. Barry for £100. He pointed out the difficulties in the way of this course, but they 'desired the matter to be completed in this way'. That was on 26 May, and that was how Tom Barry's wishes were thwarted.

The second Barry girl, Shel, tells of the immediate and drastic effect on the family of her father's death and the decision to retain Fleet Street:

> Father died in 1908 and things changed. Mother went to Tombeagh and the family was split. The younger children went with her, Kathy and I and Elgin with Auntie who remained in Fleet Street, and we went to secondary school from there. Kevin joined us in 1915 and Auntie had died in 1912.
>
> Mother installed a housekeeper and Granny Dowling in Tombeagh. I had to leave school in 1915 and go to Tombeagh to take over as the housekeepers were not reliable.[1]

Elgin remembers that the same housekeepers received unmerciful treatment from Kevin, who was always playing tricks on them.

The secondary school was the Loreto Convent Female Boarding and Day Schools on St. Stephen's Green, which all the girls attended. Shel was seventeen when she left. 'She was very well read,' says her daughter Triona, 'especially in history. She always resented the fact that she was sent down to Tombeagh'. Shel became in a sense the 'country cousin' and this divorced her from the 'city Barrys' who, as the years went by, used Tombeagh simply as a summer villa and for Christmas and Easter holidays. The move, however, did bring Shel closer to Michael.

Aunt Judith was so central to the family's life that her death in 1912 at over seventy recast the Barrys' relationship one to another. Kathy, aged sixteen and still learning leadership from Judith after her father's death, was especially downcast by this second bereavement. As Judith's clear favourite, she keenly felt the loss of her protectrix, but she now knew enough to strengthen her resolve to lend moral support to her mother and become, as she tells us, 'my mother's chief adviser in all her affairs'.

Aunt Judith was buried in Glasnevin Cemetery in a plot in which, twenty-five years later, she was joined by Kate Kinsella.

4 Schools

At the time of his father's death, Kevin was six and had just begun school with the nuns in Clarendon Street, but Mrs. Barry's decision to take four of the five younger children with her to Tombeagh meant finding a school for the boys. Elgin stayed in Dublin, where she had already begun school at the convent. The boys went to the local National School in Rathvilly where Ned Toole was the master and Lorcan Byrne was the assistant. Though it is no longer a school, the imposing building, on the right as you enter the village from Tombeagh, is still there.

Ned Toole, who signed himself Edward O'Toole, was no ordinary master and Kevin was fortunate to have had him as teacher. A keen local historian, he wrote histories of the parishes of Rathvilly and Ballon and a pamphlet on the old boundaries of the Diocese of Leighlin. He was a member of the Royal Society of Antiquaries of Ireland and did some interesting work on 'grooved standing stones in north Carlow', one of which is on the Barry farm of Tombeagh, on the south side of the road leading from Hacketstown to Rathvilly.[1]

Rathvilly had, and to some extent still has, an ethos quite different from that of Hacketstown, three miles in the opposite direction from Tombeagh. Rathvilly was a landlord's village, owned and dominated by Lord Rathdonnell of Lisnavagh House. His estate was the main source of employment, and the economy of the village depended on his prosperity.

At school, Kevin was known as a quiet, unobtrusive boy. Among his classmates were his brother Michael, Dan and John Deering of Knockavagh and Christy Byrne of the Hill. A school photograph of the five of them survives.

Ned Toole's daughter Nancy, who went to school to her father, recalled in an *Irish Press* article many years later that:

About the only time I can think of Kevin showing any signs of devilment was when he drenched my plaits with water one day. I used to carry buckets of water from the well to our home and one day I met Kevin with a pal as I was going along with two buckets full to the brim. The pair of them dipped their hands into the water and splashed it all over my long pigtails until my hair was soaked. I did not tell my father how my hair got so wet and I had to make up some story to keep Kevin out of trouble.

Michael and Kevin went to school by donkey and trap. As soon as they reached Rathvilly Moat, they often held a race with Willie Jackson of Knockboy on his way to the Protestant school in the village. By this time, Mrs. Barry had begun to send milk by train from Rathvilly to Dublin. Jimmy Barry, a kinsman, who lived with his brother Micky on the road to Ticknock, drove the milk cart for her and sometimes carried the boys from school. Micky Barry was a tailor, so the homestead was known as 'the Tailor Barry's'.

When Kevin was thirteen, he was sent back to Dublin and for three months in 1915, he attended O'Connell Schools run by the Christian Brothers on the North Circular Road. Here he first met Frank Flood, later an engineering student at University College, Dublin. Of the ten Volunteers hanged by the British during the War of Independence, two were students, Barry and Flood. It was Frank Flood who wrote from prison to his brother Alfie: 'There must be no weeping for me. I am going where I might never have reached if I had lived my ordinary life'. He was executed on 14 March, 1921, a first lieutenant in the Active Service Unit of the Dublin Brigade.

In the museum at O'Connell Schools are some reminders of Kevin's brief stay, two of his set squares and, more grimly, two bayonets taken by Kevin and Frank Flood in the raid on the King's Inns on 1 June, 1920. The school admissions register shows Kevin Gerard Barry as having attained fifth standard, having come from National School on 30 April and left the school on 18 June, 1915. His father's occupation is given as dairyman. His classmates were the sons of publicans, clerks, coachmen, builders, grocers and a staff sergeant.

There is nothing to show why Kevin left O'Connell Schools except the belief among members of the family that Kathy, now nineteen years of age and earning, decided that he should be given the opportunity afforded by a more expensive school. Aunt Judith, herself 'a bit of a lady' within the family circle and ever anxious for business success, would have heartily approved of Kathy's ambition. Accordingly Kevin was sent to St. Mary's College, Rathmines, run by the Congregation of the Holy Ghost and founded in 1890. The school has never claimed a strong Republican tradition, though Rory O'Connor was a student there. O'Connor was Director of Engineering on the General Staff of the Irish Republican Army during the War of Independence and was later executed.

Kevin Gerard Barry 'of Rathvilly' was enrolled in St. Mary's in September, 1915 in the Preparatory Grade. He left on 31 May, 1916. The school was closed by order of the General Council of the Holy Ghost Order and for some time thereafter was used for other congregational purposes. It reopened in 1926 as a secondary school.

Whatever the effect academically on Kevin of such brief sojourns in two schools, the Easter Rising coming at the end of his time in St. Mary's had an explosive impact on his nationalist sensibilities. Nurtured on tales of the Battle of Hacketstown, the pursuit of Michael Dwyer in the Wicklow mountains, the hounding to death of Parnell, and the vivid recollections of Kate Kinsella, he had already attended his first Republican function in November, 1915.

At St. Mary's, where the fathers of some of the boys were active separatists, he secured tickets for the Manchester Martyrs'* Commemoration Concert in the Mansion House. Eoin MacNeill, who at the time was president of the Irish Volunteers, took the chair at the concert, and Bulmer Hobson, a member

---

*Three Fenians, William Philip Allen, Michael Larkin and Michael O'Brien, were executed in Manchester in 1867 for the murder of Sergeant Charles Brett during the rescue of the Fenian leaders Thomas J. Kelly and Timothy Deasy.

of the Supreme Council of the Irish Republican Brotherhood, made a fiery speech.

Kathy was with Kevin at the concert where she recalled later she said hello to Bobby Bonfield and the Mac Neill boys. Bonfield (Bondfield) was a dental student from Moyne Road, Ranelagh. He was a dedicated Volunteer in the Fourth Battalion and was subsequently active in the siege of the Hammam Hotel in the early days of the Civil War. At the time of the Mansion House concert Kathy and Kevin were the only Republicans in the family. Kathy's earliest gesture of defiance of the British was at the Grafton Picture House, where she 'found it impossible' to stand up for 'God Save the King' at the end of a performance. This too was the time when numbers of the young men she knew were volunteering for service in France, but in Fleet Street 'we had a somewhat secluded and conventional life'.

The concert had a marked effect on Kevin. 'There and then', wrote Patrick Barry Moloney, Kathy's son, in *The Belvederian* (1945) 'he wanted to join the Fianna Éireann: but he was so young — 13 — that his family thought it unwise.' The Fianna had been founded in 1903 by Hobson in his native Belfast and had been reorganised at his suggestion by Countess Markievicz, who was second-in-command of the St. Stephen's Green garrison in 1916. Kevin's sister Elgin believes that, without telling the family, he *did* join the Fianna then.

And so to Belvedere.

Belvedere College is perhaps the most illustrious of Dublin's Catholic schools. The core of the Jesuit college is Belvedere House, built about 1780 by Michael Stapleton for George Augustus Rochfort, second Earl of Belvedere. Stapleton, the greatest of the native stuccadores, displays the originality of his talent in the plaster decoration of Belvedere House which, in Con Curran's words, 'offers a full conspectus of our house decoration in the Grattan period . . .'[2]

The atmosphere of the school has been described by Owen Dudley Edwards, a former student as 'one more of a masterpupil conspiracy of irony rather than the crass indoctrination of crude nationalism . . .'[3] It was the school of James Joyce.

In 1916, like other schools, it was turning out officers for the British Army in Flanders, many of them in the Royal Army Medical Corps.

Joseph Mary Plunkett, the poet executed after the 1916 Rising, went to school in Belvedere as also did Cathal Brugha, the uncompromising Republican who died fighting in the Hammam Hotel at the beginning of the Civil War. Eimear O'Duffy, the poet, and Dick Humphreys, both of the Irish Volunteers, were pupils there. Joseph Mary's brother Jack Plunkett, who with another brother George survived the War of Independence and the Civil War to fight again in the IRA campaign of the 1940s, were Belvedere boys. Another Belvedere contemporary was Dermot Fitzpatrick (Diarmuid Mac Giolla Phádraig), owner of the Dublin bookshop beloved of Republicans. A man of strong left-wing views, he was in charge of training Fianna Éireann in the War of Independence. He survived the 20s and 30s without being arrested, but was interned in the Curragh in the early 1940s.

Joyce left Belvedere in 1898. When Kevin Barry went there, 'the plump bald' Sergeant-Major Wright was still conducting drill classes. Richard Campbell, 'whom some of the boys called Lantern Jaws and others Foxy Campbell', as Joyce tells us in *A Portrait of the Artist*, did not leave until 1917. Father Joseph Mc Donnell, who figures in *Stephen Hero*, was a prefect of the Sodality of Our Lady in Joyce's time and spiritual director of the school during Kevin's years. Kevin was a member of the sodality. Sergeant-Major Wright did not confine his instruction to Belvedere. He was also the drill-master at Loreto Convent, St. Stephen's Green, when Kevin's sisters were there.[4]

The closure of St. Mary's College meant that Belvedere received thirteen extra boys on 1 September, 1916, including Kevin. They were of all ages and none was placed in Kevin's class. Total enrolment that year, 1916-17, was 237, and the fees, which in Kevin's case were paid by his mother, were four guineas a term. They had been £3 in Joyce's time.

Tom Counihan was a member of the Jesuit community at Belvedere although not yet ordained. He taught Kevin mathematics and chemistry and coached him in rugby. He was perhaps his best friend among the teaching staff. His marginal comments on Kevin's chemistry notebook demonstrate, however, that his affection for his student did not blind him to the faults he found. 'Notes unfinished', he wrote. 'Finish your notes. Sketch incomplete. Your notes are to be entered in a more careful handwriting'.[5]

French was taught by W.C. Fogarty, who spent forty years in the school (1910-50), and was much loved. His French had been perfected in the Channel Islands and French Canada. It must be assumed that he knew the limerick the boys sometimes chanted behind his back:

Fogarty's nose is long
Fogarty's nose is long
It would be no disgrace
To Fogarty's face
If half of his nose were gone

'A bright, kindhearted lad', was how he saw Kevin. In later life he recalled that one day towards the end Mr. Counihan brought a message from Kevin in prison: 'Please remember me to Mr. Fogarty'.

He was taught Irish by Lambert Mc Kenna, SJ, who in 1935 compiled the English-Irish dictionary that bears his name. Another Jesuit, Fergal Mc Grath, edited *The Belvederian* in 1919, the issue which contains the best known photograph of Kevin, wearing a trench-coat with collar turned up and with a stray lock of hair over his forehead. It was a group photograph captioned 'Pillars of the House'.

Right through this period, from 1907 to his death in 1919, William Martin Murphy was President of the Belvedere College Union. Murphy was an anti-Parnellite who had built railways in Britain, the Gold Coast and South America.

After his return, he constructed railways and tramways in Ireland and bought newspapers, including the *Irish Independent* and the *Irish Catholic*. His fame or infamy lies in his 400-strong Employers' Federation, which fought and defeated James Larkin's Irish Transport and General Workers' Union in the great lock-out of 1913. In 1915 he called a meeting of Irish employers at which a scheme was mooted to dismiss able-bodied men in an effort to force them to enlist in the British

Army. He owned the Dublin United Tramways Company, whose workers were called out on strike by Larkin and precipitated the vicious confrontation of 1913.

Kevin Barry's English master was George Dempsey, a survivor from James Joyce's days at Belvedere. For Dempsey, Kevin wrote an essay on 'Industrial Unrest' in which he launched into a vigorous tirade against William Martin Murphy:

> We are today passing through a crisis which is unparalleled in the history of the world. It is the culmination of four years of starvation, privation and misgovernment — it is the nemesis which awaited war profiteers, place hunters and grasping capitalists. It is probably the beginning of the end of aristocracy.
>
> It is interesting for us to study this huge upheaval, its causes, its effects and its possible remedies. It is interesting also because it marks the triumph of Labour, of Trade Unionism and — as Martin Murphy's rag has it — of Syndicalism. When one contemplates the immensity of the trouble — the fact that in Belfast alone 95,500 workers are out on strike — the fact that the whole city is paralysed and that the whole country could be paralysed at an hour's notice, one is amazed at the stupendousness of this system and one can understand the elation of Labour.
>
> The causes of a strike are not hard to discover. In nine cases out of ten it will be found that the cause is hunger. This itself may arise from two causes, bad wages or misgovernment. In former times it was the former. This crisis is the result of the latter.... There is no remedy for a strike except to accede to the demands of the strikers.... We here in Dublin had an experience of a strike which has been looked upon by all the world as the 'model strike'. When W.M. Murphy refused to recognise the tramwaymen as a union they went out on strike bringing out every trade union man in Dublin with them.
>
> The Socialists all over the world backed them and the foodship *Hare* was dispatched with food for the strikers; also money poured in from everywhere to keep up the

strike. The men held out doggedly till they won or virtually won, since the tramway union was recognised. Thus we received a forcible demonstration of the power of Labour and had an experience also of the power of agitation in the person of that marvellous leader James Larkin and his able lieutenant, Commandant James Connolly.[6]

Mr. Dempsey gave the essay sixty out of a hundred marks. Other than that, he refrained from commenting on its merits. The wonder is that Belvedere tolerated such inflammatory material at all in a school for the sons of gentlemen. This essay was written in 1919, Kevin's last year at school. It was the year of the second great industrial action in Belfast, which already had suffered from a massive strike in 1907.

Academically, Kevin Barry's progress was patchy. He passed junior grade, got honours and third place in middle grade (1918), and passed senior grade in his last year.[7]

More important than the grade examinations was his matriculation in the National University of Ireland in the summer of 1919. Allocated the number 1 in the examination, he got honours in Irish, English, French, History and Geography, and passed in Latin.

Socially, Kevin showed a marked capacity for friendship. In his first term at Belvedere he met Gerard Ward Mc Aleer of Dungannon, and the strong bond formed between the two ended only with Kevin's death four years later.

Gerry Mc Aleer, now a retired air commodore of the Royal Air Force and a former honorary physician to the Queen, was the only boy at Belvedere who did not have his home in Dublin. He had digs with Mrs. Tipping on the North Circular Road, beside O'Connell Schools, and does not even now know how his parents came to choose Belvedere for him — but the Tippings were from Dungannon and were friends of his father's.

Nor does he know quite why he and Kevin initially became friends. 'Perhaps it was merely because of my northern accent or because we shared the name Gerard. Kevin was always in an honours class: I was in a pass. He was a brighter boy than I was. I think I worked harder because I had to'.[7]

In fact, although Gerry Mc Aleer's marks in Irish, English, French and Latin were consistently lower than Kevin's, his mathematics was always better, and in their last year they were in the same class, Senior I.

Gerry remembers Kevin as not much smaller than himself at five feet nine inches. 'Kevin was a fairly solid fellow, broader than I was. We were both forwards in rugby. He was a demon for eating bars of chocolate at school. He would eat it morning, noon and night'.

The Mc Aleers were people of substance in Dungannon. As well as owning the Commerical Hotel, Peter Mc Aleer was an auctioneer and an undertaker. His was the Catholic hotel and his motorcar was ever in use, collecting commercial travellers from the Belfast train or following the hearse at funerals.

When Kevin was invited to stay with the Mc Aleers in the summer of 1918, it was Sam Mc Manus's car that Kevin and Gerry rode around in. Sam was a Mason and a great friend of Gerry's elder brother, Barney. 'Sam had a big motor-car, two boot shops and a sweet shop in Dungannon. He took all my family in his car anywhere we wanted to go', says Gerry.

In a letter from Dungannon to his sister Kathy, Kevin is clearly delighted, not only with Sam but with the whole set-up. 'I got several great motor drives last week. The motor man and I are great pals because he is a Meath man and looks down on all Northerners. The longer I stay in the town the better I like it. It is a great place." However, he had the misfortune to break a bicycle chain riding to Pomeroy and it cost him four shillings for a new one, thereby reducing his assets to a few pence. 'If you can spare it, send a few bob – if you haven't already sent it. . . . If you can't I can get a loan of a few bob from Gerry to carry on. I got a letter from U P (Uncle Pat) but nothing else . . .'[8]

Later there is a chatty letter to his mother, addressed 'Dear Ma'. There are two soldiers staying at the hotel. 'They are baling hay in the neighbourhood and Barney is earning 5s. per day with them. He has to write down the weight of each bale – very hard work'. He must have got the 'few bob' from Kathy – a postscript thanks his sister for her letter. And he says: 'I hope none of the family were hurt at the recruiting meeting.

There was none here yet'.[9] He put no stamp on the envelope, so there was 3d due on the letter. In other references to his mother, he calls her 'the missus' or 'the missis'.

Kevin was a substitute on the Junior Cup Team that beat Blackrock College at rugby in 1917. 'In those days', says Gerry Mc Aleer, 'that was a miracle!' *The Belvederian* of 1917 noted: 'K. Barry (forward) — though rarely brilliant always plays a good, hard game; a fair tackler; works well in the scrum'. And Gerry Mc Aleer is reported as having 'improved considerably during the year; dribbles very well, but did not shine out much — handicapped, doubtless, through want of knowledge of the game.' — a want of knowledge more than made up subsequently. Eugene Davy, later to have a brilliant international career, was a year or two younger than Kevin and Gerry, but secured his place on that junior team as scrum half — 'watches the ball very keenly and frequently comes round on the opposing half'.

The virulent influenza epidemic of October-November, 1918, took its toll of men and fixtures in the small world of senior schools rugby in Leinster. Blackrock College, the old rivals, defeated the Belvedere seniors by 36-0 in an early game and by 16-0 in the semi-finals of the Cup. Kevin was Secretary of Rugby and also a full member of the team. 'No forward deserved his place better, showed great dash, and tackled like a demon. This player improved very much during the season. A useful hooker in the scrum'. This particular team's photograph by Keogh Brothers, published in *The Belvederian*, is the source of one of the best known pictures of Kevin in the black and white striped jersey of the College. He played cricket too, though there is little on record about his prowess and no photographs can be found.

In the same season, 1918-19, Belvedere took up hurling, and again Kevin was a member of the team. The first match was played away against Terenure College. Belvedere went down by ten goals two points to two goals and one point. Gerry Mc Aleer, Eugene Davy and Jim Murphy, later to become godfather to Triona Maher, were among these pioneers of Gaelic games in a bastion of rugby. Charles Moloney, SJ remembers Kevin as his rugby secretary that year with the job of writing twice a week to the various schools to confirm fixtures. In September he gave him ten shillings to cover postage. 'What was my surprise when he came to me at the end of the football season and handed me a half-crown saying: "Sir, here is the change from your 10s".'[10]

Tom Ryan, SJ, did not actually teach Kevin at Belvedere but knew him well and came to know his family also. Many years later he still remembered his 'special quizzical smile'. When talking he would bend his head slightly and look up at a slight angle with that inevitable smile. 'He was a natural leader and drew others to him without effort but never put himself forward'.[11]

According to Tom Counihan, Kevin was not a particularly excitable person and, if anything, was always somewhat unemotional, even though he was goodnatured, and full of fun. Counihan at one point uses the word 'dour'. 'A dour kind of lad ... once he got down to something he went straight ahead'.[12] He was not one to hide his opinions from his teachers, nor did he particularly proclaim them.

He wrote an essay for his English teacher on prejudice, a subject topical at Belvedere during the war. There were two classes of prejudice which, combined, form the origin of very many of the world's greatest wars and slaughter. 'That of the white man against his coloured brother, for brother he is whether black, red or yellow, and that of the white man against his fellow white man of a different nation.'[13]

His own tolerance he may have imbibed from his mother who, as a businesswoman in the city for many years, had especially good relations with Freemasons and Jews. There were always Protestant families in the Tombeagh area, the nearest being the Thorpes. The herd on the Barry farm, John Pollard, was a member of the Church of Ireland.

Gerry McAleer's friendship with Kevin is the happiest memory of his time at Belvedere. He never saw Kevin vexed or angry, more as a person of amiable temper and 'imperturbable humour'. He was manly, 'and manliness always appeals to the best instincts of boys — so frank and so open!' No threat of punishment could ever induce Kevin to 'let down' a fellow student. '. . . he had his troubles and disappointments, and to a boy these seem great, but he took them all with the same unvarying buoyancy of spirit. He was one of the finest sports I have ever known. He was open-handed, open-hearted and generous to a fault . . .'.

Following his unremarkable progress with the grade examinations at Belvedere Kevin's excellent showing in the matriculation won him a City of Dublin Scholarship to UCD where he enrolled in the Faculty of Medicine and, no doubt, looked forward to a long and happy life as a doctor. Belvedere had exerted the strongest influence on him and, indeed, the temperate attitude of the Jesuits must have acted as a useful counterbalance to the ferment of revolution without the walls. Tony Woods, then a staff captain in the Irish Volunteers, caught the atmosphere of the city: 'Between the scraps, it was an extraordinarily unreal war, part-time civilians and youngsters pitched against a real army'.[14]

What the 'good Fathers' did not know was that Kevin Barry had joined Auxiliary C Company of the First Battalion, Dublin Brigade, of the Irish Volunteers, in October 1917, when he was aged 15. He had been part of the 'unreal war' for virtually all of his time in their care.

5 A Real Army

Augustine Birrell, the disgraced Chief Secretary for Ireland, in the last report he made to the British Prime Minister before he resigned, accurately summed up the situation after the 1916 Rising: 'It is not an *Irish* rebellion. It would be a pity if *ex post facto* it became one, and was added to the long and melancholy list of Irish rebellions.'

The course most likely to make the danger greatest for Britain – the execution of the leaders of the Rising – was precisely the course taken three days later. The country was on the high road to independence of the greatest empire the world had ever seen, and in the Autumn of 1917 Kevin Barry wanted to take his place in the fighting. Michael Collins was the Volunteers' new Director of Organisation. He used the Irish Republican Brotherhood network to put competent activists into key positions and weld the Volunteers into an efficient fighting machine 'to put them in a position to complete by force of arms the work begun by the men of Easter Week', as the executive stated.

Bob O'Flanagan recalls the fifteen year old Barry in what he believes was his first appearance at the drill hall of Auxiliary C Company, later renamed H Company. 'When not actually drilling, he was standing near the wall, looking rather a lonely figure.'[1]

Training and the acquisition of arms were the short-term priorities in which Kevin was involved. The rank and file of H Company were drawn from Dublin workers – labourers, clerks, tradesmen and students – and they trained initially at the O'Flanagan Club in Ryder's Row, Bolton Street; the Tara Hall in Gloucester (now Seán MacDermott) Street; North Great

43

George's Street, where the oath was administered, and finally 44 Rutland (now Parnell) Square, subsequently named the Kevin Barry Memorial Hall and now used by Sinn Féin as a bookshop and offices. Other meeting places were a tenement house in Abbey Street, used once when it was disguised as the Frankfort Football Club, and 46 Parnell Square, from where at least one highly successful raid for arms began. In order to avoid discovery, it was important to vary the training halls. No. 25 Parnell Square was the venue for céilí dances, which later in the evening would give way to swinging girls and 'foreign' music, a change which invariably infuriated Micheál Ó Foghlúdha, the master of ceremonies, who would try to stop the band. Bob O'Flanagan says the dancers, including Kevin at a later stage, often went to six o'clock Mass on their way home from the revelries.

All of these locations were in the north city, which was the First Battalion's area. The battalion, formed in 1913, took part in the Howth gun-running episode in July 1914. After the Volunteer split, the Irish Volunteers prepared for the 1916 Rebellion, and the First Battalion became very well equipped with Mauser and Martini rifles. On the morning of the Rising, they were addressed by their commanding officer, Commandant Edward Daly, and given their fighting positions in the Church Street area. After heavy fighting, the battalion finally surrendered having secured a convincing copy of the order signed by Commandant-General Patrick Pearse. Daly was among the fifteen leaders executed, and many of the survivors were sentenced to penal servitude in England.

The death on hunger strike of Thomas Ashe* came in September 1917, and caused a surge of recruits into the Volunteers,

---

*Thomas Ashe (1885-1917) was from Kinard near Dingle, Co. Kerry. He became a national school teacher in 1905 and was working in Lusk, Co. Dublin, from 1908 until April, 1916. He was a close friend of Seán O'Casey, the dramatist. He went to America on a fund-raising trip for the Irish Volunteers in 1914. He led local Volunteers at Ashbourne, Co. Meath, during the Easter Rising, for which he was sentenced to life imprisonment. Released in June 1917, he was arrested in August for incitement. He got two years in Mountjoy and organised a hunger strike among Sinn Féin prisoners to secure political status. He died five days later while being forcibly fed.

including Kevin Barry, whose first task was to cycle around the city on Saturdays with orders for Sunday morning parades.

John Joe Carroll,* the last surviving member of H Company, was one of the first to greet Kevin. 'It was during a parade at 44 Parnell Square that I first made the acquaintance of Kevin Barry', he recalled in 1960.

> He struck me as being a very intelligent and upright young lad, full of life and very fond of sport. He always wore a trench coat with belt and epaulets on each shoulder. He was a first-class Volunteer and it wasn't long till he was promoted Section Leader. By this time the Company had developed into a splendid fighting unit. The training was very strict and included armed patrols around the Company area and night manoeuvres around King James's Castle in Finglas (now demolished).[2]

Saturdays and Sundays were now almost working days for Kevin. On Saturday mornings there was school; then perhaps a rugby or Gaelic game with Gerry McAleer and other friends. Later on, the bicycle was taken out of Fleet Street and Kevin took a circuitous route to deliver mobilisation orders to the Volunteers, one of whom lived in Dartry on the south side. Parades were often held at eight o'clock on Sunday morning, so there was little time for sleep, especially if he had been dancing the night before.

When he joined first, his sister Kathy was told afterwards, 'everybody thought his Belvedere cap a great joke and they decided it was a flash in the pan and they would keep him until he got tired of it'. When they saw that he was serious, his officers gave him the mobilisation job, thinking he would tire of it quickly. Then they made him an NCO and his deep and lasting friendship with Bob O'Flanagan developed.

'In the Volunteers, as in everything else, he had a gilt-edged career', Kathy recalled. 'Most important people noticed him

---

*John Joe Carroll was three years older than Kevin. He was a member of No. 5 Branch of the Irish Transport and General Workers' Union. He was the father of John F. Carroll, now General President of the ITGWU and a former president of the Irish Congress of Trade Unions. John Joe died in 1987.

and liked him. Peadar Clancy* and he were very close friends. He seemed to be able to wangle himself into odd little actions and engagements both in Dublin and on holidays at home in Carlow.'

By the beginning of 1918, there were sporadic raids for arms all over the country, and arrests began for offences such as illegal drilling, unlawful assembly, raiding for arms and cattle driving. Prisoners who were Volunteers usually refused to recognise the courts and in March, Brigadier Dick McKee of the Dublin Brigade was given three months', hard labour for drilling. Kevin was introduced to the Irish Republican Brotherhood by two of his comrades in H Company, Seán O'Neill and Bob O'Flanagan.[3] At just sixteen, he was undoubtedly the youngest member of the IRB, which had been reorganised after the Rising. He was a member of the Thomas Clarke Luby circle.**

Three by-election results in 1918, though they were defeats for Sinn Féin, gave warning that the days of the Home Rule supporters were numbered. John Redmond, the leader of the Irish Party, died in March, amidst the rubble of high hopes for Home Rule.

In the same sad month of March 1918, the German offensive

---

*Peadar Clancy was Vice-Commandant of the Dublin Brigade under Dick McKee. On the night of Bloody Sunday, 21-22 November, 1920, these two and Conor Clune, a brother of Archbishop Clune of Perth, were arrested at the Gloucester Diamond, taken to Dublin Castle and shot dead in the guardroom. They died, reported the court of inquiry, from 'bullet wounds fired by members of the Auxiliary Division, RIC, in self-defence and in execution of their duty — i.e. in preventing the escape of deceased party, who was in their lawful custody'.

**Founded in 1858 by James Stephens, the Irish Republican Brotherhood as it finally came to be known, aimed to overthrow British rule in Ireland and establish a republic. Stephens designed a complex structure to preserve secrecy and prevent infiltration. As a secret oathbound society it soon incurred the wrath of the Hierarchy. Pius IX denounced the IRB after the failed rising of 1867. Soldiers of the IRB were termed the Irish Republican Army, and Clan na Gael was the movement's American auxiliary. The centenary of the rebellion of 1798 gave a boost to the IRB's sagging fortunes and members were involved in the formation of Sinn Féin and, in 1913, of the Irish Volunteers. Under Thomas Clarke's guidance, IRB members of the Irish Volunteers planned the Easter Rising.

wrought such havoc on the Allies that the British Government decided to conscript Irishmen. By uniting the country against forced levies, Lloyd George handed a new strength and purpose to Sinn Féin on a plate. Even the Catholic Hierarchy labelled conscription 'an oppressive and inhuman law'. With the arrival of a new Lord Lieutenant, Lord French, and a new Chief Secretary, Edward Shortt, a Liberal MP who in 1919 became Home Secretary, the *Manchester Guardian* prophesied that the Government was preparing for 'some very evil work in Ireland'. It was, said the paper, about to produce an Ireland 'more ungovernable except by main force, more exasperated in feeling, more alienated than any with which this country has had to deal since the Rebellion of 1798'.*

French's first move was to discover a 'German Plot', arrest seventy-three Sinn Féin leaders, and thus ensure the movement's imminent electoral success. Seditious songs were banned and a cinema prevented from showing a film of Thomas Ashe's funeral. The Government abandoned the threat of conscription, partly because the war in France was going better, and replaced it with a new voluntary recruiting campaign with the aid of well-known Nationalist MPs in uniform. The campaign was in full swing in August 1918 when Kevin Barry was on holiday with Gerry McAleer in Dungannon. There are several references in his letters home to the Sinn Féin activists who infiltrated the crowds at these meetings in order to disrupt them.[4] Despite this, upwards of 11,000 recruits signed on within three months of the inception of the campaign.

The general election called for December, a month after the end of the Great War, gave Sinn Féin two initial advantages. First, there was not time for many returning soldiers to vote; secondly, a new electoral register gave the franchise to

---

*John Fenton Pinkstone French, Lord French of Ypres (1852-1925), came from a Roscommon family living in Kent. He was C-in-C the British Expeditionary Force to France (1914) and C-in-C the Home Guard (1915-18). Replacing Lord Wimborne as Viceroy, he survived a dozen attempts on his life and in the closing stages of the War of Independence was replaced by Lord Fitz-Alan of Derwent, a Catholic. Lord French's elder sister, Charlotte Despard, supported Sinn Féin while her embarrassed brother was in the Vice Regal lodge. Another sister, Dora, was a member of the Gaelic League.

1,931,588 Irish people compared with 698,098 on the old one. This increase included an estimated 800,000 women over thirty, exercising the franchise for the first time.

From jail in England, forty-eight of the Sinn Féin candidates campaigned by statement and message for what a poster proclaimed was 'the liberation of the oldest political prisoner in the world – Ireland!' One of these candidates was the mathematics teacher who had commanded Boland's Mills in the Easter Rising, Eamon de Valera, now standing in a number of constituencies. The result of the election amounted to devastation for the Nationalist Party and triumph for Sinn Féin. De Valera defeated the new Nationalist leader, John Dillon, by a large majority in East Mayo, although in Waterford John Redmond's son Willie retained nearly the same majority he had won in a by-election a year earlier, and in West Belfast Joe Devlin handsomely defeated de Valera.

In all, Sinn Féin won 73 of the 105 seats, a sensational result and one that led directly to the establishment on 21 January, 1919, of the first Dáil Éireann, pledged to sit as an independent Parliament and appoint its own ministry.

The thrust of Sinn Féin's policy for the rest of 1919 was towards securing Ireland's right to self-determination from the Peace Conference at Versailles. If Sinn Féin had become a huge popular movement, it still held many different threads of opinion within it. At one end of the spectrum were the extreme Republicans for whom a thirty-two county sovereign State was the achievable goal. On the other, the much more moderate Nationalists who had voted Sinn Féin because they had lost faith in the Irish Party's ability to win Home Rule. It was a rainbow coalition.

Kevin Barry's own viewpoint became clear when, once a Dáil Ministry was established, the Volunteers took an oath of allegiance to the new Parliament. One night when Kevin came home, he announced to his sister Kathy that he had just taken the oath.[5]

'That's good,' she answered. 'Now you're a real army!'

'I don't know', he replied. 'Anyway, when this damned Dáil takes Dominion Home Rule, they needn't expect us to back them up'.

Kathy remembered this conversation with Kevin vividly and brought it up in one of her frequent arguments with Michael Collins in the early months of 1922 about the Anglo-Irish Treaty.

Mick listed a number of very fine soldiers who supported it and said: 'How do you know your brother would not have supported it too?' I told him this little story and, with characteristic generosity, he said: 'That is good enough. I won't say that any more'.

6 University Student

For three of the four years that Kevin Barry and Gerry McAleer were friends, Kevin was active in the IRA, yet Gerry did not know. Kevin had a remarkable ability to compartmentalise his life so that the overall effect is polychrome. McAleer had no involvement himself with the IRA and knew nothing of Kevin's extramural activities. He was also a complete teetotaller and never saw Kevin drink. Yet it is clear that Kevin and a close mutual friend, Charlie O'Neill, were fond of a bottle now and then. 'They were great dancing people', says Gerry. 'I never bothered my head going to dances, but Kevin and Charlie, and one or two others had nights out in those "low down" dance halls. If they drank, it was damn little or nil.'[1] Charlie O'Neill was a native of Dungannon and at this time was a dental student at UCD. He shared digs with Gerry McAleer in Cabra Park where there was a fellow lodger from Galway who worked in Guinness's and got blotto every Saturday night. Gerry remembers the Galway man's favourite toast while in his cups. 'Sláinte 'gus saol agat, mulligatawny, Erin go brágh, Sinn Féin, Poulaphouca, the wolf dog, the round tower, the harp, crown and feather'.

When the doors of UCD opened on 13 October for the academic session 1919-1920, Kevin Barry found himself one of a record number of medical students. The Great War had killed a whole generation of young men, both officers and other ranks, and those who had been too young to offer themselves as cannon fodder were clamouring for higher education.

In First Year Medicine, 193 students enrolled. It is a tribute to the broadminded tradition of the old Royal University that thirty-two of this number were women. The Royal, which was an examining body, had been looked upon as an interim measure before a truly national and Catholic university could be established, but it did claim to be the second university in these islands to admit women to its degrees, London University being the first. The Royal had given way to the Catholic University School of Medicine at Cecilia Street, Dublin and that body in turn had been subsumed into University College, Dublin in 1908. When Kevin Barry arrived in 1919, the medical school was situated at Earlsfort Terrace with the exception of the anatomy department which was still at Cecilia Street.

One of Kevin's contemporaries, Honoria Aughney from Tullow, said she did not even know when she went to UCD first that Kevin Barry's people were from Carlow. 'I'll tell you how we met. It was at a céilí. We were dancing "The Siege of Ennis", a dance where you change partners.

'What Kevin said was: "I didn't know the Carlow girls knew anything about dancing".

' "Yes", said I, as snooty as you like, "and I didn't know that the rugby players knew anything about it either".

'I'm sure he was glad to be rid of me in the dance. And the poor lad was probably only wanting to get into conversation'.[2]

Honoria Aughney went on to become County Medical Officer of Health for Wexford, the second such appointment for a woman. She also became a devout disciple of Canon Hayes of Bansha, the founder of Muintir na Tíre, and she travelled the country with him in the cause of community development. Gerry McAleer, who had left Belvedere with Kevin and had begun his medical studies with him, remembers that Honoria and her two sisters shared a flat in Hatch Street, all three of them studying at UCD.

Coffee in Grafton Street, dropping in to Fleet Street and having tea if it was going, enjoying Mrs. Barry's company ('she was a wonderful woman, but I loved them all'), entertaining Kevin at Mrs. Tipping's house and going to football matches and the L and H* with him and Charlie O'Neill — these are

---

*The L and H, the Literary and Historical Society of University College, Dublin, is a student debating institution that celebrated its centenary in 1958. John Farrell, who became a district justice in 1943, was auditor in 1920-21, when he had 'the assistance of the best committee of all

Gerry McAleer's memories.[3] It never crossed his mind that Kevin was living another life, a dangerous and dedicated life which he shared with many other students of the college. Edith Kaye, a fellow student, remembered Kevin and his friends walking down Grafton Street at Christmas, 1919. They were wearing false moustaches. 'The years roll back and I remember him as if it were yesterday — his twinkling eyes and wide infectious grin nearly swallowed up by that incongruous moustache. We knew, though I expect we were not supposed to know, that these lads were some of the "boys", in other words members of the Volunteers in University College'.[4]

During his one year at UCD Kevin wrote quite regularly to his friend Bapty Maher in Athy, Co. Kildare, who later married Kevin's sister, Shel. The letters give some direct and revealing insights into the young medical student and the range of time-honoured distractions from study.

'A chara dhíl', he writes to Bapty[5] from Tombeagh two days after the Christmas of 1919, 'I wrote you a letter about a month ago and I don't know if you ever got it as I'm not sure if I put the right address on it. Anyway, how are you since I saw you last? You might write to a fellow you know, now and then, and say how things are.'

He had been to Mountjoy Prison to see his friend Eddie Malone but was not admitted. His sister Kathy had tried too, but couldn't get in. They left parcels but they doubted that Eddie Malone ever got them.

'Now answer this soon and answer it to "my town house" as I'm nearly fed up here . . . Yours to a cinder, Kev.'

Three weeks later, he is in Fleet Street and still has not had a letter from Bapty. He writes:[6]

How the divil are you at all? You know you might write to a fellow once in a while. I wouldn't mind me not writ-

---

time' including James Dillon and Seán MacBride — unlikely bedfellows. In the *Centennial History of the Literary and Historical Society*, edited by James Meenan, Farrell recalls: 'In the opening weeks of that session, the membership of the L and H included Frank Flood; and Kevin Barry had, I think, been an occasional visitor. They were both well known to the members and both were my friends'. Farrell went to St. Mary's and Belvedere and was called to the Bar in 1921.

ing because I'm very busy, pictures, National Library (ahem) and Grafton (5-6 p.m.), but a fellow like you — a bloody gentleman of leisure, you know it's unforgivable.

By the way that bloody bastard never came with the suit with the result that I have to borrow one for a dance tomorrow night. Write and tell him that I say he's a —— so and so etc.

When will you be up in town? You ought to come for a céilídhe (College of Science) on the 30th Jan ... Yours till hell freezes, Kevin.

P.S. Remember me to Misses Lane, Dooley and Coyle.

From Fleet Street an undated letter[7] tells us that he went to the Commerce Dance on Wednesday night and hardly got a wink of sleep since. Miss Brown and Miss Flood had visited Fleet Street separately and 'the missus' went to see Mrs. Doyle of Westpark House. Bapty must have been depressed about something, for Kevin writes: 'Now I hope you are not moping around, as that won't do anyone any good. Try to mend the Darracq* and it will keep your mind occupied.'

In a postscript he asks Bapty to 'tell Miss Lane that I was anxiously enquiring about her health. Wouldn't I make a fine butcher uh? P.P.S. I never cursed as much in my life as coming up with dear Mrs. Bannerman. A peach of a tart got into the carriage and was swinging the glad on me the whole time and I had to look virtuous while my face was blue with suppressed curses. Excuse scrawl, K.G.B.'

Dublin was obviously a lively city for the students even after the British imposed a curfew in February 1920, under which nobody other than members of the Crown forces was permitted in the streets between midnight and five o'clock in the morning. Life simply went on. Advertisements proclaimed: 'Meet me at the Grafton Picture House', where Kevin had told Bapty Maher he could be found between five and six o'clock, presumably having tea. Mary Pickford was playing in 'Esmeralda'

---

*The Darracq was an Anglo-French motor-car with electric lighting and starting. Bapty Maher was a genius with motor-cars and could drive without using the clutch in the days before synchromesh gear boxes. He taught the author how to double declutch.

and Alice Joyce in 'The Vengeance of Durand' at the Grafton in 1920, and four other cinemas consistently enjoyed full houses. Theatre and variety shows were to be seen at the Gaiety, the Queen's ('East Lynn' twice nightly), the Tivoli, the Theatre Royal, the Empire, La Scala and the Abbey, which had Maurice Dalton's *Sable and Gold* among its shows that year.

A contemporary of Kevin's, Moira Lysaght, from a well-to-do North King Street family, says that at the time she would walk to the Abbey Theatre through Mary's Lane with her mother. They went to see the Carl Rosa company in 'Tannhäuser', the D'Oyly Carte in Gilbert and Sullivan or the O'Mara Company in 'The Colleen Bawn' or 'The Bohemian Girl'; but they never went to the cinema.

Kevin's younger sister Peggy,[8] then about twelve years old, has given us some poignant recollections of the soldier as brother:

> I remember when he had to take 'the infants' (Monty and me) to Mass, he would tell us for God's sake to walk in front of him, so that no one would think we were *with* him.
>
> I remember when Mother would have to leave us all in Tombeagh how kind he was to us 'younger ones'. He always put a few sweets or an apple under our pillows to find when we woke up.

The Barrys and the Dixons were great friends at the time. Mary, Rita and Eileen were contemporaries of the Barry girls. Their younger brother Kevin, later to become Attorney-General and a High Court Judge, was Kevin's junior in Belvedere by a year. They lived in Booterstown, Dalkey and Sandycove at different times, and were the children of Martin Dixon, a well-known builder. Eileen,[9] who became a doctor, was known to the Barry family as Chimo. She was an amateur palm-reader and would entertain the Barrys in the drawingroom in Fleet Street. One evening in 1920, she was reading Kevin's palm when she stopped and looked at him.

'You should be dead', she said.

Kevin's dancing hours were curtailed by the curfew, but his social life blossomed and few enough people except his family and his Volunteer comrades knew much about his hidden agenda.

The difficulties and provocations of the military presence was graphically expressed by Erskine Childers*, writing in the London *Daily News* at the time.

Take a typical night in Dublin. As the citizens go to bed, the barracks spring to life. Lorries, tanks and armoured searchlight cars muster in fleets, lists of 'objectives' are distributed and, when the midnight curfew order has emptied the streets – pitch dark streets – the weird cavalcades issue forth to the attack. Think of raiding a private house at dead of night in a tank (my own experience), in a tank whose weird rumble and roar can be heard miles away: the procedure of the raid is in keeping, though the 'objectives' are held for the most part by women and terrified children. A thunder of knocks: no time to dress (even for a woman alone) or the door will crash in. On opening, in charge the soldiers – literally charge – with fixed bayonets and in full war kit. No warrant shown on entering, no apology on leaving if, as in nine cases out of ten, suspicions prove to be groundless and the raid a mistake.[10]

Michael Hayes,[11] who fought in Jacob's factory in 1916, was Ceann Comhairle of the Dáil from 1922 to 1932, and later became Professor of Modern Irish at UCD, mentions some of the students who contemporaneously were active

---

*Robert Erskine Childers (1870-1922) was born in England and brought up in the house of his cousin, Robert Barton of Glendalough House, Annamoe, Co. Wicklow. Educated at Haileybury and Cambridge, he was a clerk in the House of Commons (1894-1910); was wounded in the Boer War; wrote the best-selling spy story *The Riddle of the Sands* (1903) and in July 1914, used his yacht Asgard to run guns for the Volunteers from Germany to Howth. He served in the Royal Naval Air Service in 1916 and succeeded Desmond FitzGerald as Director of Publicity in the War of Independence. In the Treaty negotiations he was on the secretariat and then strongly opposed the Treaty. At Annamoe he was arrested during the Civil War and was sentenced to death for possession of a revolver. He was executed by firing squad on 24 November, 1922. His son, Erskine Hamilton Childers, was President of Ireland from 1973 until his death two years later.

revolutionaries: Séamus O'Donovan, Major Joe Dunne, Rory O'Connor, Nicholas O'Dwyer, Kevin O'Higgins, Dan Bryan, Ernie O'Malley, Richard Mulcahy, J.J. O'Connell and of course Kevin Barry and Frank Flood. He could have added Seán MacBride, Todd Andrews, Andy Cooney, John Dowling and a number of other men who made significant contributions to the struggle for independence. Todd Andrews[12] says: 'There were a number of students who were known to be IRA men, but unless they were in the same Company or Battalion, they never spoke or associated with one another on the basis of their common allegiance'. Of Kevin he adds: 'I knew he was one of "us" although this fact in no way helped to foster our acquaintance'.

F.O.C. Meenan[13] links Ernie O'Malley and Kevin Barry as Cecilia Street students and 'two of the most evocative names in the fight for Irish freedom'. As it happens, both were also holders of Dublin Corporation scholarships.

Among Kevin's professors were some men with high reputations in their fields. John A. McClelland from Coleraine held the chair of Experimental Physics at the Catholic University School of Medicine and UCD from 1902 until his death in 1920. Hugh Ryan from near Nenagh was Professor of Chemistry, CUSM and UCD, from 1899 up to his death in 1931. He and Denis Coffey, Professor of Physiology and later first President of UCD (1909-1940), announced their engagements to be married at a joint ceremony presided over in 1904 by Sir Christopher Nixon, who a few years later attended Tom Barry in Fleet Street.

Kevin's Professor of Botany was James Bayley Butler, a Clongownian who had been born in India. He was a captain in the Royal Army Medical Corps during the Great War but kept the chair occupied by him from 1911 to 1924, when he became Professor of Zoology in succession to George Sigerson.

For Zoology, there was the eminent physician and scholar Dr. George Sigerson (1836-1925). A native of Holyhill, near Strabane, he attracted Charles Darwin's attention for his work on biology. In 1897, he was the author of an anthology, *Bards of Gael and Gall*, and he was a member of the first Senate. His daughter was Dora Sigerson Shorter, the poet, who predeceased him. Her *Sixteen Dead Men and Other Poems of Easter Week* was published posthumously. A handsome, striking figure, Dr. Sigerson suffered from a major defect – he could scarcely be heard. Douglas Hyde said of Sigerson: 'As an Irish scholar he was the last link that connected us with the era of O'Donovan and O'Curry and one of the last that connected us with the men of '48, with Kickham and with Mitchel'.

The dissecting room in Cecilia Street was described by a new student thus: 'The room is lined with small slate topped tables each bearing its load of gruesome flesh and having around it its particular coterie of interested searchers after the to them unknown. . . . Bright green paint on the walls, socialist red paint on the chairs and stools, furnish a certain amount of noble splendour to this apartment of science.'

It is tempting to attribute the high failure rate of the First Medical class of 1919-20 to the fact that the minds of many of them were far from zoology and experimental physics. But except in Kevin Barry's case, we have no way of knowing why in mid-June 1920, the board failed seventy-three candidates. Only seven of those who failed were women. Honoria Aughney and her friend Anne Stafford of Wexford were among the twenty-five successful women. Gerry McAleer joined Kevin in the ranks of those destined to repeat in September.

Professor McLoughlin certified on 24 June, 1920, that Kevin G. Barry had attended the following lectures: 48 physics lectures out of 62 delivered; 32 physics lectures out of 42 delivered; 44 out of 50 and 27 out of 30 chemistry lectures; 27 out of 36 and 11 out of 17 botany lectures, and 10 out of 10 and 11 out of 17 zoology lectures.

Considering the military and social lives he was leading, Kevin certainly was not neglecting his classes, even if he was not devoting the hours outside college to the study necessary for success in the examination.

On 1 June, 1920, before the summer examination, as we shall see Kevin took part in a raid on the King's Inns. In July, when he should have been studying for the Autumn repeat examinations, he was involved in an abortive attempt to burn the old barracks at Aughavanagh, and early in September he was still actively attached to the Carlow Brigade. He sat most of the examinations — experimental physics, theoretical chemistry, practical chemistry, botany and zoology — in the Examination Hall at Earlsfort Terrace and was due to enter for the last one at two o'clock on Tuesday, 20 September, 1920.

But, if we may anticipate briefly, on the morning of that day, the Monks' Bakery raid took place and Kevin was captured. Gerry McAleer looked for him in the Aula Maxima and was very surprised not to see him there.

And his youngest sister, Peggy, remembers:

(I wish I didn't) the day after his arrest. He hadn't been home the evening before. (I think at that period he was sleeping in Uncle Pat's but used to come in sometimes during the morning or afternoon), and Mother sent me up to Earlsfort Terrace to watch for him in UCD. I walked around it for about three hours and I think it was one of the most awful things in my life to have to go back and tell her I hadn't found him.

Even after so many years [she was writing in 1965], I am totally unable to see the whole thing objectively — to me it is still a *very* close, terrible and personal matter.[14]

By coincidence, the board of examiners met on the evening of 20 September. They passed Gerard Ward McAleer.

They failed Kevin Gerard Barry.

7 Soldier

One of Michael Collins's real achievements was the setting up of a sophisticated intelligence system. Information was just as necessary to the IRA in the acquisition of arms as in the mounting of ambushes. One of the most effective raids for arms carried out by the Volunteers was the attack on the King's Inns, situated at the top of Henrietta St., Dublin on 1 June, 1920, prior to Kevin Barry's exploits in Tombeagh later that summer. The raid was a daring blow dealt in broad daylight to an enemy whose military discipline was discovered to have slackened in that part of the city.

The King's Inns was well guarded. It was an outpost of the garrison in the North Dublin Union. On the green in front of the building, soldiers and their girl friends sat on fine days chatting, and it was possible for 'civilians' to get close to the guardroom by sitting down among them.

When Brigadier Dick McKee and Vice-Brigadier Peadar Clancy had studied the drawings of the interior, a plan was made allowing seven minutes for the whole operation and assuming a fine day on which the troops would be on the sward. The First, Second and Third Battalions of Dublin Brigade were to provide the hand-picked party under Peadar Clancy.

The men left 46 Parnell Square at intervals for Henrietta Street. Denis (Dinny) Holmes was one of them and he has told the story of the raid.[1]

Joe Dolan began the action by approaching the sentry guarding the door leading in from Henrietta Street, and asking for directions to a given office. While Dolan talked to him, the sentry, who wore a distinguished service ribbon, was surprised, disarmed and made prisoner.

Section Commander Fitzpatrick's group, who had been pretending to play cards on the green, then rushed the soldiers in the Temple Green, took them prisoner and marched them into the building. Their girl friends were placed under armed guard to prevent them from giving the alarm, and one man closed the gates.

Dinny Holmes, a second lieutenant in C Company of the First Battalion, was one of the party who followed Joe Dolan, held up the occupants of the building, and severed the telephone lines. Another section went in through the back to raid for the arms in the guardroom at the left of the building. Holmes continues the story as follows.

> One of this party was young Kevin Barry, who was a mere youngster compared to most of us, but who showed the courage and daring of a born soldier on this occasion. So far as I know, Barry had never been on an important operation before this raid, although he had taken part in many of the smaller actions, always with great credit to himself. I had drilled Kevin when, at an early age, he joined C Company of the First Battalion in 1918 [it was actually 1917 — Author], later transferring to H Company. All of us older Volunteers loved the boy, for he was gay and enthusiastic, yet very serious in his devotion to the cause, and in his rigid attention to orders.
>
> It was Kevin Barry who, in a moment of doubt, stepped forward and led the section into the building. Had it not been for his action in steadying one of the officers leading the rush, the work of all the other men might have gone for nothing.
>
> When the guardroom had been entered, the work of carrying away the arms and ammunition was done at top speed. I have a picture in my mind of Kevin Barry coming out of the guardroom with a Lewis gun hugged in his arms. His boyish face was wreathed in smiles, as he said to me: 'Look, Dinny, what I have got'. I could not help laughing, even in the excitement of the moment, and thinking that he looked like a child clasping a new toy to his breast.

While the men were at work, a cover party under Seán Prendergast, acting officer commanding C Company of the First Battalion, stood by in Henrietta Street. Section commander Paddy Kirk led another group who formed a protective cordon across the street until everyone had got away.

About twenty-five rifles, two Lewis guns, a large quantity of ammunition and other military equipment were captured and taken away in cars, the whole operation taking a minute or so less than the seven minutes allotted to it. No one was hurt and Kevin and his friend Frank Flood took a bayonet each as a souvenir.

The importance of this raid lay not only in its haul of useful guns, but in the huge boost it gave to the morale of the Volunteers in Dublin. They had demonstrated that they could with impunity snatch valuable weapons from a mighty building that lay at the core of the British administration of the country, and that they could treat prisoners magnanimously even if they wore the uniform of an army of occupation.

Soon after the King's Inns raid Kevin would have set off for Tombeagh and the summer holidays. During the summers of 1919 and 1920, he and Patrick O'Gorman (Pat Gorman) from Hacketstown, would 'knock around together'. The first time Pat ever heard the song *Come Back Paddy Reilly to Ballyjamesduff* was when Kevin sang it. 'He had a crowd of songs like *Tullynahaw*, "Giving a taste of ordher and law/To man and to baste in Tullynahaw". There were more songs about cattle driving, and *Finnegan's Ball* was another. He was the heart of a party. His brother Mick used often sing *Róisin Dubh*.'[2]

Kevin helped Mick out on the farm during these summer trips. According to Pat Gorman he was a great worker. Kevin was a stouter build than Mick though not as tall. 'I don't think he knew what fear was', was Pat Gorman's recollection.

Pat had had the distinction of witnessing some of the action in central Dublin on Easter Monday 1916, in company with Kevin Barry's uncle Pat Dowling. At one point they watched the fighting at a corner of O'Connell Street and saw the crowds looting Lawrence's toyshop. They then walked back and saw the rifles being fired from sandbags at Trinity College. They proceeded up Grafton Street to the Green and saw soldiers at the Shelbourne, and on to Jacob's where the women who were in receipt of separation allowances were shaking their fists at the rebels and shouting: 'If yez want to fight, why don't yez get out to Flanders?'

On Saturdays in the summer of 1920, Pat Gorman, Kevin and a few of the other local lads, sometimes including Mick Barry, headed off on bicycles to Glendalough or Glenmalure or other places within striking distance of Tombeagh. They would travel the route over the mountain to Glendalough and sometimes come back the long way through Rathdrum, stopping for a drink at the Woodenbridge Hotel, one of the oldest hotels in Ireland, where Eamon de Valera spent his honeymoon in 1910. Pat Gorman recalled one occasion when they were sitting drinking at a table outside the hotel, tired after the journey and with still more cycling to do before getting home. They could see a train standing at Woodenbridge station below them and Mick Barry suggested that they could get a lift in the train and cut off a good piece of the journey home. Pat Gorman volunteered to go down and talk to the driver.

So I went down anyway and oul' Jim Hayes was driving the loco. I knew him and I asked him when he'd be going. 'Ah', he said, 'I'm supposed to go now when this Dublin train passes, but you don't mind that. I see you're having a drink. Go up and finish your drink. I'll hold on till yez come down. I won't stir.' So we put the bikes in the guard's van and were carried back to Tinahely. We didn't pay either . . .

Another stopping off point was Richardson's Hotel, beside the lake at Glendalough. They preferred this to the Royal Hotel which was always full of people from Dublin and, besides, Pat Gorman was a friend of Paddy Richardson at the time. Bottles of ale were the order of the day on their expeditions although it is clear from Pat Gorman's recollections that sometimes they were not quite sure what they were drinking. There is a story told that one of their companions from Coolmana, near Tombeagh, was a week late for his dinner after one of these episodes.

Kevin wrote to Bapty Maher late that summer about one of their exploits.[3]

It was a bloody pity you didn't come yesterday. We had a good day. So good a day that my ruddy head is singing like a top and my eyes are all bloodshot. I got rid of Mike and spent the day with Gorman, but I'll never touch a drop again as long as I live. We stopped in Tinahely, Aughrim, Woodenbridge, Avoca, Rathdrum and Laragh going, and ditto coming back. I wasn't in the Bed or anywhere else. I was lying on a sofa in the Royal Hotel [Glendalough] with a Belgian girl drinking. We held up the car for 1½ hours while they were looking for us and we made them stop in Rathdrum 1 hour, Woodenbridge ½ hour and Aughrim 1½ hours, so it was 1.30 before we got into Hacketstown. We had to lift Gorman out of the car and carry him home. He was absolutely rotto. I fell off the bike twice on the way home and I was up all night drinking water.

Damn booze anyway.

Now I've gassed enough about myself but it's a pity you were not there. Scully [his friend Peg Scully] says I made a speech about Medicals and Gorman made one about Clerical Students but I'm f———d if I remember. Hoping to get a prompt reply to this and see you soon. Yours till I'm qualified.

K.G.B.

He wrote about the same binge to his kinsman and school companion Leo Doyle in early September 1920.[4] Leo had played rugby with Kevin in Belvedere and was to die tragically of peritonitis at twenty-two.

Leo old son . . . Yes, I did see you and Father Dunne* in Hacketstown but as I was drilling a company of rebels I didn't like to speak to you as Father Matt might not be pleased.

---

*Father Matthew Dunne was a family friend of the Doyles and the Barrys. He was a chaplain in the British Army, which explains Kevin's reluctance to greet him in the circumstances.

We had a great day in Glendalough altho' neither of the Deerings came — hell roast 'em. Luke McDonnell came and enjoyed himself. Gorman and I were together all day, become inebriated and generally disgraced and enjoyed ourselves. We had to lift Gorman out of the car. I met Barry O'Brien in Glendalough and Furlong at Woodenbridge. I also met two university girls, but there was a dud crowd down from Dublin.

I had a letter from Charlie Crean* today. He seems to to be enjoying himself. I suppose you are hard at work again lucky dog (???). Damn the man who invented work. He was a —— etc. I'll be up in town in about a week and I'll see you some evening outside the old College . . .

There's hell around here: 30 houses raided, 2 men arrested, 1 wounded and about 40 men 'sleeping out'. There are 6 more arrested in Baltinglass and 30 more lorries have arrived in the Union from the Curragh. So we're going to have some excitement please God . . .

Yours till I'm qualified (ad saecula saeculorum)
Kevin

Clearly, from the last paragraph in his letter, the British military net was closing tightly around Tombeagh in the late summer of 1920. Kevin's activities with the local Volunteers were a contributory factor. During the summer of 1920 he was attached to C Company of the Third Battalion, Carlow Brigade, under Matt Cullen of Vermount, Hacketstown. He had been attached to the same Company the previous summer. Cullen was chairman of Baltinglass No. 2 Rural District Council and considerably older than Kevin, whom he regarded as a very serious youth, more politically-minded than he was. Cullen farmed at Kilcarney and during the Civil War became an officer in the Free State Army.[5]

Earlier that summer, when a plan to capture the barracks in Hacketstown was mooted in C Company, Matt Cullen and Dan McDonnell went to Dublin to discuss the project with

---

*Father Charles Crean, a contemporary of Kevin's at Belvedere, was also on the Senior Cup Team with him. He became a priest in the Archdiocese of Dublin and at one time ministered in Donnybrook parish.

Headquarters and the Active Service Unit (ASU). The men they dealt with were Mick McDonnell, one of Collins' 'Twelve Apostles' or assassination squad, and Tom Kehoe.

Kehoe was a local man well known to them as the hero of many actions in the War of Independence. He later took part in the attempt on Lord French's life at Ashtown, Co. Dublin, and the unsuccessful attempt to rescue Seán MacEoin from Mountjoy Jail. He took the Treaty side in the Civil War. He was a colonel-commandant in the Free State Army when he was killed by a booby-trap on the bridge at Carrigaphoca, near Macroom, in September 1922. He is buried in a splendid mausoleum of limestone, marble and bronze in Knockananna near Hacketstown.

The ASU was quite happy that the barracks be taken — provided C Company would pay the cost. But C Company had no money, so they approached a travelling repertory company playing in the town to give one night for the benefit of the Volunteers. The actors were delighted to do so, and the show was so well advertised that the house was full. The audience little knew they were subscribing to fund an attack on the barracks.

'We appointed Kevin Barry to get up on the stage', says Matt Cullen. 'He made a very appropriate speech on our behalf and his own, thanking the show people for their kindness in giving us the night and for their performance, and thanking the people for attending in such numbers.'

Before the Volunteers could plan the attack, the barracks was evacuated, and the same night C Company burned it. It was one of the first to be destroyed. Later GHQ ordered the burning of all evacuated barracks.

Aughavanagh, a remote part of the Avondale estate that came to Charles Stewart Parnell on the death of his father, was the scene of the next action carried out by C Company while Kevin Barry was attached to it.

Aughavanagh was one of the military barracks built in 1802 to capture Michael Dwyer.* It was a gaunt, huge, rough-stone

---

*Michael Dwyer was one of the most remarkable of the United Irishmen. A Wicklow man, he was an uncle of Ann Devlin, the storied servant of

building meant to house 100 redcoats, and it was used by Parnell as a much-loved hunting lodge and mountain retreat where he was always at his happiest and most relaxed. When the Avondale estate was sold following the death of Parnell, Aughavanagh eventually came into the possession of John Redmond. Redmond not only paid over the odds for the house, but spent a lot of money making it into a comfortable home. While he led the Parnell wing of the Irish Party and, after 1900, the reunited party, he spent his leisure time in Co. Wicklow. For John Redmond, Aughavanagh was really part of his inheritance from the Chief. It became his exclusive home in Ireland, his real retreat and resting place. The active hours of his life were spent in an alien capital, and he needed Aughavanagh as a pulse through which he could know Ireland intimately. 'It was', says the writer Stephen Gwynn in his book *John Redmond's Last Years*, 'most simple, most hospitable, most unconventional and most remote.'

In July 1920, Aughavanagh was occupied by John Redmond's son, William, MP for Waterford and also by his sister Johanna and her husband Max Sullivan Greene. Green was chairman of the General Prisons Board based in Dublin Castle. (He was shot and killed by a bank robber whom he tried to catch in St. Stephen's Green, Dublin, in March 1922).

Word had reached C Company that Aughavanagh was to be occupied by the British Army and soon afterwards they received orders from GHQ to burn the house down.

Robert Emmet. Born in 1771, he was educated privately. His fame lies in the fact that after the defeat of the Rebellion of 1798 he took to the hills for five years and was pursued so relentlessly that the Military Road from Rathfarnham to the Glen of Imaal was built in 1801 and 1802 to make access easier for the redcoats. When the road system was complete, barracks were built at Glencree above Enniskerry; Laragh (Sevenchurch); Aughavanagh; Glenmalure (Drumgoff), and Leitrim in the Glen of Imaal. These barracks were to hold a field officer and, except at the Glen of Imaal, 100 men. Imaal was to hold 200. A bounty of £1,000 was offered for the head of Michael Dwyer and £250 for those of Hugh Byrne, Martin Bourke and Samuel McAllister. In the end, Dwyer surrendered voluntarily, was transported to Botany Bay and ended his days in 1825.

One wet night (Cullen recalls) fourteen members of C Company cycled to Aughavanagh, including Mick McDonnell of the Active Service Unit, Michael and Kevin Barry, and myself. When we arrived there every place was barred, but in the back there was a door with a small pane of glass in it; it was broken and Kevin Barry got in through it, head first.

Inside he found Captain Redmond with a large club raised to strike him, but the sight of Kevin's automatic vanished the pluck of the Captain. As soon as he got his speech he enquired our business.

Mick McDonnell informed him we were going to burn the barracks: he lost his speech again. By this time a female came on the scene, giving out plenty of abuse at the thought of the dirty Irish attempting to interfere with the residence of the late leader of the Irish people.

We soon calmed this hysterical woman. All occupants were ordered to pack up. The Captain asked us to go through the place and see the loss; pictures and valuable papers etc. He denied knowledge of the military coming, said that he was an MP attending the British Parliament, and assured us that he would have a very serious row there if such a thing were thought of.

The Volunteers withdrew from the Captain to have a consultation and decided not to burn the house after all, but to hold Captain Redmond responsible that if the barracks were occupied by the British troops he, Captain Redmond, would be shot. The terms were conveyed to him and the Volunteers withdrew.

In fact, Aughavanagh was occupied by Auxiliaries less than a year later without any harm coming to Captain Redmond. Happily, it now serves as a very popular youth hostel for students from all over the world.

On the way home, the weather cleared and the tired band of Volunteers sat down to rest at a hilly place called Ballygobbin. Michael Barry later recalled that Kevin stood up, looked around him at the surrounding mountains bathed in moonlight, and exclaimed: 'God, wouldn't this make you feel the country was worth living for — and dying for!'

The state of the country in July 1920 was not troubled enough to prevent English tourists from spending their holidays in Ireland. Although British troops were everywhere to be seen, more of the King's soldiers were being killed in Mesopotamia, where the Shia tribesmen were resisting inclusion in the new British Mandate of Iraq, than in Ireland. At the end of the summer, a C Company excursion to Glendalough was organised using two charabancs, long open motor vehicles with rows of transverse seats. It was Sunday, 30 August, and as Matt Cullen says, 'it was to be our last enjoyable day.'

Two nights later a general parade was called and all members were ordered to be on parade next morning at ten o'clock to collect arms from the people in the area. This parade was held on the football field in Hacketstown. That night Michael and Kevin Barry, Mike McDonald and Matt Cullen drove out in Michael's pony and trap to the New Line to cut the telephone poles. Next morning, the Company gathered to raid Jones's of Woodside, below Eagle Hill, for arms. They got some guns; then they went to the Church of Ireland rectory, where they surrounded the Rev. Charles Stuart Stamford Ellison's house. Matt Cullen later recalled the episode.

> Kevin Barry, Mike McDonald and myself went up to the hall door. We were refused admittance, demanded that the door be opened, and then saw the minister let down the window and fire from a shotgun point blank range at us. No one was injured but some of our men got a fright.
>
> We were now prepared to reply, Kevin with an automatic, Mike Mac and myself with revolvers through the window. We got back to get cover, and he kept firing out and we kept firing in for some time.
>
> We could not afford to waste ammunition as he would not give in unless we shot him. This we did not like to do without getting authority. We received orders that night to take the gun by all means. We decided not to go near the minister that night but to take him unawares. But the military took the gun that night.

The party then raided the post-car going out of the town

expecting to intercept police reports of what C Company had been up to. Kevin and Matt inspected the letters but found nothing of importance. Despite that, it was clear the net was tightening on C Company and the officers decided to go on the run. 'It was then', says Matt Cullen, 'that I got more acquainted with Kevin Barry. We were very welcome at his house in Tombeagh and many a night we stayed there'.

Shortly afterwards the Third Battalion, Carlow Brigade, was reorganised. W.P. O'Donoghue of Clonmore became commandant. He had taken part in the 1916 Rising and had been a prisoner in Frongoch Camp in Wales, where he was the only Carlow man in that 'University of Revolution'. Matt Cullen was appointed vice-commandant, Michael Barry quartermaster and Mike McDonald adjutant.

Home life in Tombeagh at this time was quite different for Kevin from life in Dublin. There was no motor-car and no electricity and old Mrs. Dowling, Kevin's grandmother, was in declining health. She lived in a little room upstairs and rarely came down. Every night she would get up and wander about with a candle inquiring 'Where's Jimmy? The boy's not home yet.' Jimmy, her son, was nearly forty-five at the time. However, apart from these inconveniences life during the summer was good. There were frequent parties and sing-songs in the Barry home attended by large gatherings of local friends, including Pat Gorman and his cousin Peg Scully who motored over from Hacketstown. In an essay in Belvedere on 'The best way to pass the Summer Holidays', Kevin had ended his piece, 'I am not going to the seaside this year but I am going down to the country which is right enough but it is a bit dull'. As he got a little older he had changed his mind.

Before he left Tombeagh to return to Dublin in September 1920, Kevin cycled the ten miles from home to Tuckmill to see Leo Doyle's cousins. (They were also *his* cousins.) When Mary Doyle opened the door, Kevin said: 'You don't know me, Mrs. Doyle, but I know you. I am Kevin Barry of Tombeagh'.[6]

Mr. and Mrs. Doyle lived with their six children in a cross-roads shop in Tuckmill and James Doyle worked as local correspondent for the *Leinster Leader* and the *Freeman's Journal*.

'Mother thought an awful lot of Kevin, the manly way he introduced himself', Bridget and Joseph Doyle recall. Joe was five years old that summer, and Bridget was not much more. They had a black pony who had just foaled and Joe used to ask every cousin who called – the Deerings, the Keatleys, the Doyles from Dublin: 'Did you see the foal?'

The children got over the wall with Kevin and went up the field. By the time they had seen pony and foal, Joe and Bridget were fast friends with Kevin.

'I stayed in Tombeagh the night before Kevin left for Dublin for the last time in September 1920', Matt Cullen recalls. 'When we got up that morning we played some hurling. He left that evening on the train from Rathvilly, and events worked quickly after that.'

Kevin at two-and-a-half

Altar-boy

From left standing, Michael Barry, Christy Byrne of the Hill, Kevin. Seated, Dan and John Deering of Knockavagh

Top from left, Shel, Mike, Kev, Kathy. Bottom from left, Monty, Mrs. Barry, Peggy, Elgin

Tombeagh

8 Tans and Auxies

The British Government rearranged its Irish administration early in 1920. Sir Hamar Greenwood, MP, became Chief Secretary with a seat in the Cabinet. Major-General H.H. Tudor replaced Sir Joseph Byrne at the head of the Royal Irish Constabulary.

Among the other changes in what was almost a clean sweep was the replacement of General Sir Frederick Shaw as General Officer Commanding the Forces in Ireland by General Sir Nevil Macready, Commissioner of the Metropolitan Police in London.

Macready was the man who in effect signed Kevin Barry's death warrant. He was the son of William Charles Macready, the famous Scottish actor-manager; had changed in 1916 the rule making moustaches compulsory for officers, and became a general only in 1918. His new post, for which he was recommended by Lord French, was the source of behind-the-scenes controversy in Whitehall because of the very high price which he demanded for his services in Ireland.[1]

General Shaw's total emoluments had been £4,342 pay and allowances (in money or kind); table money (not liable to income tax) of £1,100, and horses and forage. The GOC Ireland was also Master of the Royal Hospital, Kilmainham, and was allowed £100 for the upkeep of the gardens.

Macready's demands were three: table money of £1,500; special pension rights; and disturbance money of £5,000. 'Unless the Government are prepared to meet me in this, it will be quite impossible for me to keep my head financially above water . . .', he said.

The Prime Minister, Lloyd George, and the Lord Privy Seal,

Andrew Bonar Law, agreed; but the Chancellor of the Exchequer, Austen Chamberlain, did not approve of paying lump sums to officers to undertake dangerous and arduous duties, and Winston Churchill at the War Office said the payment could not come out of *his* budget but would have to be 'a matter of high policy'.

Macready had his answer ready. He was not a serving officer being posted to another appointment. He was going from a *civil* office to a military appointment. In the end he won all his demands, the Secretary of State for War reporting to King George V: 'Mr. Churchill with his humble duty to Your Majesty has thought it proper to offer the Command-in-Chief of Ireland to Sir Neville (*sic*) Macready, who he believes will be willing to undertake this most critical and difficult task . . .'.

This kind of thrashing about in the bath-tub, while intrinsically trivial enough, reveals the kind of constant turmoil at all levels in which the British Government was finding itself in relation to Ireland. Home Rule, reprisals and repression — these policies were being canvassed at the same time at Lloyd George's Cabinet table, where the Secretary to the Cabinet, Sir Maurice Hankey, had been converted to the view that terror must be met by greater terror.

Perhaps the truth was that Sir Henry Wilson* was the real Government of Ireland at the time. Now a field marshal and Chief of the Imperial General Staff, Wilson told Lloyd George in September 1920, that if there had to be murder, the Govern-

---

*Field Marshal Sir Henry Wilson (1864-1922) was born in Currygrane, Co. Longford, educated at Marlborough, and failed to get into Woolwich or Sandhurst. He was commissioned into the 6th Battalion Rifle Brigade of the Longford Militia, served in the Royal Irish Brigade and saw action in the Boer War. At Army Headquarters in 1914, he supported the British officers in the Curragh Mutiny, and was a staunch supporter of the Orange Order and the Unionist opposition to Home Rule. After the 1916 Rising, Wilson, 'ever the moderate', as O'Halpin says in his book, *The Decline of the Union*, 'advised General Maxwell to court-martial and then shoot' Birrell, the disgraced Chief Secretary. Wilson was publicly accused of threatening to resign if Kevin Barry was not hanged: the evidence, as will be seen, does not sustain the accusation. He became adviser on security to the new Northern Ireland Government, and was assassinated on the steps of 36 Eaton Place, London, in June 1922.

ment should do the murdering. They were discussing author-
ised reprisals and the Prime Minister danced up and down with
rage at Wilson's frankness and said that 'no Government could
possibly take this responsibility'.[2]

The Restoration of Order in Ireland Act of August, which
had a stormy passage through the House of Commons, already
gave the military authorities extraordinary powers, including
the power to intern anyone, without charge or trial, for an
indefinite period; the power to try any prisoner by court-
martial and without legal advice, except in cases requiring the
death penalty; and the suppression of coroner's inquests. The
new Act gave the Black and Tans* the opportunity, in Churchill's phrase, of 'striking down in the darkness those who
struck from the darkness'.

Three days after the Act came into force, Terence Mac-
Swiney, the Lord Mayor of Cork, was arrested while presiding
over a meeting in the City Hall. He went on hunger strike
immediately, was moved to London and lodged in Brixton
Prison. Eleven others were held in Cork Jail.

The struggle took on international dimensions. Already the
French and Italian Socialists had shown their solidarity with
the Irish people. At the second congress of the Communist
International, at which Ireland was represented by Roddy
Connolly, Grigori Zinoviev, the president, made a statement

---

*The Black and Tans were English recruits to the Royal Irish Constabu-
lary. Their name derived from the shortage of dark green uniforms,
which meant the recruits were issued with a strange medley of khaki and
green. They first arrived in March 1920, selected, in Churchill's tongue-
in-cheek words, 'from a great press of applicants on account of their
intelligence, their characters and their records in the war'. Their pay was
a handsome 10s. a day. They had no training in guerrilla warfare, but
were soon, with the regular RIC, supplied with rifles and machine-guns,
fortified barracks and new transport by their new chief, General Tudor.
By the end of May 1920, 351 evacuated barracks had been destroyed
and 105 damaged by the IRA. Fifteen occupied barracks were ruined,
and 25 damaged, and over 500 RIC men resigned in June and July 1920;
but the flow of recruits from England more than compensated for the
loss. By the time Kevin Barry was arrested, 2,000 Black and Tans had
reinforced the 8,000 members of the RIC and Gormanston had become
the Black and Tan depot.

favourable to Ireland. At the 1920 conference of the Irish Trade Union Congress, Shapurji Saklatvala brought greetings from India, and Emmanuel Shinwell read the British TUC's resolution in favour of self-determination for Ireland.[3]

In America, Éamon de Valera had gone to the land of his birth to seek recognition of the Irish Republic, to float an external loan, and to convince the American people that the US, under the Covenant of the League of Nations, 'was not pledging itself to maintain Ireland as an integral part of British territory', as he told Congress in 1964. His personal charisma and his coast-to-coast appearances proved an effective answer to British propaganda, but dissension in the ranks of Irish Americans was caused by personality clashes with Judge Cohalan and with John Devoy, the outspoken Fenian and Clan na Gael leader. The difficulties were compounded by divided loyalties, among the Irish-American leadership, to the candidates in the then forthcoming Presidential election in which Governor James M. Cox carried the Democratic colours and Warren G. Harding was the Republican choice.

Harding was elected the day after Kevin Barry was hanged. American sympathy for the Irish cause, already widespread, was deeply moved by the events of the autumn of 1920 – the deaths of MacSwiney and his comrades, the hanging of Barry, the sack of Balbriggan and the carnage of Bloody Sunday at Croke Park. Relief and help were sent in generous amounts and moral support was provided by the American Commission of Inquiry. But in de Valera's main objective – recognition of the sovereign Irish Republic – he met with no success.

As MacSwiney's condition worsened, the Cardinal Secretary of State in the Vatican reported that 300,000 Brazilian Catholics had demanded the Pope's intervention on his behalf. In a French newspaper appeared a headline: *Bravo, l'Irlande heroique: bravo le Lord Mayor de Cork*, and a German contemporary compared him with the legendary Swiss hero, Arnold von Winkelried, who sacrificed himself for his people.

At home, the escalation of violence produced a curious phenomenon as described by Bennett in his book, *The Black and Tans.*[4] 'The Bleeding Statues of Templemore', or 'the Templemore Miracle' began when a young man named Jimmy

Walsh saw the statues and holy pictures in a newsagent's house begin to bleed. Templemore, which had only a few days earlier been subjected to a Black and Tan attack during which the town hall, the markethouse and the Urban District Council offices were set on fire, became overnight a place of pilgrimage.

'A wave of adventist exultation swept the countryside', says Bennett.

> The roads to the town were blocked with farm carts, ass carts, outside cars, Fords and bicycles. Such traffic had never been seen, even for the races. Pilgrims slept in the streets and wretches past help were dragged to the newsagent's shop in the hope of a miraculous cure. An old soldier who had been shot through the right knee at the battle of the Somme, regained the use of his leg. A harness maker was relieved of his sciatica and a girl, in the last stages of consumption, rose from her stretcher and walked. Or so it was said.

This outbreak of mass hysteria touched far-off Rathvilly close to the Barry homeland, where Tom Abbey drove a full hackney car of pilgrims to Templemore twice a day.

Meanwhile the IRA was urging its members to keep up the pressure on the enemy: 'His strongholds must be attacked, his forces surprised and disarmed, his communication interrupted, his despatches seized, his activities watched, his machinery interfered with, his supplies cut off in every part of the country with such persistence, speed and ubiquity that he will not be able to get his "system" established anywhere', *An t-Óglach* exhorted.

'Flying columns' and active service units were fashioned from the hundreds of Volunteers already on the run, and action was moved from centres already at war to quiet parts of the country. The British response to this development was to form the Auxiliary Division of the RIC, a force which was to play a notorious part in the drama of the next twelve months. Recruited in London, the 'Auxies' were ex-officers with good war records. They enrolled as temporary cadets, held the rank of sergeant in the RIC, and were paid £1 a day with allowances. Jobs were scarce; these men had no calling but to arms, and they took to the mercenary's life as if it were a gift from God.

The first 500 Auxiliaries arrived at the North Wall, Dublin, at the end of July 1920. They got an abbreviated six-week police training at the Curragh, during which it was wrongly assumed that they were knowledgeable about lorries and armoured cars.

They wore large Tam O'Shanter berets with the crowned harp badge of the RIC. Their tunics, breeches and puttees at first were khaki, and they wore a bandolier across the chest, a belt with a bayonet and scabbard, and an open holster for a revolver on the right thigh, all of black leather. They were organised into companies of one hundred and sent as special units to areas of IRA activity. Kilkenny, Cork and Galway got the benefit of the first Auxiliary companies.

Brigadier-General Frank Percy Crozier*, who had trained the Ulster Volunteer Force before the war, came home from service with the Polish Army against the Red Army to command the Auxiliaries. Crozier is variously described as a reformed alcoholic, an Orange firebrand, and a volatile and excitable Irish officer. At any rate, he resigned in disgust in February 1921, having met and admired Kevin Barry in Mountjoy, as we shall see.

In September 1920, when the British Army's strength was just under 40,000, the RIC including the Black and Tans numbered 10,002, the Auxiliary Division 591 and the Dublin Metropolitan Police 1,141. The security forces, as we could call them today, were thus comprised of 50,000 men.

Against this accretion of armed might, the insurgents evolved

---

*General Crozier (1879-1937) was educated at Wellington College, served in the Boer War and retired in 1908. After working with the UVF, he was commissioned in the Irish Fusiliers and ended the Great War as GOC the 40th Division in France. He fought in the Lithuanian and Polish armies against Russia (1919-1920). As Commander of the Auxiliary Police, he served under General Tudor, who in November 1920, ordered him not to dismiss Auxiliaries for indiscipline. After incidents of destruction and death perpetrated by Auxiliaries, he resigned. 'I never could understand why Tudor took him on', said General Macready. Between 1930 and 1937, Crozier published six books including *The Men I Killed*, (1937).

a methodology that culminated in the perfection of the ambush. Although far from every ambush was a success, the troops and police using the roads felt, and were, constantly menaced. The Volunteers displayed a new skill and patience in the mounting of these attacks, and their discipline was able to accept the risks attendant on long waits in distinctly uncomfortable places until a suitable target appeared.

Near Rineen, on the road between Ennistymon and Miltown Malbay, Co. Clare, the first of these well-prepared ambushes took place on 20 September. A police tender was attacked and a District Inspector was killed.

Nearly 200 miles away, an RIC Head Constable due for promotion to District Inspector was killed in Balbriggan, Co. Dublin. And in the city itself on the same day, the raid for arms in which Kevin Barry was arrested cost the British Army the lives of three soldiers. 'The coincidence of these three attacks', says Townshend, in his book *The British Campaign in Ireland*, 'was remarkable, and their consequences were, in the favourite adjective of the Irish press, sensational'.

In Balbriggan on the night of the constable's death, police broke into, looted and burned four public houses, and burned or damaged forty-nine houses and a hosiery factory. Two 'reputed Sinn Feiners' were killed, reportedly by bayonet, but the Balbriggan reprisal was quite outdone in savagery next day in Clare, when the RIC found the results of the Rineen ambush. In Ennistymon, Lahinch and Miltown, twenty-six buildings including Lahinch Town Hall were burned. Among the four people killed was a boy who was helping to put out the fires.

Three days later, Sir Henry Wilson noted in his diary: 'At Balbriggan, Thurles and Galway yesterday the local police marked down certain SFs as in their opinion the actual murderers or instigators and then coolly went and shot them without question or trial. Winston saw very little harm in this but it horrifies me.'[5]

Courts-martial were a feature of daily life. General Macready reported to the Irish Situation Committee of the British Cabinet on 26 September that thirty-one people had been tried by court-martial in the preceding week. Sixteen had been found

77

guilty of having arms, ammunition or documents. Sentences handed down ranged from two years' hard labour to a £2 fine.

In succeeding weeks, 72 were court-martialled and 47 convicted; 78 court-martialled and 71 convicted, and 44 court-martialled and 36 convicted. In the next situation report, No. 48, the number of courts-martial was down to 24, with 11 convictions, and General Macready commented: 'I am . . . of the opinion that under the surface the situation is developing against the extremists'.

His complacency was shortly to be shattered.

9 The Best-Laid Plan

A report that a Lancashire Fusilier in the North Dublin Union had smuggled out two rifles was the genesis of the Volunteers' raid on the British Army lorry at Monks' Bakery in Church Street on 20 September, 1920.

John Joe Carroll,[1] a member of H Company who had taken part in the successful raid on the King's Inns, went with another Volunteer, James Douglas of C Company, to North Brunswick Street. They had an appointment to meet a civilian go-between and arrange to buy the rifles.

Their business done, they fixed a meeting with the intermediary for the next day in a public house in Dominick Street. In the meanwhile, they told the OC of H Company, Captain Séamus Kavanagh, what they had been doing, and got his approval. The end result was that they bought only one rifle, a Canadian Ross with aperture sights, for £1.

But while they waited in North Brunswick Street, they noticed an army lorry with troops which had pulled up outside Monks' Bakery at 79-80 Old Church Street. They saw two NCOs and about eight armed privates and they watched carefully as the NCOs entered the bakery yard. For two or three days, John Joe Carroll and James Douglas returned and watched the lorry arrive to collect the bread ration at about eleven o'clock. John Joe later inspected the yard and saw that the clerical staff, Mr. Molloy and Miss Byrne, were housed on the left with a telephone (Dublin 1084) just inside the office of Mr. Feely the manager. There was a door opposite, leading down a corridor to a retail bread shop in 38 North King Street. John Joe noted that this would offer a useful retreat route. He drew a rough sketch of the position of the lorry and the layout of the yard.

Captain Kavanagh was attracted by the prospect of disarming the troops and burning the lorry. But Church Street was outside H Company's area and he had to seek permission to go ahead.

Twenty-four men were selected to take part in the raid, and two to man the van that hopefully would carry off the captured arms.[2] Two of the Volunteers, James Douglas and Tom Kissane, were not members of H Company. Douglas was a C Company man and Kissane was a member of the Active Service Unit. Kissane, who was a brother of Dr. Edward Kissane, later President of St. Patrick's College, Maynooth, was a medical student at UCD who had dropped out to become a full-time paid member of the ASU. He had red hair and gold-rimmed spectacles and shared lodgings at 11 Great Denmark Street with Captain Kavanagh, Michael Knightly,* and Joe Griffin, then an IRA intelligence officer.

Kevin Barry had come back from Carlow some days previously to repeat his examinations and decided to stay at his Uncle Pat's house on the South Circular Road in case Fleet Street was raided. But he came home for a meal now and then and was there for dinner on Sunday 19 September, the day before the raid.

Mrs. Barry remembers that she and Kathy were going out to visit the Dixons in Sandycove on that Sunday evening. When they left, Kevin was joking with Kate Kinsella and singing *The South Down Militia*, a popular song by Peadar Kearney who wrote the National Anthem.

---

*Michael Knightly of Tralee was then a reporter. He had fought in the GPO in 1916 and was imprisoned in Frongoch. He was arrested in a raid on No. 11 Great Denmark Street and was in Mountjoy when Kevin Barry was preparing for his death. In October 1921, he was one of the staff of bodyguards, couriers and secretaries that accompanied Michael Collins to London for the Treaty negotiations. Among them were Ned Broy, Emmet Dalton, Seán MacBride, Erskine Childers and the enigmatic John Chartres. A former editor of Dáil Debates, Michael Knightly acted as official censor of newspapers during the Emergency (1939-1945).

You may talk about your King's Guards,
Scots Guards an' a',
Your Black and Tans and Kilties
An' the fighting forty-twa
Also our brave Auxiliaries --
A most ferocious band --
But the South Down Militia
Is the terrors of the land.

As soon as he had arrived back in Dublin from Tombeagh Kevin had heard of the plan to attack the bread-ration lorry. He had an examination at two o'clock on the appointed day, but as the raid was timed for eleven in the morning he reckoned he would have plenty of time for both events, and he so convinced his commanding officer.

Séamus Kavanagh gave him permission and also, since Kevin had left his own .45 revolver in Tombeagh, arranged with Tommy O'Brien, the company quartermaster, to issue him with a .38 Mauser Parabellum on the morning of the raid.

On Monday, 20 September, 1920, the raiding party assembled at nine o'clock in the O'Flanagan Sinn Féin Club in Ryder's Row, Bolton Street. Séamus Kavanagh and Tom Kissane arrived from 11 Great Denmark Street. Kevin came a little late from church, where he had received Holy Communion. He was bawled out by Captain Kavanagh, who said: 'Well, this is the only gun I have for you'. It was a .38 Mauser automatic pistol made in 1915 and numbered RJR 995 KN2.[3]

The plan was illustrated in detail on a blackboard and positions were allocated. Seán O'Neill, who was second in command, section leader Kevin Barry, and second lieutenant Bob O'Flanagan were to follow the lorry into Upper Church Street and hold up the soldiers. Simultaneously Harry Murphy, Thomas (Tucker) Reilly and Christy Boy Robinson were to close in on the lorry from the Brunswick Street side.

Séamus Kavanagh would join the action from Lenehan's pub across the street accompanied by Frank Flood, Kevin's student friend, Liam Grimley and Mick Robinson, also UCD medical students, and Tommy O'Brien.* Tommy McGrane, a first lieutenant, Frank O'Flanagan, John Joe Carroll, Dave McDonagh and James Douglas were to enter the bakery by the side entrance in North King Street.

Armed with grenades, Paddy Young and Jim Moran were detailed to take up position at the corner of North Brunswick Street to prevent a surprise attack by enemy troops. This was crucial since the Lancashire Fusiliers occupied the North Dublin Union only a couple of hundred yards away and they could be expected to act at once if they heard gunfire.

To avoid interference from troops stationed in the Royal (now Collins) Barracks, Maurice Higgins and Tom Kissane, also carrying grenades, were to wait at the North King Street corner and cover the road to the river. To cover any withdrawal from the north, John P. Kenny, John O'Dwyer, Eugene Fox and Tom Staunton were to take up positions on Constitution Hill.

A van driven by Davy Golden with Jimmy Carrigan as helper would wait in Coleraine Street to pick up the arms.

It was a simple plan. Occupy the bakery, isolate the short stretch of Upper Church Street — fifty-seven yards precisely, as the Royal Engineers' cartographer calculated it later for the court-martial; close in on the lorry and disarm the men on it. It had worked at the King's Inns; it should work again. A whistle blast** would signal the withdrawal and the Volunteers would have added more guns and ammunition to their armoury and dealt another blow to the morale of the enemy.

By ten thirty every man was in place. They arrived from different directions and mingled with the crowd on the street. Some bought newspapers in the nearby shops to pass the time.

The lorry was late. Three times a week it came from Collins-

---

*Liam Grimley and Mick Robinson became medical doctors. Tommy O'Brien later kept the Kevin Barry Memorial Hall and Memorial Committee going, says Kathy Barry.

**Bob O'Flanagan said there was an agreed signal for retreat.[4] Seán O'Neill and Patrick Young did not agree. It is a small point, especially as in the general confusion a whistle blast would have been difficult to hear. But the Barry family believed that there was a pre-arranged signal and that it was not given. Otherwise, they held, Kevin might have got away.

town Camp* where the 2nd Battalion, the Duke of Wellington's Regiment, was stationed; and it was due at eleven o'clock.
This time, as Bob O'Flanagan of Derry recalls, 'we had to mooch
around the neighbourhood for practically an hour'. Some of
them wrapped their newspapers around their revolvers.

Half an hour after eleven, the ration lorry turned the corner
from North King Street and about forty yards on it stopped
just beyond the wide entrance to the bakery. Lance-Sergeant
Archer Banks[5] got out from the seat beside the driver, dropped
the tailboard, and went into the bakery with two unarmed
fatigue men, to see if the bread was ready. Bandsman William
Smith and Bandsman Frank Noble were his ration party.

Seán O'Neill moved to the left as planned; Kevin was in the
centre at the dropped tailboard, and Bob O'Flanagan on the
pavement side.

In the back of the lorry there were then five armed men,
Privates Henry Washington, Matthew Whitehead, G. Dalby,
P. Newton and M. Cleary, all with rifles and fifty rounds. Pri-
vate Thomas Humphries, also armed, was in the front with
Private C. Barnes, the RASC driver.

'They were sitting around the edges of the lorry', Bob
O'Flanagan recalled.[6] 'They had their rifles between their
knees'.

Seán O'Neill reported: 'We ordered them to drop their arms,
and they all did so. But one of them saw that he was not
covered, took up his rifle again and fired – probably only a
warning shot'.

Firing then became general. The window of Clarke's dairy
next door was penetrated by a bullet and Mrs. Clarke moved
a baby in a pram to the safety of the back room. Mrs. Chatham
in a flat on the second storey of No. 114 became weak and
collapsed on the floor.

Bob O'Flanagan had good reason to remember one part of
the action. 'There was one fellow sitting with his back to the
cab. He seized his rifle, raised it and fired. He's the fellow that
got me. The discharge from the rifle set fire to my cap and

---

*Now Dublin Airport.

the bullet took part of my scalp on the right side. We were looking up and they were firing down on us'.[7]

Kevin Barry's gun jammed. He knelt down beside the lorry to free it, then stood and fired again. The Parabellum jammed again on the fifth round and he knelt once more to free it. He was still working at it when he sensed a change in the atmosphere and found that he was alone. He dived under the lorry hoping to get away in the confusion.

In the meanwhile, Sergeant Banks was well down the passage when he heard gunfire. A man facing him fired two shots without hitting him and the sergeant ran into the manager's office where he saw an armed man in a blue serge suit. He struck out at the man and hit him, but got hit in turn with the man's revolver. The man made off and the manager, Mr. Feely, advised Sergeant Banks: 'You stay here. If you go out you'll get shot'. He stayed. Bandsman Noble, who was in the passage, saw three men pointing pistols at the lorry and four or five others had pistols in their hands. One man in the yard fired down the passage and Noble was hit in the ankle. Bandsman Smith was hit in the right elbow.

Private Barnes, the driver, had jumped down to see to his engine when a man approached him and fired a pistol in the air. A number of men then fired and Private Humphries was wounded.

Private Dalby saw four men approach the lorry from the rear. One of them, he told the court-martial later, was the accused, Kevin Barry. They drew pistols and shouted 'Hands up!' and 'Hand over your arms'. 'Without waiting further they opened fire', said Dalby. 'The accused was seen to fire into the lorry in the direction of one of the soldiers, who immediately fell. The guard of the lorry then opened fire and one of the attacking party was shot. Private Washington was then dead in the lorry'.

Private Whitehead was the soldier who, Private Dalby said, had succumbed to a bullet fired by Kevin Barry.

When everything went silent, John Joe Carroll recalled later, 'firing broke out in the yard, with people rushing all over the place, the three of us who were inside decided to make our getaway as quickly as possible.'

In the confusion I had great difficulty in locating the passageway which led to North King Street. Eventually I found the door I was looking for and luckily it was not bolted.

Then I found myself in a long narrow corridor. I ran to the end of this corridor to another which was also un-bolted and found myself in the bread shop in North King Street.

When the girl behind the counter saw me she nearly fainted – none of the customers spoke. I put my gun in my pocket and left the shop and proceeded down North King Street as quickly as I could.

The area was immediately surrounded by several hundred troops and everybody in the vicinity was held up and questioned. When I got as far as Bolton Street, I realised I had left my cap behind. There were no marks of identification on it, so I felt fairly safe. I heard afterwards that when detectives from Dublin Castle arrived at Monks', each employee had to try on the cap in turn, but it evidently did not fit any of them, for no arrests were made among the staff.[8]

Like John Joe Carroll, the other Volunteers did not expect to get out of Church Street alive. How Bob O'Flanagan managed to stay on his feet even he could not explain. Blood poured down the side of his face. He thought his brains were coming out and that he was finished.

I was making my escape and bullets were digging up the street. A hawker in a pony and trap suddenly wheeled into the line of fire out of North King Street. At Church Street Chapel I saw a man with a cab and hailed him. Jimmy Moran ran all the way after me with my cap, which had dropped on the street. He was afraid my name was on it. Part of the scalp was still in the cap.[9]

He went to Jervis Street Hospital and a student doctor poured iodine into the wound and stitched it. When he came out half an hour later, Frank Flood was in the waiting room covering the entrance in case of a British raid for wounded Volunteers.

Later that night a doctor washed and re-stitched the wound. Bob O'Flanagan spent the next two months in hiding recovering from his head wound.

He did not see Kevin ducking under the lorry. 'You saw nobody only the fellow over you with the rifle. But the .38 ammunition was always a bloody nuisance; it was always jamming'.

The general confusion and disorder meant that shooting was erratic particularly on the part of the surprised British soldiers. Casualties among the Volunteers were consequently not as heavy as they might have been. Apart from Bob O'Flanagan's head wound, Seán O'Neill and Harry Murphy were hit and wounded but not severely.

That night the H Company men returned to the Church Street area to patrol it and protect the people from reprisals. But Father Albert* emerged from the Capuchin Friary and appealed to them to go home. There would be no reprisals, he said. And there were none.

The British suffered devastating casualties. Private Washington was killed outright, shot through the mouth and throat. Private Humphries died later of abdominal wounds, and Private Whitehead also received fatal injuries. The three were

---

*Father Albert Bibby was born in Kilkenny in 1877. He entered the Capuchin Order at Rochestown, Co. Cork, and was ordained in Church Street Friary, Dublin, in 1902. A graduate, he taught philosophy and theology there. He spent years in Church Street, loved and respected by the poor. He was a member of the Columcille branch of the Gaelic League and visited the Gaeltacht several times. During the 1916 Rising the Capuchins were active in Commandant Edward Daly's area and one of them carried the surrender order from Patrick Pearse. They brought consolation to the wounded and dying and then ministered to the leaders about to be shot. Arrested in 1920 by the Black and Tans, Father Albert was taken to Dublin Castle. Later, in Mountjoy, he visited Kevin Barry, and when the Civil War began, he and Father Dominic O'Connor were in the Four Courts, where he gave general absolution to the garrison. The two priests also ministered to the men in the Hammam Hotel under Cathal Brugha. For their Republican sympathies, Albert and Dominic were exiled to the United States in 1924. Albert died in Santa Barbara, California, in 1925. In 1958, their remains were returned to Ireland. The President and the Taoiseach greeted them and followed in procession to Rochestown, where they were reinterred.

taken first to the North Dublin Union nearby and then, with Whitehead in a deep coma and Humphries in an agony of pain, to King George V Hospital (now St. Bricin's) near the Royal Barracks. It was 12.30 p.m.

A telephone message was sent at once from Dublin District of the British Army to General Macready in General Head-quarters, Ireland, Parkgate. The transcript, made almost certainly by Colonel H. Warburton for General Macready, reads:

> Six armed civilians attempted to hold up a party of the Duke of Wellington's Regiment entering the North Dublin Union Bakery this morning between 11.30 and 11.45 am. The civilians opened fire killing one soldier and badly wounding two others. The picquet of the Lancashire Fusiliers turned out and captured one civilian who was armed with a revolver. The remainder of the civilians had scattered.

The telephone clerk added a scribbled note: 'Dublin District are making further enquiries'.

General Macready's mind was made up at once. He wrote clearly on the text of the telephone message a succinct note to Lieutenant-Colonel H. Toppin, Assistant Adjutant-General, Dublin District Headquarters. He initialled and dated it.

'Colonel Toppin', it read. 'Try for murder'.

10 Interrogation

Lance-Sergeant Archer Banks had one foot on the tailgate of the ration lorry, which was about to drive away when an old woman shouted, 'There's a man under the lorry!' She was Mrs. Garrett,[1] mother of two grown girls, and she owned a little coal and vegetable shop on the corner of Church Street and North King Street. It is fairly clear that Bandsman William Smith, who had been wounded, and Sergeant Banks, for whom discretion had proved the better part of valour during the action, saw Kevin at about the same instant as Mrs. Garrett.*

The soldiers climbed down off the lorry and surrounded Kevin. Sergeant Banks arrested him and later deposed that Kevin said: 'We were after the arms — we were told by an officer'. Banks handed Kevin over to the Lancashire Fusiliers, who threw him into the back of the lorry beside the dead soldier, Private Washington, and the two wounded men of the Duke of Wellington's Regiment, Privates Whitehead and Humphries. Two civilians carried Bandsman Noble to the Richmond Hospital, and Bandsman Smith walked there without assistance. The hospital was just inside the Union gates.

As the lorry drove towards the North Dublin Union, the

---

*Kathy Barry states: 'Incidentally, I should mention that some months after his execution we were most distressed to hear that this woman had been driven mad and was in an asylum as a result of the blame attached to her by her neighbours . . .' John Doyle of Ballywaltrim, Bray, was working in Kavanagh's shop beside Lenehan's public house on the day of the affray. He was a customer of Mrs. Garrett's and says that she was quite old and died quite naturally a few years afterwards. He dispels the myths that arose after the event; for example, that the woman who warned the soldiers was later run over by a lorry herself.

Lancashires jabbed at Kevin with their bayonets, but they did him no harm. A few minutes later, he was in the guardroom of the barracks.

Although Kevin Barry's own account of the next few hours was not given until 28 October, it is such a dispassionate record of his interrogation that its proper place is here. It took the form of a sworn affidavit and the circumstances under which it was made will come to light later.

I, Kevin Barry, of 58 South Circular Road in the County of the City of Dublin, Medical Student, aged 18 years and upwards, solemnly and sincerely declare as follows:

(1) On the 20th day of September, 1920, I was arrested in Upper Church Street in the City of Dublin by a sergeant of the 2nd Duke of Wellington's Regiment and was brought under escort to the North Dublin Union, now occupied by the military. I was brought into the guardroom and searched. I was then removed to the defaulters' room by an escort with a sergeant-major. The latter and the escort belong to the 1st Lancashire Fusiliers. I was then handcuffed.

(2) About a quarter of an hour after I was placed in the defaulters' room, two commissioned officers came in. They both belonged to the 1st Lancashire Fusiliers. They were accompanied by three sergeants of the same unit. A military policeman, who had been in the room since I entered it, remained. One of the officers asked my name, which I gave. He then asked for the names of my companions in the raid or attack. I refused to give them. He tried to persuade me to give their names and I persisted in refusing. He then sent the sergeant out of the room for a bayonet. When it was brought in the sergeant was ordered by the same officer to point the bayonet at my stomach. The same questions as to the names and addresses of my companions were repeated with the same result. The sergeant was then asked to turn my face to the wall and point the bayonet at my back. I was so turned. The sergeant then said he would run the bayonet into me if I did not tell. The bayonet was then removed and I was turned round again.

(3) The same officer then said to me that if I persisted in my attitude he would turn me out to the men on the barrack square, and he supposed I knew what that meant with the men in their present temper. I said nothing. He ordered the sergeant to put me face down on the floor and twist my arm. I was pushed down on the floor after my handcuffs were removed by the sergeant who went for the bayonet. When I lay on the floor one of the sergeants knelt on my back, the other two placed one foot each on my back and left shoulder and the man who knelt on me twisted my right arm, holding it by the wrist with one hand while he held my hair with the other to pull back my head. The arm was twisted from the elbow joint. This continued to the best of my judgement for five minutes. It was very painful. The first officer was standing near my feet and the officer who accompanied him was still present.

(4) During the twisting of my arm the first officer continued to question me as to the names and addresses of my companions and also asked me the name of my Company commander and any of the other officers I knew.

(5) As I still persisted in refusing to answer these questions, I was allowed to get up and I was again handcuffed. A civilian came in and he repeated the questions with the same result. He informed me that if I gave all the information I knew, I could get off. I was then left in the company of the military policeman; the two officers, the three sergeants and the civilian leaving together.

(6) I could certainly identify the officer who directed the proceedings and put the questions. I am not sure of the others, except the sergeant with the bayonet. My arm was medically treated by an officer of the Royal Army Medical Corps attached to the North Dublin Union the following morning and by the prison hospital orderly afterwards for four or five days.

(7) I was visited by the court-martial officer last night and he read for me a confirmation of sentence of death by hanging to be executed on Monday next and I make this solemn declara-

tion conscientiously believing same to be true and by virtue of the Statutory Declarations Act 1835

(Signed) KEVIN GERARD BARRY

Declared and subscribed before me at Mountjoy Prison in the County of the City of Dublin this 28th day of October, 1920

(Signed) Myles Keogh*
A Justice of the Peace in and for the said County

Kevin was fortunate that he was in the hands of the British Army. Had he been taken and interrogated by the Black and Tans or the Auxiliaries, it is doubtful whether he would have suffered only the injury which put his arm in a sling for three weeks. It was a time of terror and reprisal everywhere, and with feelings running high following the casualties inflicted on the troops, he could have fared far worse. Three days later, Sir Henry Wilson[3] recorded in his diary: 'Tudor made it very clear that the police and the Black and Tans and the 100 Intell. officers are all carrying out reprisal murders'.

Kevin was removed from the North Dublin Union to the Bridewell police station for the night. From there he was taken to Mountjoy Prison, where he spent the six weeks until he was hanged.

While he was held in the Bridewell, he had a visit from Pat Dowling. He was having considerable pain in his arm and complained to his uncle about it but then he said that somebody would probably come and look after it soon.

Kathy Barry was at work in Abbey Street when she got a telephone call about four o'clock from Pat Dowling's manager to say that the shop and house in the South Circular Road had just been the target of an intensive military raid. Every item of Kevin's property had been seized and taken away. Pat

---

*Myles Keogh, LRCP, LRCSI, JP, was a surgeon dentist at 4 Lower Mount Street and 157 Strand Road, Merrion. He was a justice of the peace and quite a socialite; what was disparagingly called 'a Castle Catholic'. He had dined on occasion with the Lord Chancellor of Ireland, James Campbell, and the Joint Under Secretary for Ireland, James MacMahon, both of whom will figure later. He had been High Sheriff of Dublin in 1917.

Dowling made strenuous efforts later to have this property returned by the British Army. Kathy records that among the items taken and never returned were 'a perfectly new suit of Donegal tweed, a spare wristlet watch and a couple of good fountain pens'. She does not remember the manager's name. He was new and had replaced Tom Cullen, who had just joined the Active Service Unit. He told her he understood that Kevin had been arrested. 'From that moment', she says, 'I knew by some obscure instinct that Kevin was finished'.

She left her office and went home to Fleet Street, where her sister Peggy's birthday party was in full swing. She told her mother of Kevin's arrest and after they had made the children's tea, they dressed in their best and made the rounds of the prisons and their contacts between teatime and curfew. In that way they learned of Kevin's imprisonment.

Michael Knightly later recalled the very human and predictable pattern of activity that emerged soon after the action at the bakery.[4]

Knightly had asked Tom Kissane early that morning to call later and tell him how the raid went. He got worried when Kissane did not turn up and decided to go immediately to 11 Great Denmark Street where he found Kissane lying on a sofa, a very disappointed man.

Kissane complained, 'I told Seamus Kavanagh that the job would not be that easy, but he though differently. . . .'

Knightly then gave Kissane a description of the captured youth exactly as he had heard it from Paddy Quinn, the journalist who had seen Kevin in the lorry.

'It is Kevin Barry', said Kissane.

Could Kevin stand up to torture? 'Yes', Kissane replied and wanted to know why Knightly asked the question. Knightly continued, 'If he breaks down it might be serious for all of you. In any case you had better take precautions. Change your clothes and get out'.

Kissane said he had only one suit of clothes so Knightly asked him to at least remove his glasses which were remarkable in that one of the lenses was cracked down the middle. Kissane did so but soon afterwards when they were walking towards Findlater's Church he got frustrated.

'To hell with it, I can't see', he said, and put them on again.

That evening Kathy called on Knightly looking for information about her brother. She had been directed to him.

I explained that her brother was a prisoner and unhurt. She seemed relieved. I said: 'Of course you understand the position is serious. Two Tommies are dead and he is likely to be tried for his life.' She said she understood that, but she was glad that he was all right for the moment.

A few weeks later I was a prisoner in Mountjoy. I became friendly with my warder and inquired if Kevin Barry was uninjured when brought to prison.

He said no, that his arm was in a sling. I asked him was he sure of that and he said: 'Yes. There is a record of it in the books.' So it was obvious that poor Kevin had his arms twisted to get him to disclose information, and that he had held out against his torturers.

1077, Kevin Barry, eighteen and a half, with dark hair, blue eyes and fresh complexion, was committed to Mountjoy Prison on 21 September, 1920. The Committal Book is not to be found, but the General Register of Prisoners gives his address as 58 South Circular Road and his next-of-kin as his uncle, Patrick Dowling. It also records that he was a student, single, a Roman Catholic and could read and write. He was charged with offences under the Defence of the Realm Regulations. The column containing further remarks states simply that he was executed on 1 November, 1920.

As a remand prisoner, he was entitled to have meals brought in by his family, and he exercised that right. The Property Book, also missing from Mountjoy, would have given details of what he was wearing and carrying when he was admitted; but we know from other records that he wore his well-loved trench coat. His other property was the subject of some argument after his death, as will be seen.

Uncle Pat Dowling was Kevin's earliest and most frequent visitor. The family in Fleet Street was wary of visiting him, hoping that the British might feel that a mistake had been made. Kevin was acutely aware of the danger to his family. That is why he gave the South Circular Road as his address and Uncle

Pat as his next-of-kin. Many years later Kathy Barry explained the family's position in her statement to the Bureau of Military History.*

> Paddy Flanagan told me that Army orders were that none of us was to go near Kevin, that there was a hope that the British might feel that a mistake had been made, and that only my uncle and outside friends, who were not connected with the Republican movement, should visit him ...

Kathy had taken charge within the family at this time of crisis and anguish. She did not in fact visit Kevin until after the court-martial, and to the best of her knowledge neither did the other members of the immediate family. That is excepting her mother.

Mrs. Barry did visit Kevin, incognito. Kathy tells us that her mother went to Mountjoy heavily veiled, giving the name 'Miss McArdle', her mother's maiden name. His arm, she saw, was in a sling. At this time, Kevin's friends went in large numbers to see him, and no interest was taken in his case by the general public. Mrs. Barry, who dressed in borrowed clothes, was accompanied by Kathleen Carney, later Mrs. Vincent Gogarty of Drogheda, who was a close friend of Sir James MacMahon's family.

---

*The Bureau of Military History was established in 1947 to record for posterity the actions of those who took part in the fight for independence from 1913 to 1921. Its records were not to be made public for twenty-five years, a period since extended by various Ministers. They still have not been released (1989). The Bureau, which was at 26 Westland Row, was closed in 1957. Its chairman was Richard Hayes (1878-1958), the scholar and politician from Bruree, Co. Limerick. He was Film Censor from 1940 to 1954. Other members of the bureau were R.J. Hayes, Director of the National Library; Denis Gwynn, the historian; James Hogan, Professor of History at UCC; Sheila Kennedy, lecturer in history, UCG; G.A. Hayes McCoy, the military historian and Professor of History, UCG; Major Florence O'Donoghue, Republican, author and Army officer (1940-1945), who built up the Bureau's reference library; Professor Séamus Delargy, the folklorist, and P.S. O'Hegarty, the writer and member of the IRB. Kathy Barry Moloney made some of her testimony on Kevin Barry available to her brother-in-law, James O'Donovan, when he was researching his unpublished book on Barry.

Mrs. Barry's visit was on 1 October. The same day Kevin wrote to Gerry McAleer, 'The missis was up today and she is looking awful.'[5] His letter was typical. It might well have been written from the comfort of Fleet Street.

> Congrats on your exam. I believe I stuck, but that does not worry me. How did all the others do? I suppose they did well. You are all swanky second medicals now. When will you be up again? I believe Vin* is coming up on Monday next. I'll write to him and to Jack [Jack Henry, a fellow medical student, who served as a doctor in World War II and lives in England] soon.
>
> By the way, tell Mrs. Tipping I'll settle up with her when I get out — if I ever do so. The missis was up today and she is looking awful.
>
> Uncle Pat was up nearly every day and I had several other visitors including Paddy [Paddy Collins, a civil servant].
>
> When you are writing to Charlie O'Neill, explain why I can't answer his letter. Tell C. O'N. [same] to beware of wine and women when he starts his medical career or —. Remember me to Barney [Barney McAleer] and all at home. Also to all the boys in the College and to such of the girls whose acquaintance you can claim.
>
> Now goodbye and the best of luck.
>
> Yours till I'm qualified.
>
> Kevin

He had established himself well with the warders early on in his imprisonment. He gave one of them a tip, Busy Bee, for the race due to run on Wednesday, 22 September.

---

*Vincent Shields, a law student, native of Dungannon and fellow lodger in Tippings with his brother Frank, a dental student, who later practised in Dungannon. Vincent Shields became a distinguished solicitor in Loughrea, Co. Galway, where he joined the practice of Paddy Hogan (1891-1936), the Volunteer who became a Sinn Féin T.D. for Galway in 1921 and was an outstanding Minister for Agriculture from 1922 to 1932.

11 Malice Aforethought

When the body of Private Washington and the two wounded soldiers, Whitehead and Humphries, arrived at King George V Hospital at 12.30 p.m. on 20 September, Sir William Taylor and Colonel F.J. Palmer, RAMC were waiting to receive them. Taylor was Surgeon Consultant to the Forces in Ireland and an eminent Dublin surgeon. Private Whitehead was the more gravely injured and, without any preparation, he was operated on.

No bullet was found, although there was no exit wound. An attendant, John Morgan, who had seen fourteen years' service in the Royal Irish Fusiliers, found a bullet on the floor when he was cleaning up. This bullet, Colonel Palmer later stated under oath, came out of Private Whitehead. 'I have a conviction amounting almost to a certainty', was how he put it.

The point is important because the prosecution had to decide with which death to charge Kevin Barry. Private Whitehead died at ten to three that afternoon. Private Humphries, whose chances of survival were rated more highly, lingered on until nine-thirty the following night. In the meanwhile, General Headquarters of the IRA did not share the public's lack of interest in Kevin's case. Although all eyes and hearts were on Terence MacSwiney's* fast to the death in Brixton Prison,

---

*Terence MacSwiney (1879-1920) was born in Cork and was a graduate of the Royal University. He was a member of the Gaelic League and the Irish Volunteers. He represented Mid-Cork in the First Dáil and succeeded the murdered Tomás MacCurtain as Lord Mayor of Cork. Arrested in August 1920, he embarked on a hunger strike which captured international attention. He died on 25 October after seventy-four days of fasting. His best known work (he was also a poet) was the essay *Principles of Freedom*, published posthumously. He was Commandant, Cork No. 1 Brigade.

GHQ got in touch with Kathy Barry[1] through P.J. O'Flanagan, owner of the Wood Printing Works at 13 Fleet Street, editor of *The Irishman*, and brother of Bob O'Flanagan who was wounded in the Monks' Bakery raid.

O'Flanagan's first communication with Kathy, as we have seen, was to advise against the family visiting Kevin in prison for the moment. Kathy goes on in her later statement to the Bureau of Military History.

On Thursday at lunchtime [September 23rd], Paddy Flanagan sent for me again, and in his office I met Seán Ó Muirthile,* who told me that the case was to be handled by G.H.Q. . . . Meantime we were not to show ourselves as connected at all with Kevin; there was still hope of confusing the British.

Next day Friday 24 September, Ernest A. Aston,** who was

*Seán Ó Muirthile of Cork was secretary to the Supreme Council of the IRB. With Diarmuid O'Hegarty, he helped to revitalise the IRB after 1916. With Cathal Brugha, he helped to rebuild the Volunteers. With Neil Kerr, he helped to send de Valera secretly to the United States in 1919. He became Quartermaster-General of the Free State Army in 1922. He was dismissed from the Army in 1924 because of his IRB activities. He had a ship's chandlers business in Cathedral Street. Michael Hayes tells an amusing story about Ó Muirthile when the British HQ at Parkgate was handed over in 1922 to a unit under the command of General Richard Mulcahy. It was the last barracks to be vacated. Outside the gate, a British sergeant-major marched up and down restlessly, ignoring the excited crowd that had gathered. When Mulcahy's unit arrived, the sergeant-major looked carefully at his watch. 'You're three minutes late', he complained. Before Mulcahy could reply, Seán Ó Muirthile who was with him retorted: 'Blast ye to hell! You've been here for seven hundred years and three minutes more won't do any harm'.

**Ernest A. Aston was a prominent Dublin consulting engineer, a Protestant Home Ruler, a member of the League of Nations Society and a strong advocate of proportional representation. He and Lieut.-Commander J.F. MacCabe, whose exploit in sinking a German submarine during the Great War has gone down in British naval history, went to see Lloyd George to seek a reprieve for Kevin Barry, an episode described later. Aston, MacCabe (who was a civil engineer with the Local Government Board) and Frederick Purser Griffith made up the team that created the garden suburb of Killester, built after the Great War as housing for ex-servicemen. Aston had offices in 28-29 Upper Abbey Street and 65 Middle Abbey Street. He lived at Woodleigh, Upper Castle Avenue, Clontarf.

Kathy's employer, was told by Sir Hamar Greenwood, the Chief Secretary, that Kevin would be tried for murder and probably sentenced to death.[2] Aston had gone to Greenwood through the intervention of Sir Henry McLaughlin, KBE, the building contractor, who was a prominent Irish Freemason and, says Kathy, 'an extraordinarily decent human being'.

'The boy is only a child', said Aston to the Chief Secretary, 'I know him well'.

'He may be a child in years', Greenwood replied, 'but he is a dangerous man. He has a long record as an IRA man'.

Kathy Barry[3] recalls that within a week of Kevin's capture, she called into the Wood Printing Works and met Seán Ó Muirthile. He told her GHQ had placed the case in the hands of Éamon Duggan* the solicitor. Since the charge would be murder, it would probably be necessary for Kevin to recognise the court and be defended.

'I saw Mr. Duggan then and on several occasions later. A cold legal person, he complained that he found Kevin difficult — he did not want to recognise the Court'. Duggan explained to her that he himself was acting under GHQ orders and that Kevin and the Barry family would have to follow his instructions.

At the Parkgate HQ of the British Forces in Ireland there was intense concentration on the Barry case. Reports were being written and telephone messages dispatched in preparation for the execution of the first victim since Sir Roger Casement was hanged in August 1916. Kevin Barry's position in the pantheon of Irish heroes lies in this — that he was the first Volunteer captured by Crown Forces since the Rising. His youth, the fact that he was hanged and not shot like the 1916 leaders, and the instant popularity of countless ballads and poems composed in his memory, all help his story to endure. But his primacy lies in the decision of General Macready to try him

---

*Eamon Duggan (1874-1936) was born in Longwood, Co. Meath. He became a solicitor in 1914, fought in the GPO in 1916 and was interned. He became Director of Intelligence in 1918 and was elected for Louth-Meath in the First Dáil. A signatory to the Anglo-Irish Treaty, he became Minister of Home Affairs in the Provisional Government. He did not contest the 1933 election and was elected to the Senate, where he became the last member to take the Oath of Allegiance before it was abolished.

for murder, thus reversing the policy followed after the 1916 executions had provided the British with a pyrrhic victory.

Captain R.S. Chomley, Adjutant of the 2nd Battalion the Duke of Wellington's Regiment, made a formal report on the day of the raid.[4] It adds nothing to our knowledge of the events. Next day Captain R.F. Bridges of the King George V Hospital staff conducted a post-mortem on the body of Private Washington and established that he had been killed by a .45 pistol bullet.

On Wednesday 22 September inquests held by the City Coroner, Dr. Louis A. Byrne, on the three soldiers brought in verdicts of death 'by bullets fired by persons unknown'. Colonel Toppin received a most unsatisfactory handwritten note from Major C.G. Hetherington, a staff officer at GHQ, saying: 'This is the only report I can find about the affair in Dublin on Monday. It should have gone to you before. – Not my fault! It is obviously very incomplete . . .'

He is referring, presumably, to the telephoned account of the raid. A court of inquiry was held about the matter but had to reassemble later because somebody had forgotten to have the witnesses sworn 'in accordance with GHQ instructions', according to a handwritten report by Colonel S.D.N. Browne of Dublin District.

On Friday, Colonel Toppin forwent his weekend leave, ordered a file opened, and sent a 'secret and pressing' message to Dublin District asking how the Barry case stood, adding: 'The G.O.C.-in-Chief desires that this case would be put forward in a thorough manner as soon as possible.'

Capt. A.H. Barrett gave up his Sunday to pen a 'secret and urgent' communication to the Chief Commissioner of the Dublin Metropolitan Police, Colonel W. Edgeworth Johnstone, giving him full statements from all the military engaged and a sketch-plan, 'for the assistance of the Law Officers'.*

---

*The references to British documents on the court-martial of Kevin Barry used in this book are new. What seems to have happened is this: A voluminous file – R.O.2609 (Restoration of Order Section) in the GOC's office at Parkgate, and the correspondence in the file of Dublin District – 59/169/A1 (A2, etc.) were gathered into one file in Dublin Castle and labelled: 'Kevin Berry – Civilian'. Some time in 1921, and

Also active in the case at this time was Geoffrey Granville Whiskard ('Whiskers'), one of the bright young men brought over from London in the reform of the Dublin Castle administration early in 1920. Involved also was James MacMahon,* the Joint Under Secretary for Ireland, one of the few who survived from the previous régime, mainly because he was an Irish Catholic. His appointment, in Sir Warren Fisher's words, was believed to be 'a source of satisfaction to the Roman Catholic Hierarchy'. MacMahon's daughter Molly married Walter Doolin, a private secretary on the Castle staff. In 1974, Molly Doolin told the historian Léon Ó Broin:[5] 'We did not like Whiskard. He was a poor type of Englishman, impudent and uppish'. Sir Geoffrey Whiskard became High Commissioner to Australia in 1935.

---

he does not say whether it was before or after the Truce of 11 July, James O'Donovan 'acquired' this material, which he tells us is now 'deposited in the National Library of Ireland and will be available for inspection on the publication of the present work (or the author's previous decease). How these documents reached their present destination cannot yet be divulged'. James O'Donovan, the present writer's father, had worked from 1948 to 1964 on a book to be entitled *Ireland's Kevin Barry*. He failed to have it published and he died in 1979, the last surviving member of the General Staff of the IRA in the War of Independence. *Leaba i measc na naomh go raibh aige*. If he had not taken this material, it would lie in the public Records office in London awaiting release in 1995 under the seventy-five-year rule that applies to legal papers. A letter from O'Donovan to the Library Director makes an 'unconditional gift' of the 'originally captured British file' once two photostats of each of ten of the documents have been given to O'Donovan.

*James MacMahon (1856-1954) was a Belfast man, educated in Armagh and at Blackrock College. He was Secretary of the Post Office from 1916 to 1918 and from then until the *Götterdämmerung* was Under Secretary for Ireland, the senior civil servant in the administration. He was retained in the purge of Spring 1920, but was made *Joint* Under Secretary with Sir John Anderson. MacMahon was very close to the Hierarchy. Cardinal Logue was a good friend and he and other bishops often stayed in the Under Secretary's Lodge in the Phoenix Park. MacMahon's assistant, Sir John Taylor, was believed to dominate MacMahon. The *Irish Independent* of 24 April, 1920, wrote: 'Taylor has virtually superseded MacMahon in authority because he is a Catholic − in fact he is ignored'. But a later report said: 'MacMahon is again to have his old influence on the Irish administration'. Molly Doolin, understandably, dubbed Taylor 'a rotter'.

On Tuesday, 28 September, Whiskard wrote to General Macready's office on behalf of Lord French: 'His Excellency is advised that the offender in this case should be prosecuted by Court Martial for murder', a decision already made eight days earlier by the GOC.

Two days later, 30 September, Kevin Barry was taken from his cell to a room in Mountjoy in which the hard-working Captain Barrett, the Courts Martial Officer for Dublin District, had gathered together in relays the sixteen witnesses who would appear at the trial. They there and then made sworn statements and some of them were cross-examined by Kevin.

This process lasted through Thursday, Friday and the following Monday, with Captain Barrett informing GHQ that the Summary of Evidence should be ready by Monday, 4 October.

Kevin asked twenty-six questions, and declined to question eleven of the witnesses. Of Private Dalby, he asked: 'How was I dressed?' Dalby answered: 'Raincoat, dark suit and a cap'.

'What colour was my cap?'

'I don't know.'

Nothing of consequence emerged from Kevin's cross-examination of the witnesses, and he did not succeed in pinpointing any but minor discrepancies in the prosecution's evidence. For example, Sergeant Banks said he was wearing a soft hat with a black band, not a cap. But Kevin did not pursue the point.

General Macready received a long letter dated 5 October from Colonel Henry Davis Foster MacGeagh in the Judge Advocate General Office, London. He said Kenneth Marshall, the Deputy Judge Advocate, would act as Judge Advocate at the trial. Macready should detail a barrister among his legal officers to assist in conducting the case for prosecution. It would be 'a convenience' if the trials (they were contemplating charges against Kevin of murdering all three soldiers) 'could be fixed to begin early in a week so as to avoid, if possible, counsel being detained in Ireland over the week-end'.

On the same day, Captain Barrett submitted, in 'very secret' form, the Summary of Evidence to General Macready. He said that Kevin's pistol and 'all relevant rounds of ammunition' were in his possession.

The charges were drafted in Dublin and submitted to London. Two of them having been dropped during the trial, it is enough to quote the charge that formed the basis of the general court-martial:

Committing a crime within the meaning of Regulation 67 of the R.O.I.R., that is to say, MURDER, in that he at Dublin in the County of the City of Dublin on the 20th day of September, 1920, feloniously, wilfully and of his malice aforethought did kill and murder No. 4603629 Private Matthew Whitehead, a soldier of His Majesty's Forces.

The charge sheets were signed at Dublin Castle by Colonel A.H. Spooner of the Lancashire Fusiliers. A flurry of messages crossed the Irish Sea every day from now until the execution, enough work to justify the beaverings of some seventy British officials involved in the case. This figure does not count chaplains, warders, guards and stenographers at the lower end of the social scale; nor the Lord Lieutenant, the Director of Public Prosecutions, the Secretary of State for War and the Judge Advocate General at the upper end.

On 12 October, Captain Barrett informed Éamon Duggan as Kevin's solicitor that he hoped to have the Summary of Evidence and the charge sheet by next day. He told Kevin too. And he informed them both that the trial had been ordered for Wednesday, 20 October. He made a mistake. He told Duggan in writing that the prosecution would employ counsel. Colonel Warburton said Kevin too should have a full week's notice of counsel's appearance, but Barrett sent Kevin an amending note only on 16 October. He claimed that he already had given him verbal notice.

'Mr. Duggan', says Kathy Barry[6] of these events 'was much perturbed.' He had tried without success to get the British to alter the date of the court-martial from 20 October. He had to leave Ireland on that day in connection with a case which had gone to the House of Lords. He said he would make a final effort, and if he failed to get the date altered, he would have to hand the case to another solicitor.

On Monday 18th, I learnt that Seán Ó hUadhaigh,* solicitor, of Little, Doyle and Woods, wanted to see me. I went there and he asked me to go out and see Tim Healy** with the Summary of Evidence. G.H.Q. wanted Tim Healy to defend if he thought he could save Kevin's life. Healy read the Summary of Evidence and told me, with tears, that there was no doubt that they meant to hang Kevin.

Kathy Barry's account goes on with her account of the meeting with Healy.

(a) The case was watertight and he could hold out no hope of a successful defence unless he were to plead insanity, a course which I took it upon myself to reject out of hand.

(b) Kevin would stand a better chance by being allowed to follow his inclination and refuse to recognise the court — thus throwing on the English conscience the onus of hanging an 18-year-old prisoner of war who had not been defended.

(c) He could hold out no hope that even this would succeed because of the 'badness' of Lloyd George. If

---

*Seán Ó hUadhaigh (John K. Woods) was a Dublin solicitor. He was a friend of Éamon de Valera, Chairman of the Irish Aero Club — he made the first flight to the Aran Islands in 1935 — and was largely instrumental in establishing Aer Lingus, of which he became the first Chairman. He was a nephew-in-law of Michael Cusack, the Irish-speaking Clareman who founded the Gaelic Athletic Association in 1884.

**Timothy Michael Healy — 'the gift-tormented T.M. Healy', as Dangerfield has called him — was born in Bantry, Co. Cork, in 1835. He emigrated to England, became a railway clerk in Newcastle and parliamentary correspondent for *The Nation*. He was elected MP for Wexford in 1880 and was Parnell's secretary during his American tour. Called to the Bar in 1884, he became an expert in agrarian law. He broke with Parnell in 1886 over the Galway by-election and played a leading role in the Chief's downfall. He represented the employers in the 1913 lock-out, refused to defend Casement in case the public would identify him with 'the traitor', and was made first Governor-General of the Irish Free State in 1922. Healy lived at Glenaulin, Chapelizod, where Kathy Barry saw him. When he was Governor-General, the Vice Regal Lodge inevitably came to be called 'Uncle Tim's Cabin'.

Bonar Law were Prime Minister, there might have been some hope, but as things were, there was none.

He actually wept most of the time, and very kindly sent me home laden with hot-house fruit for mother.

Colonel Warburton[7] said in a memorandum that 'the Chief' (Macready) 'wants a good President' for the general court-martial. It took some days for agreement to be reached on the court. In the meanwhile Lieut. E.F.R. Sample of the Royal Engineers, who was an architect in York, prepared a 1/16 scale map of the Church Street area. The lorry did not appear on the map because the position of the lorry was to be the subject of evidence to be given in court. The map was made in Beggar's Bush Barracks and nine copies of it were made by the Sun Print Process. Special passes for Kevin's counsel, solicitor and family were prepared.

The 'good President' sought by General Macready was Brigadier-General Cranley Charlton Onslow, Officer Commanding the 25th Provisional Infantry Brigade. He was to sit with six members – Colonel Hubert Peel Yates of the 2nd South Wales Borderers; Colonel C.F. Phipps of the Royal Garrison Artillery; Colonel E. Morton of the 1st Cheshire Regiment; Colonel F.C. Pilkington of the XV Hussars, and Colonel B.H. Chetwynd Stapylton of the Cheshires. The additional member, nominated by the Lord Lieutenant, was Major Signey Johnson Watts, an Assistant Legal Officer who was a barrister.

The 'waiting members' were Major C.L. Price, Major E.B. Cotter and Major T.F.K. Dunne, all of the Royal Garrison Artillery.

These names, though they were a closely-guarded secret at the time, mean little enough now. But there are two points of interest. First, only three of the nine were on the first list devised; and secondly, the regulations stated that the ranks of the members could be much lower than the ranks of those actually chosen. It was, in short, a very senior court, and it was expected to sit for three days.

Marshalling the evidence in a four-page letter from the Judge Advocate General Office to General Macready, Colonel Foster MacGeagh instructed that an additional six pieces of evidence must be given on top of what was already in the Summary of Evidence, and he ordered the services of 'a competent short-hand-writer'. Another difficulty arose here. The RIC's short-hand staff was depleted and it was only on the day before the trial that Lieut. Walsh produced a shorthand-writer from some-where.

Marlborough Barracks* was proposed by Captain Barrett as the venue of the court-martial. It was near Mountjoy, thus reducing the security risk. He received a letter on 19 October from Seán Ó hUadhaigh protesting against the exclusion of the public (which the solicitor assumed)** and against the in-adequate time allowed to him to prepare a defence. Ó hUad-haigh asked again for the adjournment already applied for by Duggan. It was much to late to change anything.

---

*Marlborough (now McKee) Barracks was built between 1888 and 1892 on a site chosen because it was near to the railway and port, and to training facilities for the cavalry it was intended to house. It was the newest Dublin barracks and merited an article in the *Irish Builder* in October 1891. Brickwork façade, tall chimneys, broken gables, turrets, cupolas and parapets give the barracks a character unique in Irish mili-tary architecture. It was renamed in the mid-1920s after Brigadier Dick McKee (1893-1920), whose bust by Laurence Campbell, RHA, was placed in the hall of the Officers' Mess in 1950. Radio Éireann's call-sign, 2RN, came from a mast erected in the barrack area in 1926, and issued from there for about five years. The Army Equitation School was founded and located in McKee Barracks in 1926. It is the oldest unit in the barracks.

**According to instructions from the Judge Advocate General Office: '. . . Other members of the public may be admitted up to the extent of the accommodation available, but with such precautions as to search as the Officer Commanding XV Hussars may consider necessary . . . The Court should be closed to press and public until the trial actually begins with the arraignment of the accused.'

12 No Questions

Wednesday, 20 October, 1920 was wet. It was raining heavily when Mrs. Barry and her entourage arrived by cab.[1] In the cabs were her brother, Pat Dowling; Seán Ó hUadhaigh, the solicitor acting for Kevin; Father Augustine, OFM Cap;* Eileen O'Neill, a young Dublin friend of Kevin's; Gerry McAleer, his almost constant companion for four years; and Joe Farrell,** a close friend of the family and an engineering student at the College of Science.

---

*Father Augustine, OFM Cap, was born John Hayden at Waterloo, Blarney, Co. Cork. He went to the Seraphic School in Kilkenny, an experimental juniorate for aspirants to the Capuchin Order. Augustine was a close friend of an tAthair Peadar Ó Laoghaire, described as 'the creator of modern Irish prose'. The growing Capuchin tradition of nationalism and republicanism — not shared, it must be said, by all members of the community, some of whom served faithfully and honourably as chaplains in the British Army in France — reached its full flower during the 1916 Rising, when Albert, Augustine, Jarlath, Sebastian, Columbus and others succoured the wounded and brought spiritual comfort to the dying during the week. They went to see Pearse in Arbour Hill and helped to convince insurgents in outposts that the surrender order was genuine. As the executions proceeded, the Capuchins offered the consolations of religion to the leaders. Fathers Augustine and Albert paid several visits to Kevin Barry in Mountjoy. Augustine died in 1954.

**Joe Farrell, who called himself O'Farrell after he married, was shot and wounded in action during the War of Independence. He became an engineer in the Electricity Supply Board, where he later helped Kathy Barry to find a job. There was no telephone in Fleet Street and Joe Farrell had easy access to a telephone. He was thus able to help the family in a practical way in their hour of need. Gerry McAleer, who knew Joe very well, says: 'He was a terrific IRA man, a gunman'. It is surprising that the authorities so easily allowed him into Marlborough Barracks. The Farrells were from Portlaoise.

Everybody entering Marlborough Barracks that morning, including the newspaper reporters, was closely searched. Mrs. Barry and the rest of her group were held up at the gate for some time, but then were admitted to the court.

In spite of the delay at the gate, Kevin's relatives and friends were in the room before the court assembled. At ten o'clock precisely, the members of the court-martial took their places at the long elevated table, the Judge Advocate, Kenneth Marshall, Esq., CBE, wearing the traditional wig.

The minutes ticked away, but no prisoner appeared. 'At 10.20 there was a kind of subdued hysteria at the table', says Kathy Barry. 'We all felt puzzled, but beautifully detached. Then at 10.25, Kevin was brought into the room by a military escort. This was the first time that I had seen him since his arrest a month earlier. He looked well and very cheerful, and desperately amused when he saw the tableful of British officers.'

The reason Kevin was twenty-five minutes late for his own trial was that the armoured car bringing him from Mountjoy Prison to Marlborough Barracks had broken down on the North Circular Road. It had stalled and would not start again, and the escort became increasingly agitated until a relief car arrived. The whole episode hugely entertained Kevin, who as a result was the coolest man in the court room when the hearing began.

The order convening the court was first read, and Kevin was given a chair. He was arraigned on the charges by the Judge Advocate, and immediately Seán Ó hUadhaigh asked for a quarter of an hour's adjournment in order to consult with his client, as he had had no opportunity of doing so earlier. The President, Brigadier-General Onslow, granted the request.

When the court resumed and the accused was called on to plead, Kevin said: 'As a soldier of the Irish Republic, I refuse to recognise the court'.

'That is a plea of not guilty', said the President, who gravely explained the prisoner's perilous situation. Kevin did not reply, but Seán Ó hUadhaigh spoke.

'Another professional gentleman was instructed in this case', he said, 'but he had to go away and it was only yesterday that I was instructed. This is the first opportunity I have had of consulting the accused. But as he has declined to recognise the court, my functions have come to an end'.

Seán Ó hUadhaigh then engaged in a neat piece of opportunism. According to one daily newspaper of the next morning,[2] before he withdrew from the case he lodged a complaint which the President ordered should not be published 'for the present'.

Prosecuting counsel said on a point of order that his learned friend did not represent the accused in the case, and the present was not the occasion or the place to make the observations which he had made.

Mr. Ó hUadhaigh: 'My reason for doing so is to draw the attention of the court to it before I retire, as I feel sure it will be investigated.'

President: 'We are here for one purpose only, but if you send this complaint to me personally, I will take notice of it'.

Mr. Ó hUadhaigh: 'I will do that. I merely wish to draw the court's attention to the matter, as the accused, not recognising the court, might not call attention to it himself. The accused is a minor and I was retained by his family. As such, I bring the matter under the notice of the court. That is all. . . .'

President: 'Am I to understand that you are retiring from the case?'

Mr. Ó hUadhaigh: 'I cannot force my services on the accused as he declines to recognise the court. The attitude he takes up is that the act he did was an act of war, and I do not see how I can take any further part in the proceedings'.

He then withdrew from the court, but sat with the family for the rest of the day.

What Ó hUadhaigh had raised out of the blue was that Kevin had been ill-treated by British officers while he was in custody. Surprisingly most of the newspapers chose to ignore completely this fascinating exchange between Brigadier-General Onslow and Seán Ó hUadhaigh at the time. And the Barry family, who were there throughout the exchanges, made no subsequent mention of Ó hUadhaigh's 'complaint'. The British authorities, as we shall see, became quite heated about this affair *after* Kevin was dead, claiming that Ó hUadhaigh had tricked them by pretending to represent Kevin when in fact he had withdrawn from the case.

Opening the case, Percival Clarke, KC, who had with him Major D.R. Osborne, said: 'This is the first case of its kind which has to be tried by such a tribunal as is now sitting, and which is unfortunately rendered necessary by the conditions through which the country is now passing.'

Counsel then outlined the prosecution's case, giving a long, detailed and objective account of the 'Church Street Shooting Affray', as that day's *Evening Herald* called it. Perhaps the principal point with which Kevin's counsel would have taken issue in the opening statement was the type and number of rounds in the German automatic found on Kevin.

'The magazine', said the Crown counsel, 'contained two live cartridges, while in another chamber was another cartridge. The two rounds found in the magazine were flat-nosed while the one in the chamber was a round-nosed bullet. The flat-nosed bullet had a nickel casing and the round-nosed one a copper casing'.

Throughout the hearing the Crown called sixteen witnesses. As each one ended his evidence, the President turned to Kevin to ask: 'Any questions?' Each time Kevin replied: 'No', and again took up the *Evening Telegraph* he had been reading.

Eventually he lost his patience, put down the newspaper and said to General Onslow: 'Look! I have told you I don't recognise the court. I have no interest in what anybody says here. You are only wasting your time asking me'.

Onslow, a tall man with a dark melancholy face and a lot of dark hair, was taken aback and said mildly: 'It is my duty to ask you if you have any questions. I think as a soldier you can appreciate that'.

Kevin relented a little: 'I don't see why I should facilitate you but if it is any consolation to you – no, I have no questions.'

The parade of witnesses continued, all telling more or less the story as it happened, no one connecting Kevin directly with the death of Matthew Whitehead during the morning.

At one o'clock it was time to adjourn for lunch. Kevin was taken away. The Barry family and their friends went to the City Arms Hotel in Prussia Street half a mile away.

For some time after lunch, evidence was given that the bullet found in the body of the deceased soldier and those in the pistol taken from the accused corresponded. The pistol, which had recently been discharged, was a German automatic of the year 1915.

Three soldiers had died in the action at Monks' Bakery, from single bullet wounds in each case. It was of importance to the British military, though not paramount, to establish that the gun that Kevin Barry was caught with and the remaining bullets in that gun corresponded with the bullets that killed one, two or all three of the soldiers.

The strenuous efforts made by the Judge Advocate's office and the Courts Martial Officer to link Kevin, his gun and the death of one soldier, Private Matthew Whitehead, involved eliminating – though only at the last minute, during the court-martial – the charges of murdering Privates Washington and Humphries, both killed by bullets of a calibre different from Kevin's .38.

It should be remembered that, although a transcript of the court-martial was made, it is not available to us. The witnesses at the court-martial bore no names and the newspaper accounts of the evidence given are not extensive and are based on the reporters' judgements of what was important. We know that the press was not present at all material times during the course of the hearings. Indeed only one reporter – from the *Free-man's Journal* – took his courage in his hands and reported the exchange between the President, General Onslow, and the Barry family's solicitor, Seán Ó hUadhaigh, about the ill-treatment which Kevin had suffered at the hands of British officers.

What is available to us is the Barry file, removed from Dublin Castle by Jim O'Donovan in 1921, which contains the evidence taken by Captain Barrett in Mountjoy from sixteen witnesses, preparatory to Kevin Barry's court-martial. These were the same witnesses who later appeared at the court-martial, so we have their first full statements and we know who they were from this source. Kevin was able to cross-examine these military, medical and ballistics experts in Mountjoy and in some cases he did so. Later he had decided not to recognise the court and so asked no questions. Had he agreed to be repre-

sented by counsel, it would scarcely have affected the out-
come, but we would have seen a strong spotlight trained on
the witnesses' statements about the bullet that allegedly killed
Private Whitehead.

Regrettably the bullet has disappeared. Jim O'Donovan
stated in his unpublished typescript *Ireland's Kevin Barry* that
in circuitous ways all three bullets — the one that allegedly
killed Whitehead, the one that allegedly killed Humphries and
the one found at Church Street that is believed to have killed
Washington — had found their way into his possession in later
years. Now, all that can be found is a mis-shapen piece of lead
in an envelope marked 'Washington'. The envelope, on which
the seal has been broken, forms part of Ms. 8043, in the
National Library. Whether it *is* the bullet that killed Washington does not matter because it is of lead, Whitehead allegedly
was killed by a copper bullet.

We may now look at the evidence, available to the court-
martial on the afternoon of 20 October, relating to the bullet
that allegedly killed Private Matthew Whitehead. Lt.-Colonel
F.J. Palmer, RAMC, who assisted Sir William Taylor in the
operations on Privates Whitehead and Humphries, had been
called to the King George V Hospital on 20 September to see
'a seriously wounded man, Pte. Whitehead', and he described
what he saw:

> The wound of entry was in the left lumbo (*sic*) abdominal
> region of the abdomen. *The bullet was lodged in the
> body* (author's italics). There was no wound of exit.
> When the abdomen was opened four perforations of the
> bowel were stitched up. There were several bleeding ves-
> sels which required tying and the abdomen was full of
> fluid and clotted blood. Blood clots were scooped out
> with the flat of the hand. *No bullet was found at the
> time* (author's italics).

Colonel Palmer, under Sir William Taylor, then attended to
Private Humphries. A charge of murdering Humphries was
prepared against Kevin, but was dropped at the trial, so there
is no need to elaborate on his operation. But Palmer goes on
to say:

In my opinion the bullet found by the attendant and handed to me could only have come from Pte. Whitehead and was probably swept up unnoticed in a mass of blood clots during the operation. Later on, the operating theatre attendant Morgan handed me a golden coloured bullet which I now identify. It bore marks of having been fired.

This version, taken by Captain Barrett in the hospital, differs from the one Colonel Palmer gave under oath at the prison a day or two later. It is proposed to use author's italics again in this excerpt. When Private Whitehead was being operated on, Palmer says, *'no bullet was found at the time'*. He died in the wards about fifteen minutes later, while Humphries was being looked after.

Palmer goes on:

After [Pte. Humphries] had been operated on the Theatre was cleared out, and [the word 'and' is crossed out by Foster McGeagh in the Judge Advocate General Office in London] one of the two operating theatre attendants handed me a bullet [the next 12 words have been crossed out] which he said had fallen from the operating table in cleaning up. There was no time to clean up the Theatre between the operations. The Theatre previously to the first operation was absolutely clean. I recognise the bullet now produced as a revolver bullet of a kind unknown to me. The casing is of a golden colour. It presented the appearance of having been recently fired. The grooves on the bullet were slightly blackened. I kept the bullet in my possession until I handed it to Captain A.H. Barrett, Courts Martial Officer, Dublin District. *I have a conviction almost amounting to a certainty that the bullet came out of Pte. Whitehead* and was swept out unnoticed from his abdomen in a handful of blood and clot. The reason I came to this conclusion is that there was no wound of exit in the case of Pte. Whitehead, whereas in the case of Pte. Humphries there was a clean wound of entrance and exit.

Colonel Palmer was cross-examined by Kevin Barry in Mount-joy, who asked one question:

Q. Was the wound in Private Whitehead on the left side of the abdomen?

A. Yes.

John Morgan, the civilian theatre attendant who found the bullet, says in his evidence that after the operation on Private Whitehead there was left on the table

> a quantity of swabs, blood and possibly some pieces of flesh. After the second operation, I helped in clearing up. Whilst cleaning up I heard something fall off the table close to me. The theatre and floor were absolutely clean before the first operation. *About an hour after the second operation I found a bullet similar to the one produced, on the floor between the table and the window. I put it in my pocket. I gave the bullet to Colonel Palmer when I came off duty* (author's italics). I noticed when I picked up the bullet it had grooves in it. It is not a rifle bullet. It is a copper coloured bullet. It could have been fired from a revolver or pistol. I am an ex-serviceman late 1st Battalion Royal Irish Fusiliers. I have 14 years' service in before I left.

Kevin asked no questions of John Morgan, whose evidence is undated.

On Tuesday 28 September at King George V Hospital, Colonel Palmer handed Captain Barrett 'a bullet found in the operating theatre after the operations on the two deceased soldiers. It is a copper coloured pistol bullet,' says Barrett.

> I proceeded the same afternoon to the North Dublin Union and in the presence of the Adjutant, Lt. Lonsdale, Lancashire Fusiliers, I opened the sealed packet contain-ing the revolver and ammunition found on the accused and compared the bullet received from Colonel Palmer with those in the packet. The bullet is of the same calibre.
>
> I sent for the Armourer Sergeant of the Lancashire Fusiliers and on his arrival he stated as his opinion that the bullets were the same. Two of the rounds in the packets are flat nosed — one is not. The flat nosed bullets

have not been flattened after manufacture, but were cast flattened. The bullet found in the operating theatre fits the pistol, which is a Mauser automatic, 1915 pattern.

Captain Barrett continued:

In my presence the Armourer Sergeant stripped the pistol and upon looking through the barrel one observes sufficient superficial fouling to indicate that the pistol has been recently fired through. There are six grooves in the barrel of the pistol forming the rifling and there are also six grooves on the bullet found in the operating theatre *which shows that a bullet with six grooves is intended to be fired through a pistol with the same number of riflings in order that when fired it may take up its twisting action* (author's italics).

The three rounds taken out of the pistol were found in the pistol. There was also in the parcel an expended revolver bullet of a different pattern which I was informed was picked up by the lorry.

I put the pistol reassembled by the Armourer, together with the three rounds found in it and the spare round picked up by the side of the lorry, in the parcel and sealed it up myself in the presence of the Adjutant and the Armourer.

The sergeant's name is Armour Sergeant [Edward] Clarke.

Colonel H. Toppin, who had been given General Macready's original order to 'try for murder', wrote to Headquarters, Dublin District, on 30 September giving detailed instructions on the case. Three of his orders are given here. He says: 'Herewith Government file 31707 in the case of Murder of Ptes. Washington, Whitehead and Humphries . . .'

2. Great care should be taken to clear up exactly where this pistol was found and the opportunity of seeing it being found which each witness possessed.

3. Great care should also be taken to clear up the transfer of the three cartridges from one witness to another

and as to the person to whom they were finally handed over . . .

5. As regards the bullet which appears to have been taken from Pte. Whitehead's body, it will be necessary to produce either a musketry or an Ordnance Officer expert as to its corresponding to the bullet found in the pistol, if this is so. The question as to the grooves is also one for an officer expert. It appears that the grooves in a bullet are formed by its being forced through the rifled barrel.

Thus Colonel Toppin displays more knowledge of ballistics than Captain Barrett, who seems to consider that a Mauser bullet is cast with its grooves already formed.

Toppin's concern about the handing over of the pistol and the transfer of the cartridges was to some extent excessive. The Courts Martial Officer, Captain Barrett of Dublin District knew his job and had been careful to rehearse his witnesses before bringing them to Mountjoy where they faced the prisoner. On 24 September, Lance/Sergeant Archer Banks deposed: 'Just before the revolver was handed over to the adjutant, the driver showed it to me and also three rounds of ammunition which he stated he had taken from the revolver. *The bullets had their noses pared down*' (author's italics).

An earlier reference to filed down bullets was made on the day of the raid by Captain and Adjutant R.S. Chomley of the 2nd Battalion the Duke of Wellington's Regiment at Collinstown. He was not on the scene, but that does not prevent him from expressing his certainty about Kevin's guilt: 'Pte. Washington was killed by the man who is now a prisoner. He was hit in the mouth and throat . . .'

More to Colonel Toppin's point, he says:

The sergeant [Banks] came out of the bakery at this moment and noticed one man lying under the lorry. He obtained a rifle [another witness tells us it was the dead soldier Washington's gun] and ordered him to come out. The civilian dropped his revolver, a German automatic, on the ground. The revolver was found to have one bullet in the breach [*sic*] and one in the magazine *with the ends filed* (author's italics). He was recognised by Ptes. Dolby and Cleary as being the man who shot Pte. Washington . . .

Ten minutes later at the North Dublin Union, Sergeant W.H Brain of the 1st Lancashires received the pistol.

Outside the hospital [the N.D.U.] the driver of the lorry handed me a German automatic pistol which I now identify. I examined it. I opened it. I took out the magazine which is in the stock. The magazine contained two bullets. After taking out the magazine I drew back the breach [*sic*] and found one round in the chamber. I identify the ammunition now produced . . . The two in the magazine were flat nosed and the one in the chamber was round nosed. They were copper coloured.

At the court-martial, the ordnance officer, then unnamed, whom Colonel Toppin had considered essential to the case, gave evidence. He was Lieutenant Thomas Watters of the Royal Army Ordnance Corps, Islandbridge, and he said:

The pistol produced to me is a 1915 Mausa [*sic*] pistol. The barrel shows that it has been fired through. It has not been fired for a fortnight. I say this because of the state of the superficial fouling. I cannot say the number of shots that has been fired through it. It is not a British issue.

The magazine would carry at least eight rounds. The three rounds produced fit the pistol. Each is of a different mark. I cannot say which is the Government of issue. The expended round fits the pistol. The grooves on the expended round prove that it has been fired as these are caused by the rifling of the pistol. The bullet has six grooves, there are six grooves in the pistol. The bullet was fired out of a pistol of the same calibre and pattern as the one produced.

Kevin declined to cross-examine this witness.

Captain Barrett had done his work well. On 5 October, a fortnight before the court-martial, he stamped 'Very Secret' on a letter which he signed for the Brigadier-General Commanding Dublin. The addressee was GHQ Ireland (that is, General Macready) and he said: '. . . The pistol in question together with the round found in the operating theatre are now in possession of my Courts Martial Officer . . .' The CMO was of course, Barrett himself.

In this fashion then, the court-martial evidence on the afternoon of 20 October relentlessly and methodically linked Kevin's automatic specifically with the death of Private Matthew Whitehead. The witnesses had an easy time of it. There was no cross-examination.

Also before the court were copies of a plan of the area in which the attack took place, drawn to scale by Lt. E.F. Ronald-Sample, of the Royal Engineers, who himself appeared before the court and gave evidence. The position of the lorry was not marked on the plan because it would be the subject of evidence.

After the completion of the ballistics evidence the court ordered that Kevin be taken out into the yard. The family was also told to go there. Kevin was allowed to talk to them. Presumably the court used this time to arrive at a finding. The timing of the various accounts varies. Certainly at this point the Judge Advocate had not yet summed up the evidence. At any rate, Kathy took the opportunity to have 'the first conversation I had had with him since his capture — the family had been told by the IRA not to visit him . . .'

He told me what had happened on 20 September. His gun jammed on the first shot. It was not his own, which he had taken with him to Tombeagh when he went on holidays. He had only come up to town for an exam, and had insisted on being included in the Monks' Bakery job, which should have been well over before his exam at 2 p.m.

The gun had been issued to him for the occasion, and he said it had just been reconditioned. When it jammed he discarded the first round, fired two rounds, and it jammed again on the fourth. This time he could not free it quickly, so he knelt down beside the lorry for shelter, while he struggled with the jammed gun. [In another account, Kathy's evidence is significantly different: 'He

117

explained to me that, when he stood up after discarding the third round, he lifted a flap of the lorry, fired and got this man. The gun jammed again on the fifth round. . . .']

His whole attention was concentrated on the job of freeing it. Suddenly he noticed a silence, or a change in the noises. He looked around and saw none of the I.R.A. party. The signal for retreat was to be a whistle, but no whistle had been blown.

He thought the best thing to do was to dive in between the wheels of the lorry and take a chance of getting clear when it drove away. The soldiers were all in the lorry, and the Sergeant had one foot on it, to get in, when a woman shouted (probably hysterically, he thought): 'There's a man under the lorry'. The soldiers swarmed down and captured him. He had not succeeded in freeing the gun.

Father Augustine later recalled the interval in the yard where Kevin stood by a wall and spoke to the priest: 'He was his own calm natural self, not in the slightest degree perturbed, and apparently not in the least interested in what was taking place around him . . .'[3]

During the entire court-martial proceedings Mrs. Barry remained entirely calm and needed no support. Kathy sat on her right side and Father Augustine on her left. Augustine recalled the scene in the court-room.

We sat together at the side of the room in which the court-martial was held, and our chairs were on a line with Kevin, whose right cheek and face we could see clearly, being only about ten feet away. He sat on the chair before the presiding Judge, leaning back easily against its support, his head bent in meditative mood, his chin resting, as it were, on his chest. He seemed quite indifferent to everything that was passing, and even now [1948] I remember vividly thinking how extraordinary it was that he could be so unemotional in such strange circumstances.

Soon after the Court resumed following the interval in the yard, Kathy was asked to take her mother home. Seán Ó hUadhaigh was afraid that sentence might be passed that evening and he did not want Mrs. Barry there for that. The others waited until the end.

The Judge Advocate summed up the evidence, which he said was not disputed. Then he came to the heart of the matter:

> It is not necessary to prove that the accused set out with malice aforethought to kill Private Whitehead. It is sufficient to prove that he was killed while a felony, in which the accused took part, was being committed.

It was a curious statement from the Judge Advocate though perhaps understandable since the evidence had not been challenged. Curious, in that the specific charge against Kevin was actually that he 'feloniously, wilfully and of his malice aforethought did kill and murder No. 4603629 Private Matthew Whitehead'. It was a catch-all summary, required despite the painstaking assembly of technical evidence.

At this point a departure from the usual court-martial procedure was made. The Barry trial was the first of its kind and the court was to some extent making up the rules as it went along. In the ordinary course, the members of the court would have arrived at a finding or verdict. The accused would have been formally and publicly arraigned, standing to attention as the President announced the finding. Evidence in mitigation would have been heard. And sentence would have been pronounced. Alternatively, the President would have stated that sentence would be awarded later. The press would have been present for this most important exercise of the duty of a general court-martial.

As it happened, the newspaper reports of the court-martial end with the Judge Advocate's summing up, the *Evening Herald* adding only: 'The court closed and sentence will be promulgated'.

In its report next morning, the *Irish Independent* said: 'We learn unofficially that Barry has been lodged in the condemned cell in Mountjoy Jail, and the sentence of the court-martial (whether confirmed by the competent Military Authority or not we cannot say) that he is to be hanged has been intimated to him'.

The press, it seems, had been ordered from the court; the finding of guilty had been passed, and Kevin was told that sentence would be handed to him later. He was taken back to Mountjoy in the armoured car.

At about eight o'clock that evening, after a long day throughout which Kevin remained nonchalant, Captain Barrett came in to his cell and read him the sentence of the general court-martial: 'To suffer death by being hanged'.

13 The Condemned Cell

Kathy recalled that the next morning the prison refused to accept Kevin's breakfast, which was sent in every day.

> We knew then that he was sentenced, and later in the day he said that the sentence was handed to him on the evening of the 20th by the Court Martial Officer, who burst into tears and left the cell hurriedly.[1]

It was, says Kathy Barry in another account, Kate Kinsella who brought Kevin's breakfast in to him.

> All his meals had been sent in from a restaurant from the beginning, but he had asked one of his visitors to tell us that the breakfast was not as good as Kate's and after that she had taken his breakfast up every morning. She was back before 8.30 and her own early associations with the Invincibles gave her the clue — which we lacked — to this refusal of the prison authorities to accept his breakfast . . . I shall never forget the sound of her loud crying when she got inside the hall door.

After the court-martial, Kevin's uncle, Pat Dowling, had gone back to Fleet Street and straight on by taxi to Mountjoy to see if he could learn anything. While he was outside, he saw the armoured car passing in with Kevin, but he could get no information.

The condemned cell in Mountjoy is spacious and was, by prison standards, well appointed. It is the width of three ordinary cells, one-third of it then being taken up by a lavatory, with a spyhole. It stands at the end of D Wing, and is only a matter of yards, through a barred door, away from the hanghouse.

When Mountjoy was built in 1847, all the cells had lavatories. Over the years they were damaged and eventually done away with. The condemned cell, where Kevin was lodged from 21 October until his death, was the only cell with a fireplace. He heard Mass the next Sunday in the prison chapel, where there is a special barred space beside the altar for men awaiting execution. Desmond McCarthy, in a forceful article in the *Westminster Gazette* on 30 October, stressed that Kevin would be hanged two days later 'unless the prisoner is allowed the usual interval of life between sentence and execution – three Sundays'.

One of the condemned man's rights – there has not been a hanging in Mountjoy since 1954 – is to choose two prison officers to be with him at all times. There was a special payment for warders who took on this duty; most of them did not take the payment, or used the money to have Masses said for the repose of the soul of the executed man.[2]

Edward Charles Stewart Proctor, from Killeshin, Co. Carlow, was one of Kevin's choices as permanent company as far as the scaffold.[3] Mrs. Mag Leonard, Ned Proctor's daughter, says he was on day duty (seven a.m. to five p.m.) on the morning of the execution. Kevin gave him a rosary beads as a keepsake, which Mag Proctor Leonard now holds as a cherished possession.

Another privilege afforded to the condemned was a special issue of food. Convicted prisoners normally got 8 ounces of bread for breakfast; 1½ pints of stirabout containing 3 ounces of Indian meal and 3 ounces of oatmeal for dinner, and another 8 ounces of bread for supper.

On 22 October Captain B.J. Hackett, MC, RAMC, who was the Medical Officer at Mountjoy, ordered a diet 'recommended for the prisoner Kevin Barry under sentence of death'.

Breakfast: 1 lb. bread, ¼ lb. bacon; 1½ oz. butter; ¼ oz. tea; 1 oz. sugar. Dinner: 2 lbs. potatoes; ½ lb. bread, ¾ lb. beef (¾ lb. of fish on Fridays in lieu of meat) and one small bottle of stout. Supper: 1 lb. bread; 1½ oz. sugar; 1 pint milk.[4]

'The prisoner may be supplied with cigarettes', wrote Dr.

Hackett in the Medical Officer's Book. A week later, Dr. Hackett or his Assistant Visiting Medical Officer, Dr. W.A. Cooke, ordered: 'Fruit in season; grapes or apples may be supplied to prisoner Kevin Barry under sentence of death. Half a pound of grapes or a pound of apples may be supplied at a time.'

The doctors had discretion in the matter of diet and were unaccustomed to prescribing for condemned men. It was nearly twenty years since John Toole had been hanged for the murder of his wife on 18 March, 1901.

The people of Ireland, waiting only for the end of Terence MacSwiney's protracted hunger-strike, still did not know the result of Kevin's trial. But Mark Sturgis,* one of the new boys brought over from London to stiffen up the running of Dublin Castle, noted in his diary on Thursday, 21 October, 'The Bakery Gun Boy, Kevin Barry, is sentenced to death.'[5]

---

*Sir Mark Beresford Russell Sturgis, who played a relatively major part in the drama of Kevin's last days, was born in 1884. He was a Special Commissioner of Income Tax when he was drafted in to the reformed Dublin Castle. Sir John Anderson became Joint Under Secretary, and A.W. ('Andy') Cope and Mark Sturgis became Joint Assistant Under Secretaries. 'The exercise', O'Halpin notes in his book *The Decline of the Union*, 'involved the grouping together of some of the most promising officials in Whitehall'. Sturgis in 1914 married Lady Rachel Montagu-Stuart-Wortley, daughter of the 2nd Earl of Wharncliffe. He lived at No. 4 Upper Castle Yard, too small to accommodate his wife and family. Rachel made frequent visits from London to go racing, have lunch at Jammet's and go to dinner at the Chief Secretary's and Vice Regal Lodges. There they met people such as Lady Eva and Olein Wyndham-Quin (the Dunraven family name). In mid-October, 1920, Sturgis noted in his diary: '. . . Everybody has been shooting everybody while I've been away — quite gay! ' On 3 November: 'His Ex, Burkes, Lady Massareene dined with Helen [Lady French], also Lord Dunraven, his Secretary, and Mrs. Blennerhasset, whom I have not seen since I stayed with them at Tralee before the war. D [Dunraven] is wonderful for his age, 80 — he looks years younger and quite all there except that he is deaf. He said he would declare himself a Republican if he wasn't afraid to — this is not to be taken too seriously'. On 9 November: 'I like this life most awfully and find the Vice Regal lot most pleasant and delightful, though Helen and Dicky [Lord French] are of course the makings of it, — but Gawd knows whether I shall *ever* settle down happily in a London office again — here one is up to the neck in intrigue, plot and

He had substituted 'Gun Boy' for 'murderer'.

On Friday evening, 22 October, the *Globe* in London announced the death sentence as 'official', and next day the *Freeman's Journal* vainly sought confirmation at Dublin Castle. But it was late on Wednesday, 27 October, before the prisoner himself was given final confirmation of the sentence and informed that it would be carried out on the following Monday.

On the same day, Ernest Aston, Kathy Barry's employer, was told by Sir John Anderson,* the Joint Under Secretary, that the execution would not be delayed. The frantic and belated movement for reprieve began as people suddenly realised that, unless they did something, Kevin was going to hang.

Sometime before noon the next day, Thursday 28 October, Kathy Barry got word that she was to go immediately to the Wood Printing Works, where Brigadier Dick McKee told her that she was to take Seán Ó hUadhaigh and a Justice of the Peace into Mountjoy that afternoon and tell Kevin that 'on Dick's order, he was to make a sworn affidavit concerning his torture in the North Dublin Union.'[6]

I was to take the affidavit straight from Mountjoy to

---

counter-plot with a small spice of danger all mixed up with the life of something like a big country house in the old days . . .)' The reader might agree with A.W. Cope who in December 1922, gave James Mac-Mahon a preview of the New Year's Honours List. Sturgis was to get a KCB though 'for the life of me I can't see what Sturgis did either for coercion or peace'. By the 1930s he was back where he came from. He was Presiding Special Commissioner of Income Tax.

*Sir John Anderson — Jonathan to his friends — was born in 1882 and enjoyed a long and successful career in the public service. He was chairman of the Board of Inland Revenue when he was appointed Joint Under Secretary for Ireland. In 1922 he went to the Home Office and ten years later was made Governor of Bengal. He was an MP and Cabinet Minister in 1938 and was Home Secretary when the war began. He introduced the eponymous air-raid shelter before he became Chancellor of the Exchequer. He was created Viscount Waverley in 1952 and died in 1958, full of honours. In Ireland he is remembered as the man who induced the British Government to finance the establishment of the B Specials in Northern Ireland. Molly Doolin, earlier referred to, found him 'a bit of a stick; I could never warm to him'.

Arthur Griffith's* office in Pearse Street, where Dick would be waiting. He had arranged that Desmond Fitz-Gerald,** the Dáil Minister of Propaganda, would be there to collect it and give it next day to the Press with the object of having it published in the world Press, and particularly in the English papers, on Saturday, October 30th.

Dr. Myles Keogh was secured by Seán Ó hUadhaigh and the three went to Mountjoy. 'Kevin was reluctant to make such a fuss', says Kathy, 'but on being told that it was Dick McKee's order, he made the affidavit', which has been reproduced in full earlier. The handwriting on the original document is Seán Ó hUadhaigh's.

Kathy says that this interview was held in the boardroom of the prison, as were all interviews after the death sentence had been pronounced. Her recollection is confirmed by her surviving sister, Elgin, who remembers that there was always a fire burning in the grate — 'at least there was that'. Elgin also says there was no difficulty in arranging visits. 'It was

---

*Arthur Griffith (1871-1922) was a Dublin man educated by the Christian Brothers at Strand Street. He was a Celtic revivalist, printer and journalist and went to South Africa at the invitation of John MacBride, to whom he introduced Maud Gonne in Paris. His concept of dual monarchy was widely studied and his theory of economic self-sufficiency for a self-governing Ireland was adopted by Sinn Féin in 1905. He left the IRB in 1910, but joined the Irish Volunteers and took part in the Howth gun-running (July, 1914). He was imprisoned several times and when de Valera went to America he became Acting President of Dáil Éireann. He led the team of Plenipotentiaries to the Anglo-Irish negotiations. He supported the Treaty, accepted the bombardment of the Four Courts in the Civil War, and died of a cerebral haemorrhage on 12 August, 1922.

**Desmond FitzGerald (1889-1947) was born in London of Kerry and Cork parents. He was an early friend of the poet Ezra Pound; a journalist and politician, fluent in six languages, and he organised the Irish Volunteers in Kerry with Ernest Blythe. He fought in the GPO, was imprisoned and was substitute Director of Publicity during the War of Independence. Minister for External Affairs from 1922 to 1927, he was appointed Minister for Defence until 1932. Poetry, drama and philosophy were among his interests and he was also a member of the Seanad from 1938 to 1943. His son, Dr. Garret FitzGerald, was Taoiseach in the early 1980s.

Kitby [Kathy] who looked after all that. I was too young.'
(She was sixteen.)

Kathy remarked on the interest in the proceedings shown
by the two Auxiliaries on guard that day, and tells us that a
couple of times during the taking of the affidavit 'when Kevin
seemed to be at a loss for a British military term, one of the
Auxies supplied it. They were most friendly and co-operative
with him and deeply respectful with us.'

From Mountjoy, Kathy arrived in Pearse Street about five
o'clock. Griffith and McKee were there, and FitzGerald was
due at five thirty. McKee had to go shortly before six and left
impressing on her the vital importance of publishing the affidavit on Saturday. FitzGerald came about six thirty and Kathy
handed him the affidavit. Because his typist had gone home
he feared that he would have no copies to give to the journalists he was meeting that night. Kathy had the key to Aston's
office and the use of an excellent typewriter and a duplicator,
but FitzGerald refused her offer of help and told her to leave
the matter in his hands.

Desmond FitzGerald carried out his orders, but the newspapers did not carry the affidavit until the day of Kevin's
execution. It appeared in the Irish newspapers; verbatim in
some of the English papers, partially in others. The *Daily
News* and *Leader* carried the whole text. *The Times* noted:
'We have received, apparently from an official Sinn Féin source,
what purports to be a copy of an affidavit sworn by the boy
Kevin Barry . . .' The paper then published a condensed version of Kevin's account, and the affidavit, as we shall see,
became the subject of heated exchanges in the House of Commons on 5 November.

'A Message to the Civilised Nations of the World' was issued
by President Griffith on Friday, 29 October, and appeared in
international organs of opinion next day. Griffith cited three
recent instances in which the standards observed by the IRA
at the very least conformed to the civilised behaviour laid
down in international law:

(i) Twenty-five British soldiers were disarmed at the King's
Inns, Dublin, on June 1st and immediately released;

(ii) after a fight in Cloyne, Co. Cork, in which one Volunteer was killed and two were wounded, the whole of the opposing force was captured, disarmed and set free;

(iii) Brigadier-General Lucas was taken prisoner by the Volunteers and during six weeks of captivity was afforded all the privileges due to his rank as a prisoner of war.

The Dáil Government was using all the resources of its publicity machine to mobilise public opinion in favour of the reprieve of Kevin Barry. In a powerful letter to the *Westminster Gazette*, Erskine Childers wrote, in part:

> This lad, Barry was doing precisely what an Englishman would be doing in the same circumstances and with the same bitter and intolerable provocation — the suppression by military force of their country's liberty. To hang him for murder is an insulting outrage, and it is more: it is an abuse of power: an unworthy act of vengeance, contrasting with the forbearance and humanity invariably shown by the Irish Volunteers towards the prisoners captured by them when they have been successful in encounters similar to this one . . .
>
> To hang Barry is to push to its logical extreme the hypocritical pretence that the national movement in Ireland, unflinchingly supported by the great mass of the Irish people, is the squalid conspiracy of a 'murder gang'. That is false; it is a natural uprising; a collision between two Governments, one resting on consent, the other on force. The Irish are struggling against overwhelming odds to defend their own elected institutions against extinction.

When Honoria Aughney,[7] by now a Second Medical student, heard that Kevin had been sentenced to death, Nora Brick*

*Nora Brick of Caherbreagh, Tralee, Co. Kerry was, according to Síghle Bean Uí Dhonnchadha, 'a most attractive looking girl'. She got a first-class Arts degree, became a prominent member of Cumann na mBan working with Austin Stack, and married Éamonn Bulfin. Bulfin, a tall,

suggested to her: 'We'll go down to Church Street and we'll get a Mass said for him'. Honoria Aughney says:

> We wrote a note to Kevin in Mountjoy telling him we were having a Mass said for him. I had a letter back from him. 'Nora Brick' wouldn't have meant anything to him so I had signed the note '*Aichnaidh*' [Aughney] which he would be able to recognise.
>
> I think the letter was sent on to me in class one day by Gerry McAleer. It said: 'Thanks very much for having the Mass said. Tell the boys to carry on. There are good times comin'. One of the lasses in Dominican Hall [the student hostel] said: 'You should cut off that and give us all a little piece of it'. But I kept it until my maid or someone threw it out years later.

The British authorities did themselves no service when they chose 1 November, All Saints' Day, for Kevin's execution. F.W. Doheny, of The Parade, Kilkenny, wrote on Saturday, 30 October, to Sir Hamar Greenwood pointing out the unsuitability of selecting a Catholic Church holiday, and citing two local precedents for changing the date. In the case of Kevin Barry, Mr. Doheny told the Chief Secretary, 'the impossibility of carrying out the sentence on the date publicly named may well be permitted to act as a balancing factor in favour of the life of this very youthful prisoner'.

Quite apart from the outcry against hanging a man on a church holiday, the British forgot, or perhaps simply ignored, the effect of executing a young man on a day when every church in the country would be full to the doors several times over. The saying of Masses would be continued for six hours and more, creating a groundswell of public protest where the Catholic Irish were at their most susceptible, in church.

The most charitable interpretation of this monumental

---

elegant man, of Derrinlough, Birr, Co. Offaly, was a son of William Bulfin, author of *Rambles in Eirinn*, and nephew of Frank Bulfin, TD, who voted for the Treaty. Éamonn Bulfin went to Pearse's school, St. Enda's, and, as a member of E Company, 4th Battalion ('Pearse's Own'), fought in the GPO in Easter week. His sister Catalina ('Kid'), who worked with Nora Brick under Austin Stack, married Seán MacBride.

lapse from common sense is that Monday, 1 November, 1920, was selected without thought for its religious significance. The English made a martyr of Kevin Barry.

Belvedere, 1917

Belvedere, 1919

Pillars of the House, 1919. Kevin is third from left

9 Tombeagh, 1919. Kevin and Michael

Portrait from photograph. Artist unknown

Richardson's Hotel, Glendalough

14 The Quality of Mercy

The reprieve movement had very little time. Ernest Aston enlisted the help of Commander Jack MacCabe and they set off for London to plead with Lloyd George. They brought with them a photograph of Kevin which had been given to Aston by his secretary, Kathy Barry, who explains the circumstances: 'Mr. Aston believed that it was only at the highest level that Kevin's execution could be stopped and he asked for this photograph. I was so terrified of letting Kevin down that I refused the photograph until I could get IRA permission. I was told it was perfectly all right to give the photograph, since Mr. Aston understood our attitude'.[1]

Aston had asked Kathy for the photograph on Monday, 25 October, and set off for London that night. He came bouncing back from London and was in his office on the Saturday morning. 'It is all right', he told Kathy, 'the reprieve is through'. When she looked doubtful, he said: 'I have Lloyd George's personal word of honour.'

> This was so funny that I laughed [says Kathy]. He looked a little hurt, but said very patiently: 'I'll put it another way. If I weren't satisfied, I wouldn't be here. I'd still be in London.'
>
> I was so sorry that I had been ungracious, but I explained to him my deep instinct that Kevin was to die on Monday morning. He said: 'Don't be morbid! Run home now and tell your mother the good news. There is nothing in the office that can't wait'.

That was on Saturday, 30 October. The hangman's new ropes had arrived in Dublin Castle the day before. Even before that, on Thursday as the affidavit was being prepared by Seán Ó hUadhaigh in Mountjoy, Lloyd George was presiding over a Cabinet meeting ('Conference of Ministers') in Mr. Bonar Law's room in the House of Commons. Hamar Greenwood was there too, and Tom Jones acted as secretary. The minuted record of the meeting is characteristically dry.

> The attention of the conference was called to the case of a young man, aged 18 years and nine months, who had been sentenced to death by a court-martial for taking part in an attack on military in Ireland. He was to be hanged on the following Monday, and an appeal for mercy had been received by Mr. Devlin* on the ground of youth.
>
> It was pointed out to the conference that three soldiers had been murdered in the raid in question, that the prisoner had been found with a revolver, which had been fired, in his hand, with one bullet in the barrel and two more in the magazine, and that it was precisely young and irresponsible men of this type who were the main cause of the present disturbance in Ireland.
>
> The Conference agreed:
>
> That they could not recommend any commutation of the death penalty.[2]

Kathy Barry and David Lloyd George were *ad idem*. But what of Kevin's attitude to the movement for reprieve and the attitude of his family? When Kathy visited him for the first time in Mountjoy — after the court-martial of 20 October — he told her about having been handed the death sentence by the British Court Martial Officer and continued.[3]

'Mind, there's to be no appeal.'

---

*Joseph Devlin (1872-1934) was born in Belfast, where he got little education but strong working-class support for his political action. Nicknamed 'Wee Joe', he was the spokesman for the Catholic population and a life-long opponent of the Orange Order. He was a pillar of the Ancient Order of Hibernians, and was Home Rule MP for West Belfast from 1902 to 1918. He supported Larkin's Belfast strike of 1907, and in the war encouraged Irishmen to enlist in the British Army. He led the Ulster nationalists from 1918 and did not enter the new Stormont Parliament until 1925.

'You know we wouldn't do that,' Kathy said.

'Well I depend on you to see that nobody in the family lets me down.'

Elsewhere, Kathy adds:

> On that morning he said to me: 'The sentence has to be confirmed and they tell me here that there is a hope it may be changed to shooting. I must say I'd rather be shot.' He said he was living in luxury on the fat of the land, that he had been told he had only to ask for any kind of food and drink and it would be supplied ... He was allowed four visits every weekday, two in the morning and two in the afternoon, and up to three persons at each ... One afternoon that I visited him, he was much annoyed because some girls had got in and some of the family had been turned back. He said: 'I don't want my past appearing any more. I'd rather see my family while I can'.

The reprieve machinery rolled on. Joe Devlin and T.P. O'Connor* called on the Prime Minister and believed that he favoured a reprieve. Devlin expressed the belief in a letter to Ned Toole, Kevin's old schoolmaster in Rathvilly. Toole had sent Devlin a telegram and Devlin replied by letter on 29 October. Devlin said Lloyd George had tears in his eyes while they talked. British newspapers such as the *Westminster Gazette* (29 October) called for the use of the prerogative of mercy. The *Sunday Times* thundered to its readers: 'An example has to be made'.

To Kathy Barry that Friday, 29 October, seemed a whirlpool nightmare of 'dashing round and dealing with all kinds of people.' Some people came to ask the family to sponsor a petition for a reprieve; others to offer sympathy and ask if

---

*T.P. O'Connor (1848-1929) was a native of Athlone, a journalist and MP for the Scotland division of Liverpool (1880-1929). He supported the Land League and Parnell, though he fell out with Parnell over the divorce case. He was Father of the House of Commons in his old age, and in 1917 became the British Official Film Censor. In 1902 he founded *T.P.'s Weekly* and as editor turned down a job application from James Joyce. He wrote biographies of Disraeli and Parnell and published his memoirs the year he died.

there was anything they could do; others to enquire why no rescue was being organised — 'these were mostly people who would not know one end of a gun from another'. Kathy is adamant about her family on the question of reprieve, 'none of us had anything to do with appeals for reprieve, nor did we feel there would be any reprieve'.

My personal concern was to see that Kevin's wishes were carried out and that no word or action of his family could be twisted into letting him down. He had laid this as a charge upon me, so that in addition to my own personal inclinations, I felt I had the sanction of his wishes.

I remember dashing down Anglesea Street and meeting Alderman James Moran, later Senator Moran [1925-34] — a very nice man but not a Republican. He looked very distressed and, to cover up the awkwardness of the moment, he said: 'You are in a great hurry!' I said 'Yes, Alderman Moran, I am up to my neck organising the successful execution of my brother.' It was only when I saw his look of shock that I realised it had been a cruel thing to say to a man who was on the opposite side of the great gulf fixed at that time between Republicans and those we called pro-Britishers.

On the Saturday afternoon, the aged and ailing Archbishop of Dublin, Dr. Walsh,* and the city's Lord Mayor, Larry O'Neill, called on General Macready at the Royal Hospital, Kilmainham. He referred them to Anderson at the Castle, who in turn sent them to the Viceroy, Lord French. According to the newspapers, French told them that their view would be 'transmitted to the proper authorities'. But in his own diary, French recorded: 'The Archbishop (R.C.) of Dublin

---

*William Joseph Walsh (1841-1921) was Roman Catholic Archbishop of Dublin from 1885. He was a Dubliner and a strong nationalist whose appointment was opposed by the British Government. An authority on bimetallism, his major work, *Bimetallism and Monometallism*, was published in 1893, translated into German that year and into French the year after. He was an ardent Sinn Féin supporter and was Chancellor of the National University of Ireland until his death. He was succeeded as Chancellor by Éamon de Valera.

and the Lord Mayor called and urged me to remit the death sentence – I refused . . . The Lord Mayor rang up several times up to 10 p.m. I hear that in the small hours of the morning he applied by wire to the P.M. but with no success.'[4]

The Lord Mayor afterwards told the Barrys that the Archbishop had made a very real sacrifice in approaching the British authorities. He had made it a rule when he became Archbishop of Dublin that he would not have anything to do with Dublin Castle. Larry O'Neill felt that Dr. Walsh's breach of his own code would carry great weight in the Castle. It did not.

Lord French's aide-de-camp was an old Stonyhurst boy who, because of that, had a helpful interest in the cause of a young man who had similarly been educated by the 'Black Militia'. The Lord Mayor, also a product of the Jesuits, derived some faint amusement from the coincidence, but despite being received graciously the Archbishop was restive about being sent from Billy to Jack. So much for the power of the Hierarchy.

When Larry O'Neill telephoned Lloyd George at midnight on Sunday, the Prime Minister was at his residence in Hythe, Kent. This time he was firm. The Government would not grant a reprieve under any circumstances.

Whose was the right to commute the sentence, to exercise the royal prerogative? Mark Sturgis was never busier in his young life, but he had time for a revealing entry in his diary for Saturday, 30 October:

> A chasse, entailing many wires, yesterday evening about the prerogative of mercy. The case of Kevin Barry must go to the Lord Lieutenant or in his absence the Lords Justices – in this case Campbell,* the Lord Chancellor.

---

*James Henry Mussen Campbell, first Baron Glenavy (1851-1933), was born in Terenure and educated at Kingstown School and Trinity College. After a brilliant academic career, he was called to the Bar in 1878 and took silk in 1890. An MP from 1898, he became Solicitor-General, Attorney-General, Lord Chief Justice, and Lord Chancellor of Ireland (1918-1921). He was the first chairman of the Senate of the Irish Free State (1922-1928). O'Halpin, in his work *The Decline of the Union*, says: 'Campbell distinguished himself only by his importunity, greed and opportunism'.

Anyway, the result is that French is returning himself tonight. There is, I believe, no question of remitting the sentence.

Two grim-looking ropes arrived from Pentonville via the Home Office yesterday. The execution is fixed for Monday morning. Rather a pity no one noticed it is All Saints' Day. Great play will be made about Barry's youth, 18½.

The *Freeman* calls him *Master* Barry of course, but he is quite as old as a large chunk of the British Army and the three soldiers he and his party killed were all under 19, so there's not much in that. I think the Shinns would gain more sympathy as 'Sportsmen' if they were a little more logical about all this – they seem to see nothing absurd in making their proudest boast that they are a rebel army attacking a tyrant and yet using every sort of plea for mercy whenever one of their brave soldiers is up against it. Just as the local authorities see nothing ridiculous in pledging themselves to Dáil Éireann, signing resolutions to protest their abhorrence of England and her Government, and then come screaming for our money and protesting the hardship of stopping their grants.

Jonathan [Sir John Anderson] has gone off to England – this afternoon the old Archbishop of Dublin with the Lord Mayor called upon J [Anderson]. They did not base their plea for reprieve upon any individual factor in the case – Barry's youth or anything like that, but solely on the bad effect his execution would have upon the populace – it is the old argument that has been used over and over again: 'Don't exact this penalty or you make peace impossible.'[5]

Sturgis, who with Basil Clarke* had been charged by Macready to 'do anything we like' to sharpen up the British propaganda

---

*Basil Clarke (1879-1947) was a *Daily Mail* war correspondent, then Director, Special Intelligence, Ministry of Reconstruction, 1918. He was Director of Public Information in the Ministry of Health (1920-1923) when he was seconded to the Irish administration from 1920 to 1922. He was knighted in 1923. By the end of September 1920, says

machine, ends his lengthy entry: 'I can't see any reason to let him off if we are ever going to execute anybody — he was one of the party who attacked the bread lorry in Upper Church Street when they killed three soldiers and Barry was identified as the man who shot the first soldier dead. He was caught hiding under the lorry, pistol in hand. This was on September 20th.'

A man who had not known Kevin at school felt it his duty to do what he could for the prisoner. Father Frank Brown,[6] the well-known photographer, joined the staff of Belvedere after Kevin left. He had been a chaplain in the British Army, was a brother of Father Stephen Brown, SJ, and a nephew of the Bishop of Cloyne. Francis Mary Hegarty Brown had served with Lord French and knew him well, so his appeal was personal. But it was no more effective for that.

Shortly after eleven on Sunday morning, less than twenty-four hours before the execution, Kathleen Carney came to Fleet Street in great excitement. She said that the Under Secretary for Ireland, James MacMahon, wanted Mrs. Barry to send a personal telegram to King George V. If she would draft the telegram, MacMahon was waiting to send it off at once. 'My mother was furious', says Kathy, 'and as a matter of fact it was a couple of months before she could bring herself to be more than polite to Kathleen. It fell to my lot to soften the sharpness of my mother's refusal and to ask her to explain to Mr. MacMahon that, while we appreciated his personal kindness, there was a definite principle at stake — the principle for which my brother was glad to die.[7]

In his book, *Annals of an Active Life*, published in 1924, General Macready recalled the case of Kevin Barry.

Every kind of effort was made to secure a reprieve, though there were no circumstances in the case to justify consideration ... At his trial, counsel being employed on both sides (*sic*), it was clearly proved that one at least of

Sturgis, 'he was clearly established as the head of the news bureau'. But he had great difficulty getting a supply of information from the Crown forces, and was defended by Anderson against Macready's criticisms: 'I do not think that he or anyone ought to be expected to create propaganda out of his own inner consciousness'.

the soldiers was killed by him . . . A great point was made
by those who agitated for a reprieve, of the youth of
Barry, but, as I pointed out to Dr. Walsh, the Archbishop
of Dublin, who came to enlist my sympathy, the victims
of the crime were also mere youths, one being younger
than Barry, and they too, left mothers to mourn their
losses. Barry met his fate with fortitude, the victim of
those who preached assassination under the guise of patri-
otic sacrifice.

Among the appeals was one from a group of seventeen ex-
officers of the British Army studying at Trinity College,
Dublin. One of them was Thomas McGreevy, scholar, poet
and critic, friend of Beckett, Joyce and Jack B. Yeats and
(1950-1964) Director of the National Gallery of Ireland.

The Barry's friend Eileen Dixon went around with Frank
Morrin organising a doctors' appeal with Harry Meade and
Dr. Jim Maginnis.

Madame Charlotte Despard,* who was a sister of the Lord
Lieutenant and a source of some embarrassment to him because
of her blatantly Republican activities, told Heavey[9] in
1923 that she made 'a frantic journey from some European
capital to Dublin in an effort to use her influence with her
brother Sir John French (*sic*) to have the execution called off.
She told me she was certain that if she had reached "John"
in time, the execution would not have taken place'. Put not
your trust in princes, even if related.

On a normal Sunday morning, the Vice Regal Lodge was a
green haven of quiet and seclusion, reflecting its origin as the

---

*Charlotte Despard (1844-1939) was a close friend of Maud Gonne
MacBride. (The people of Dublin fondly called them 'Maud Gone Mad
and Mrs. Desperate'). Her views were left wing and she worked with
Hanna Sheehy-Skeffington, Helena Moloney, Peadar O'Donnell and
Frank Ryan. She lived in Roebuck House for many years. In 1932 she
established a workers' college in Eccles Street, in a house that was also
the headquarters of the Irish section of the Friends of Soviet Russia.
Predictably, in March 1933, the house was attacked by the 'St. Patrick's
Young Men's League'. She died lonely and penniless in Whitehead, Co.
Antrim. Maud Gonne gave the oration in the Republican Plot in Glas-
nevin Cemetery, Dublin, where Charlotte Despard is buried.

house of the chief park ranger, Nathaniel Clements, who built a simple three-bay house in 1751. The British Government bought the house in 1782 and made additions suitable for the use of the Lord Lieutenant. It failed as a stately mansion and, in spite of the classical trimmings, still looks today like a rambling rustic house, pleasant and unpretentious.

Sunday, 31 October, brought early visitors. When General Macready arrived, he found that Mark Sturgis and Geoffrey Whiskard were already there. They had brought the Kevin Barry papers from Dublin Castle at ten o'clock. All three went into Lord French's study.

The Lord Chancellor of Ireland, Campbell, had sent a letter to Lord French and had also sent telegrams to the Prime Minister, Mr. Bonar Law, and Sir Hamar Greenwood:

> Most earnestly urge reprieve of Barry on ground of boyhood and that he acted under duress. — Also because his is first capital conviction under new procedure — Chief Justice [Thomas Francis Molony] concurs. Feeling here for reprieve universal in all classes as certainly making for better atmosphere — while refusal gravely accentuates difficulties. Earnestly recommend reprieve accompanied by official warning that in future law must take extreme course.

The Lord Lieutenant began by going fully into the case. He did not, Sturgis noted in his diary, review the evidence, upon which the confirmation of the Judge Advocate General had satisfied him.

> But he heard the story from Macready and read us a letter he had received from the Lord Chancellor. Whiskard read him the Lord Chancellor's minute on the paper recommending reprieve and I read him Anderson's minute reporting the visit of the Archbishop and Lord Mayor.
>
> His Ex. asked Whiskard whether the age of the condemned man would of necessity mean a reprieve in England and was told No. Macready said that it was a clear case of the sort where the soldiers and police rightly expected us to exact the full penalty.

His Ex. said he entirely disagreed with the Lord Chancellor's opinion and that his reasons seemed to him bad and he wrote on the papers: 'After a most careful and exhaustive examination of this case, I can see no just reason to exercise the prerogative and the law must take its course. — French 31/10/20'[10]

Sturgis goes on with his account of the meeting to say that all present were conscious that a life was at stake and that the proceedings were thorough and in no way perfunctory.

I can say without doubt that we four in the room had no doubt but that the decision was the right one. I have sent Macready a note since urging him to try to stop his Ex. from rambling about the country on his horses, anyway for a few days . . .

I hear Barry is quite calm and unrepentant, not at all like a boy driven into a deed by the orders of others. He will be hanged at 8 tomorrow morning.

'A noteworthy fact', Sturgis remarks in a way that shows clearly that he kept his diary with an eye to publication, 'is that this is probably the first time a Lord Lieutenant has disregarded the advice of the Lord Chancellor of Ireland'.

When Sturgis got back to the Castle, he found a telegram from Sir John Anderson saying that, after the Cabinet had heard his report on the Archbishop's visit, the Ministers were 'quite firm that mercy would simply be called cowardice and do less than good'.

Thick and fast came the petitions for mercy that Sunday. Greenwood received a telegram from two mature students back from the war. 'Ex-Officer students University College Dublin petition reprieve of death sentence passed on their young fellow student Kevin Barry'. It came from H.V. Gill, DSO, MC, and Major J.B. McArevey, MC. Among the UCD staff, Professor J.S. McArdle,* who held the chair of surgery from 1904 to 1928, busied himself on Kevin's behalf.[11]

---

*J.S. McArdle was born in 1859. In July, 1914, he addressed a parade of the National Volunteers at his home in Ballyteigue, Co. Wicklow, with quite belligerent remarks about being ready to defend the country

Nor was the Lord Chancellor the only man in the administration to ask Lord French to reprieve Kevin. James MacMahon, who with W.E. Wylie was known as 'the Irish side' in the Castle, added his voice:

> Your Excellency, for the past 24 hours I have been importuned from all sides of politics in the country to bespeak your Excellency's favour for reprieve of the convict Barry.
>
> Though no one of the people who have expressed themselves as anxious for his reprieve finds any excuse for his crime, all unite in the belief that his execution, however just it may be, will produce effects in the country as disastrous as those which followed the equally just executions that followed the Rebellion of 1916.[12]

That contorted plea was made on Sunday, 31 October. Next day MacMahon got a curt note from French, who 'felt myself compelled to refuse to exercise the prerogative'. He was tidying up. Kevin was already dead.

In America, Éamon de Valera made a statement on the death of Terence MacSwiney. He and Governor Al Smith held a huge Sunday memorial meeting at the New York Polo Grounds. 'President de Valera', says McCartan in his book, *With de Valera in America*, 'sorrowed nobly for MacSwiney and reflected his glory'. He got a twelve minute ovation. De Valera, conscious that he was focusing America's attention on the Irish question at a critical time in US domestic politics, knew that John Devoy and Judge Cohalan would have preferred to see Irish power used to defeat Woodrow Wilson, his League of Nations and his party. They need not have worried. A few days later, the Democrats went into the wilderness from which they did

as a rank-and-file member. Surgeon Boyd Barrett, who was also on the platform, said that as McArdle had disembowelled many members of the aristocracy, he should be made Minister of the Interior. McArdle was well known in Dublin drawingrooms and as a racing man, which inspired Oliver St. John Gogarty to write:

> Let Surgeon McArdle confirm you in hope
> A jockey fell off and its neck it was broke
> He lifted him up like a fine honest man
> And he said he is dead; but I'll do what I can

not return until Roosevelt's triumph twelve years later. Sir Henry Wilson recorded in his diary that the British Prime Minister was restricting reprisals in Ireland until after the American election, but this was hard to reconcile with the extraordinary timing and implications of the deaths of Barry and MacSwiney.

In his statement, de Valera expressed the depth of his feeling in words — his own and Yeats's — that were unusually emotive for him: 'MacSwiney and his comrades gave up their lives for their country. The English have killed them. Tomorrow a boy, Kevin Barry, they will hang and, he alike, he will only regret that he has but one life to give. O God!

They shall be remembered forever,
They shall be alive forever,
They shall be speaking forever,
The people shall hear them forever.*

---

*A contemporary recording of de Valera's statement was made in a New York studio. T.P. O'Neill, de Valera's biographer, says the President went there alone and suddenly realised that he was in a strange part of town without a bodyguard. As a result of that experience, Harry Boland gave him a Remington revolver. Mike Burns of RTE, who was in New York in the course of research on Project Y (the code name given by RTE to the collection of material to be broadcast when de Valera died), discovered the recording, which is now in RTE's archives. Maurice Moynihan, who edited *Speeches and Statements by Éamon de Valera 1917-1973*, makes no reference to the recording. The lines are from W.B. Yeats's play *Cathleen nī Houlihan* (1902).

15 Rescue?

T he Barry family's co-operation in any rescue attempt was not sought at any time until 30 October. This statement was made categorically by Kathy Barry[1] but it does not mean that no attempt to rescue Kevin was devised.

There is some controversy about the seriousness of GHQ's endeavours. Perhaps it should be said that once the sentence was handed down there was a ring of steel around Mountjoy which made any effort to bring Kevin to safety more than difficult and dangerous. Michael Collins' anguish as the inexorable end came nearer was palpable.

Any attempt at extricating Kevin from the condemned cell was tempered by the tide of rumour which swept the city that he had been reprieved. Lloyd George with his half promises and the tears which, as the cynics said, he could turn on as easily as a housewife turns on the kitchen tap, helped to build the uncertainty that sapped the would-be rescuers' determination.

But serious concern there was, among the rank and file of the Volunteers. John Joe Carroll, who had been with Kevin on the Monks' Bakery raid, says that after he was found guilty, 'the thought in everybody's mind now was, would any attempt be made to rescue Kevin from Mountjoy?'[2] Carroll goes on:

Unfortunately no serious attempt was ever made. True, the Big Shots made a bit of a demonstration — they had men from Dublin Brigade waiting around the vicinity of the prison on several occasions but no one received any instructions and the whole business fizzled out.

One plan was to cause a breach in the prison wall. This was to be effected by means of a home-made bomb. The men would then enter through the hole in the wall and no one knew what would happen after that. It's an extraordinary thing that the H.Q., with all its contacts inside Mountjoy and its secret service men inside Dublin Castle, could not plan any move with even the remotest chance of success.

The rank and file were ready and prepared to play their part in any attempt but the 'Brass Hats' were only play-acting and had no intention of risking their skins in any serious attempt at rescue.

In my opinion there was only one thing that could offer any hope of success and that was to attack the escort on its way to Dublin Castle (*sic*) for the court-martial. Surely I.R.A. intelligence must have known the route the escort would take, but this seemed to have been conveniently overlooked. Not a single shot was fired at Mountjoy Jail while Kevin Barry was in the condemned cell waiting for the end.

Writing forty years later, Carroll bitterly concludes: 'The political boys behind the scenes had the last word. Kevin Barry was more valuable dead than alive'.

There *was* a plan, says Cronin in his book *Kevin Barry*, to seize a British armoured car during the court-martial. A one-armed British officer commanded the car, which was near a bank at Doyle's Corner, Phibsboro, making a payroll collection. Volunteer Willie O'Connell* was killed in the attempt, which was directed by Brigadier Dick McKee and carried out for the most part by members of D Company of the 1st Battalion. The failure was attributed to the men's dislike of firing on a handicapped officer. At any rate, when the turret had been closed it proved impossible to seize the car.

For the second attempt, timed for the Saturday, 30 October,

---

*According to *The Last Post* (Cumann na n-Uaigheann Náisiúnta, Dublin, 3rd edn. 1985), Liam O'Connell of Lombardstown, Co. Cork, was killed in action at Phibsboro, Dublin, on 14 October, 1920. This was six days before the Barry court-martial and there is some doubt that it was connected with it. Volunteer O'Connell was buried at Glentane, Co. Cork.

two days before the execution, Michael Collins was at the planning meeting in the hall of the Dublin Typographical Provident Society in Lower Gardiner Street. A large number of Dublin printers were members of the IRB and the DTPS hall was a focal point of Dublin Brigade activities.

Charlie Byrne, the OC of D Company, was in charge. With him were Frank Flood, Barry Byrne, Paddy Kenny and Seán O'Neill. Collins supplied three snipers: Jimmy Conroy, Frank Teeling and Paddy Halpin from GHQ. They were to 'take out' the sentry inside the main gate and engage the guard of Auxiliaries. Paddy Doyle — who like Frank Flood had been on the King's Inns operation with Kevin and was hanged with Flood in Dublin in March 1921 — with Gussie Byrne and Phil Leddy was to hold the Circle in the prison while Kevin was taken from the boardroom, where visits were conducted. Davy Golden and Jimmy Carrigan (who had manned the van in the Monks' Bakery action) were to wait at Berkeley Road in a commandeered car to take Kevin to safety.

Kathy Barry[3] had come home early to Fleet Street after Ernest Aston told her to bring the 'good news' of his meeting with Lloyd George to her mother. Frank Flood and Paddy Kenny, both of H Company, came in with a stranger who turned out to be Captain Charlie Byrne. Earlier that week, members of H Company had spoken to Kathy and her family of attempts, and they had tried to dissuade them — not because they believed in the possibility of reprieve, but because they could not encourage the risk of losing other valuable IRA lives in what would probably be an unsuccessful attempt to save the life of a member of their family.

At that time [Kathy says] the British were freely using the formula 'shot in an attempt to escape' in order to cover up the murder of I.R.A. prisoners. We believed that this would provide them with an easy way out of the difficulty in which they undoubtedly, that week, found themselves, of hanging an 18-year-old prisoner of war.

I must stress that these were our opinions freely expressed to members of the H Company, but until the Saturday morning no member of the family had been asked for active co-operation.

Captain Byrne told Kathy to take with her one girl who could be relied upon for courage and initiative. They were to present themselves at the gate of Mountjoy and ask for a visit at exactly three fifteen in the afternoon. From observation and experience he estimated that they would be admitted about three thirty. He would allow ten minutes for possible delays inside and then attack.

The job for myself and the other girl was to tackle the two Auxiliaries and prevent them from shooting Kevin before entry to the boardroom of the rescue party. The warders, he said, they had 'made arrangements for'.

He explained that the whole affair must be over by 3.50, because the military guard on the jail was changed at 4 p.m. At or slightly before the hour a British military lorry would drive in with the guards who were going on duty. Kevin, and the rescue party, must be well away before then. The accurate timing of the job was of supreme importance.

Kathy tried to argue with Charlie Byrne that lives would be lost in vain.

'It's an order from Headquarters', Charlie said.

'Can't you get them to reconsider it?'

'I've got my orders. I must carry them out'.

'But you'll all be killed', Kathy pleaded.

Charlie's reply was crisp and conclusive: 'It'll be a pleasure; that's what we're in the army for'.

Frank Flood asked Kathy somehow to let Kevin know about the attempt but she refused, saying that it would be unfair to raise hopes of rescue since Kevin was so happy at the prospect of death for the Republic. Kevin read the papers and knew all about the reprieve movements. 'He had a firm belief that he would not be reprieved. He enjoyed the fuss the papers were making. Frank was bitterly disappointed at my refusal . . .'

On her own initiative, Kathy decided that, since it was more than possible that the other girl and herself would be killed, it was 'only fair' to take one of the family. Kathy, who had been left 'a little property' by her father, made her will and had it signed and witnessed by two servants. One of the servants was Kate Kinsella, to whom the whole story was told.

I asked Kate to pray hard and to explain the position to Mother if I were arrested. I did not mention the matter to Mother, but I discussed it with my sister Elgin. She was only 16 years of age — Shel, who was next in age to me, had had to go to Tombeagh; Monty, a younger sister, with her. Our youngest sister Peggy was Mother's greatest consolation. My brother Michael was out of the question, since I had been told to take a girl. Elgin insisted on coming, and I knew that her courage and initiative were at least as good as my own.

At the prison, the Volunteers joined the crowd milling around the main gate. When the wicket was opened to admit visitors, the IRA men could see the sentry on his beat inside the second set of gates. The Auxiliaries had a guardroom to the right, out of sight.

Kathy and Elgin handed in their names at precisely three fifteen. They had spotted some of the Volunteers outside and mixed with the relatives of other prisoners at the inner gate. Kathy recognised Charlie Byrne but gave no sign.

Ten minutes later the girls were still awaiting admission when a Ford car drove in and 'a tall priest* whom we did not know at that time stepped out and asked for a visit to Kevin Barry. He was admitted before us.' At three forty Captain Byrne edged over towards them and out of the corner of his mouth muttered: 'I'm afraid I'll have to call it off. That priest upset everything.' Just then the priest came out, and they were admitted.

When Kathy and Elgin had been searched by the warders, they were taken through the second set of gates past a line of Black and Tans drawn up in formation and into the main hall, which was crowded with Auxiliaries.

One of the Auxiliaries in the boardroom was standing at a window on the east side of the room, to the right as you face the fireplace. The other Auxiliary was seated

---

*This was Father C. Brennan, a curate in Hacketstown. Kevin made reference to his visit when his sisters arrived in the boardroom.

near the west wall on the other side of the fireplace. Kevin was at the fire.

We sat in the best position we could choose, pulling our chairs as near as we dared to the Auxiliaries. When the clock struck four, we knew the rescue bid had been abandoned.

When they left Mountjoy, Kathy and Elgin found only one man waiting for them. Tom Keating was standing on the North Circular Road. A member of H Company, he began to cry as soon as he saw the Barry girls.

In the tram, they were coming down North Frederick Street when Elgin began to cry 'silently and hopelessly', her sister says. She had been bright and gay all through the visit and was able to postpone her reaction while in the sight of the enemy. Kathy did not attempt to stop her. 'Even in those days, the psychological value of tears after shock was well known.' She took Elgin into Paddy Flanagan's office at the Wood Printing Works so that she could recover before they went home. Several members of the rescue party came into the office while Kathy and Elgin were there. 'Their distress was terrible', she remembers, 'but they assured us that there would be another attempt'.

16 Over the Top

Gerry McAleer[1] visited Kevin on 28 October, the morning after he was given confirmation of the death sentence.

'Who signed the confirmation?' Gerry asked him.

'I'm blessed if I know', Kevin replied.

'Was it Macready?'

'For all I know or care it might have been Charlie Chaplin', said Kevin.

Gerry McAleer is convinced that Kevin really did not care, that the calm unconcern with which he took his sentence was typical of his whole character, as the students knew it, that he was meeting death as he met life, with courage, but with nothing of the braggart. 'He did not believe that he was doing anything wonderfully heroic . . .'

Gerry was feeling down at the meeting and probably looked it. But Kevin was having none of it.

'I'd like to leave you something', he broke in.

Gerry's eyes were still cast to the floor and Kevin pretended to misinterpret his glance.

'I would leave you the shoes only I couldn't very well walk barefoot to the scaffold'.

Did he ever take anything seriously? Gerry McAleer has no doubt in his mind about this. 'He did – his country and his country's cause. Beneath his carefree laughter lay a heart that loved, and a brain that planned for, Ireland.'

The strain however was beginning to tell on Kevin. It showed in his last letter to Gerry; in his admission of fear to Father Augustine, and in the slightly hysterical note that he wrote on the title page of his well-worn copy of Kickham's *Knocknagow*. He was resigned to death; he entertained no hope of reprieve, and he placed no false hopes on any attempt by his comrades to pluck him from prison. But the peace he made with God was uneasy. He would have preferred to live.

'Jerry old dear', he uncharacteristically opens his last letter.[2]

I was glad to see you yesterday looking so fit and well, also the boys [Charlie O'Neill and Jack Henry]. But I'll hardly get a chance of seeing you any more, hence this epistle. I will write to the boys if possible but in any case I am more glad than you can imagine to have seen the three of you together for old time's sake.

Now Jerry I can't indulge in heroics nor can I curse, so this is a very tame letter — not at all like the ones you used to get from me, but you will make allowances.

Give my best wishes to any Old Belvederians you meet. You know that it is unnecessary to state you have all my best wishes for success in everything — even love.

There are several people in the College I would like to write to but have neither time nor energy. But when the 2nd Meds are assembled tell 'em, boys and girls, that I wish them every success and ask them to say a prayer for me when I go over the top on Monday.

P.S. Goodbye now and remember me to all at home.

Your pal, Kevin.

The letter dated 30 October 1920, is written in a firm bold hand, the writing still schoolboyish and the implement a purple pencil. The censor's mark is illegible, but the embossed 'G.R.' stands out on the small single sheet.

Father Augustine saw Kevin twice in Mountjoy.[3] He was told by a priest acting for Canon John Waters, the prison chaplain, that Kevin wished to see him. He left Church Street Friary on the afternoon of 29 October. As he walked along the corridor that led to the room in which Kevin was confined, he saw him in the distance leaning against the jamb of the door, looking and smiling at him as he advanced.

I remember it all with strange vividness even now [1948] and have often thought since that his sweet and charming smile brightened my way and quickened my step. We met and clasped hands as brothers, for there was a wonderful affection in my heart for that gallant boy who was so soon to lay down his life for the glory of God and the freedom of Ireland.

I spoke to the official who had accompanied me and also to the sentry, with the result that the latter stood outside the door the whole of the time I was inside doing all I could as a priest for Kevin, who was a most devout Catholic with grand childlike faith and piety. After I had finished my priestly duties, we had a long intimate talk during which he told me much. He was wonderfully calm, in perfect peace, thinking of his mother and sisters as well as of the coming sacrifice. With a feeling of affectionate pride I left [him] in that quiet gentle mood and, gripping his hand, promised that I would see him again early on the morrow.

True to his word, Father Augustine was back at the jail early on Saturday morning and found Kevin in the same beautiful disposition. He spoke to him of St. Francis of Assisi, and received him into the Third Order,* giving him the scapular and cross. After that, he was singularly happy, and there was not the slightest trace of any fear.

Judge, therefore, my astonishment when, from out of the heart of our brotherly conversation, he said, looking straight into my eyes: 'Father, I'm praying for courage'. I replied with great earnestness, having my left hand on his right shoulder, and thinking of the *manner* of his

---

*The status of a tertiary, that is, 'a member of the Third Order', was originated by St. Francis of Assisi. His own order was the first; the order of Minorite nuns ('Poor Clares') founded by St. Clare, was the second. The third (1221) was a sort of middle term between the world and the cloister. The members, men and women, were bound by rule to dress more soberly, fast more strictly, pray more regularly, hear Mass more frequently and practise works of mercy more systematically than ordinary people. They were also (as Augustine no doubt told Kevin) to abstain from dances and theatrical entertainments, to eschew all quarrelling and contention, not take up arms except in defence of the Church or their native land, and to take no unnecessary oaths.

going: 'And you'll have it, Kevin. Before they touch you, St. Francis will have hold of you by his *cord*, and will welcome you to Heaven.'

Soon after, about 20 minutes to 10, clasping his hand and drawing him to my heart, I left him in silence and in peace, having given him a final blessing. He knew I was going to assist at the Solemn Requiem Mass for the repose of the soul of Terry MacSwiney whom I had married in Bromyard, Herefordshire, in 1917.

After the Mass I saw Máire and Eithne, Terence Mac-Swiney's sisters, for a few minutes at the Gresham Hotel, then returned to the Friary, Church Street, and travelled down to Cork by the afternoon train with Arthur Griffith and some others who have since passed away. *Beannacht dílis Dé len a n-anam.*

General Crozier, who commanded the Auxiliary Division of the RIC ('I held a camouflaged command as a policeman trying to do a soldier's job without the moral support afforded to soldiers in war-time'), played a central role in this last scene of the drama. In his book, *The Men I Killed*, he wrote that he had a great deal to do with the last hours of young Barry's life as it was his duty to supply a party of auxiliary policemen (ex-officers all), under a Regular Army officer of the Reserve of Officers, to watch over the lad in the prison cell so that the condemned prisoner might not commit suicide and thus cheat the hangman of his fee.

He visited Barry only once. When he did so he was reminded of the last hours of Johnny Crockett who was executed in Flanders. According to Crozier the setting and the circumstances were different. Crockett did what he did, in desperation, perhaps, to escape the cold and wet of a fire-trench during a grim winter campaign. Barry did what he did while fired by the desire to free his Ireland from what he considered an unfair yoke; with his eyes wide open to the facts and consequences, he was prepared to forfeit his life in combat or by execution. Crozier goes on:

Neither of these lads whined. Had I had the opportunity I might have given Barry the chance I gave Crockett —

of getting drunk in his last few hours . . .

In France I made Crockett drunk to get him out of his misery. In Ireland some of the men who had most to do with Barry's last hours made *themselves* drunk to get them out of *their* misery. Fortunately, I am a teetotaller.

Crozier makes the point that as no hangman could be found to hang Barry, 'we had to bring one all the way from England, in disguise, and in great secrecy'. In fact, Ireland has not had her own hangman in modern penal history.

John Ellis*had executed Sir Roger Casement at Pentonville – 'the bravest man it fell to my unhappy lot to execute', he said at the time. He came to Dublin with his assistant, Welles, and lodged overnight in Mountjoy. Their first task was to inspect the new ropes brought in from Pentonville. Then Ellis used the spyhole in the condemned cell to calculate the drop, which depends on the height, weight and age of the prisoner. When he had chosen the rope he wanted, he shackled it to the chain in the roof of the hanghouse, let it hang all night with a sandbag, slightly heavier than the condemned man, and retired to bed.

---

*John Ellis succeeded Henry Pierrepoint[4] before the war. He and Henry's brother, Tom, were then the Home Office approved executioners, though Ellis claimed seniority. Using two assistants, Ellis hanged Mrs. Edith Thompson and her lover at Holloway in 1922. It was a *cause célèbre* in any case, but when the sickening details of the botched execution became known, the uproar was such that Ellis, after 203 executions, retired fourteen months later. In 1924, he attempted suicide by shooting and some time later succeeded. He was succeeded by Tom Pierrepoint, who usually took his nephew Albert with him when he worked. The fees for the first ten years of Albert's working life were unchanged from his father's day – £10 for the executioner and two guineas for the assistant.

17 Last Visits

Kevin in the meanwhile was passing the time between visits by inscribing his name in Irish and English and his exact address – Condemned Cell, Mountjoy Prison – on the title page of *Knocknagow*.[1] Opposite he wrote: 'K.G. Barry M.S. [Medical Student]. A dangerous criminal. A decided menace to the British Empire.'

> Captured 20th September, 1920
> Tried 20th October, 1920
> Hanged 1st November, 1920
> Up the prisoners of war
> Amongst the many crimes put down to this dangerous man is that he did put pepper in the cat's milk and steal a penny from a blind man, besides wilfully, feloniously and of his malice aforethought smiling derisively at a policeman.

Among Kevin's early visitors on Sunday were a couple of Jesuits accompanied by one of the Barry girls. The Belvedere men were Father Michael Quinlan and Mr. Tom Counihan. They had been rehearsing little things to say and were distinctly nervous when they got to the boardroom. When Kevin saw them he burst out laughing.

'I have the laugh on you fellows now', he said. 'You are going to spend the rest of your long lives hoping for a good death. I am going to have a good death tomorrow morning'.

The same Volunteers who had been ready to attempt a rescue on Saturday met on Sunday in the Connolly College, North Great George's Street. They changed into British Army battle-dress in readiness for a march on the prison in the guise of reinforcements. Then they learned that real reinforcements had arrived at Mountjoy and that plan, too, had to be abandoned.

On Sunday also, Dick McKee and Oscar Traynor* planned to visit Kevin disguised as priests. Jack Plunkett,** who liaised between the Dublin Brigade and the Barry family, takes up the story:

> The day before Kevin's execution I was summoned to meet a member of G.H.Q. staff and a member of the Dublin Brigade staff who were considering the possibilities of rescuing Kevin.
>
> I was sent to the Barrys' house in Fleet Street to ask that Mrs. Barry would not take the visit that was arranged for her, but that the visit be reserved for two priests.
>
> The Barrys considered that such action would be thought very suspicious by those who were guarding Kevin; they pointed out that they were just about to leave for Mountjoy to take the visit at the prescribed time, and they asked me to go back and confirm either the existing arrangement or the new one for the priests. It had been understood that I was to return and report in any case.[2]

Plunkett returned to Brigade HQ and after some delay was given a message that had been left with a junior officer for

---

*Oscar Traynor (1886-1963) was born in Dublin and fought in the Easter Rising. He led the Dublin Brigade after Dick McKee was executed in November 1920, and commanded the burning of the Custom House. He was in the Four Courts garrison during the Civil War and was a founder member of Fianna Fáil. He was a minister in Fianna Fáil Governments from 1936 to 1961.

**Jack Plunkett was a brother of Joseph Mary Plunkett, executed after the Easter Rising, and of George Plunkett. They were sons of George Noble Count Plunkett, who was Minister of Foreign Affairs in the First Dáil Ministry. Jack and George were lifelong Republicans who had many spells in jail and many brushes with authority. Walter Mitchell says: 'I preferred Jack to George, who was a bit of a bulldozer in his own quiet way'. Todd Andrews whiled away the hours before release from Newbridge in 1924 by discussing with Jack Plunkett Thomas Aquinas's distinction between faith and reason. Plunkett's hobby, according to Andrews, was tinkering with motor-car engines in the enormous garage of the big Plunkett house in Ballsbridge.

him. This was to the effect that the original visit of the Barry family was to go ahead, as there was not time for the rescue attempt, and that another attempt would be made later.

When he got the message at HQ Plunkett headed back and met the Barrys as they got off the tram opposite the Mater Hospital. He gave the message to Kathy as they passed. Mrs. Barry and Michael were a pace or two in front. Plunkett was on his bicycle.

Kevin had a steady stream of callers that day, the last visit being allocated to his mother, Kathy and Michael. Inside the first gate on the wide roads to right and left, Kathy could see lines of soldiers and Black and Tans. The Tans were not normally in Dublin, which was Auxiliary territory.

In the boardroom were General Crozier's two Auxiliaries, but also a number of warders, some of them armed. A chief warder sat at the large table with a revolver before him. Rescue was not going to be easy for anyone attempting it, though the fact that some of the warders were in tears makes it difficult to tell whether sympathy might have overcome duty. Conversation was not easy. Mrs. Barry was quiet though composed, and Michael Barry was, in Kathy's words, 'at no time a great chatterer'.

'Just before we got in for the visit', Kathy recalls, 'hundreds of students of U.C.D. had arrived with Father Albert to recite the rosary outside the jail. Shortly after we met Kevin, we mentioned this to him.'[3]

'If I could only see them again', he said.

Kathy then said that she had been asked by Cumann na mBan* to tell him they would be outside in the morning to pray.

'Tell them that is foolish. They'll all be shot,' was Kevin's reply.

---

*Cumann na mBan was the women's division of the Irish Volunteers. It was founded at the same time, November 1913, and was led by Countess Markievicz and Mrs. Kathleen Clarke. The majority of its members opposed the Treaty and during the 1920s, led by Maud Gonne, they supported the Irish Republican Army and some of the radical movements of the period.

It suddenly crossed my mind that when Cumann na mBan marched away in the morning he, who was now talking to us, would be dead. For a moment or two I could think of nothing to say, and there was a silence. Some of the warders were crying. Kevin sat with one leg over the other. Suddenly he began to whistle *Steady Boys and Step Together*,* swinging his foot to the rhythm and giving me a sideways smile. We all rushed into conversation and gradually we were all talking quite naturally.

Just before five o'clock the Deputy Governor, Mr. Meehan, came in and said: 'I'm sorry, Mrs. Barry, but I'm afraid you'll have to leave now'. They said goodbye.

The last words Kevin said to Kathy were: 'Give my love to the boys in the Company'. He then kissed her. At the door they turned and he was standing at the salute. He wore his trenchcoat that day with the collar turned up at the back, as was his habit. He had a white scarf.

Mother was magnificent. She was battling with her tears but she did not break down. In the corridor outside we met Canon Waters, the Chaplain, for the first time. He expressed some doubt as to whether Kevin actually realised that he was to die in the morning. He could not understand his gaiety. Mother said: 'Canon Waters, can't you understand that my son is actually proud to die for the Republic?' He became more flustered and we parted. We were upset by this encounter because he was the chief chaplain and the nearest thing to a friend that Kevin would see before his death, and he seemed so alien.

---

*The song *Step Together* was written by M.J. Barry; the music was especially composed for the book *The Spirit of the Nation*, ballads and songs by the writers of *The Nation*, the journal founded by Charles Gavan Duffy in 1842. After Thomas Davis's death in 1845, the chief writer was John Mitchel. *The Spirit of the Nation* was printed in full in January 1845, when Davis wrote of the original shorter sixpenny book: 'It is to be found everywhere, from the English Admiral's cabin to the Irish peasant's — from Dublin to Boston, to Sydney, and to Calcutta'. John Edward Pigot (1822-1871) may have composed the music of *Step Together*.

When the family came through to the front gate of Mount-joy, the crowd of students had been joined by hundreds of citizens. Father Albert was still there. He asked, on the spur of the moment, to be allowed to see Kevin. This was permitted. The Barrys waited until he came out.

When Albert[4] met Kevin, they spoke first in Irish, Kevin sitting on a chair with his hands in his overcoat pockets. He was 'visibly affected' when the priest told him of the Masses that had been celebrated for him and of the Rosaries and other prayers and hymns which his fellow-students were reciting outside the prison.

Kevin sat up when he heard this and said eagerly: 'I wonder could I see them once more?'

He thought of giving Albert a written message to take to the students, but when the policeman said that any written message would first have to be submitted to the Governor, he decided on a verbal message instead. He said to Albert: 'Remember me to the students of my university, especially those in my own class, and tell them all to hold on.'

Albert recalled that Kevin spoke quite naturally and without any kind of heroics. In fact, he joked about some newspaper stories he had heard attributing to him the saying that 'he was proud to die like Roger Casement' and laughed heartily at them! 'I never made such a remark', he said.

'Tell them outside', he said to Albert in parting, 'I want no pity, but prayers'.

Kathy Barry says that the actual words Albert quoted were: 'Hold on. Stick to the Republic'. News of a reprieve was all over the crowd and 'strings of people asked us for information'. But when the Barrys left for Fleet Street at about five thirty, there was no news to give the people. One woman turned back to a friend and said loudly: 'Everybody in Dublin knows it except his own people!' Kathy says: 'I knew from her tone that she thought we were trying to make ourselves important.'

The gathering of people outside the jail formed the nucleus of a crowd which spread up and down the North Circular Road. By seven o'clock, it had assumed such proportions that the British sent out armoured cars to patrol the North

Circular Road. It was this crowd and the armoured cars, Kathy was later told, that caused the calling off of the final desperate plan to breach the wall of Mountjoy and rescue Kevin by storming the jail.

For the 'final desperate plan'[5] on All Hallows' Eve, Dublin Brigade mobilised C, H and D Companies of the 1st Battalion. C Company covered the front of the prison from the Mater Hospital side. H Company's long line ran from Doyle's Corner to the Parnell Monument with orders to prevent enemy reinforcements from getting through once action had begun. D Company at Killarney Parade was to breach the prison wall with a land mine, then fight through to the condemned cell and take the prisoner out.

To distract attention, Kevin's own comrades in H Company, Frank Flood, Seán O'Neill, Paddy Kenny and John O'Dwyer, were to open fire on the guard at the main gate. Dublin Brigade HQ at Connolly College timed the operation for eight o'clock.

The materials for the explosive charge were prepared in a stable at the back of the north side of Merrion Square. Jack Plunkett[6] was in charge and he had guards posted all around him. The mine was not quite ready when a message came to say that the attempt could not go on, at least for the present. The British, it was reported, had arranged for one of his guards to shoot Kevin if there was any disturbance.

About seven o'clock on the Sunday evening, a Halloween without joy for the Barrys, Tom Counihan[7] got a visit from some of the family at Belvedere College. Counihan was a Jesuit scholastic, still three years off ordination. Aged twenty-nine, he had been Kevin's maths and chemistry teacher, his rugby coach, and above all his friend in the Jesuit community. Kevin wished to see him, they said, and he was puzzled and a little fearful. He sought the advice of the Rector, Charles Doyle, SJ who told him that he must go: 'you cannot refuse the request of one of your pupils in his hour of greatest need'.

'It was dark and forbidding as I turned in along the entrance to the large gate', says Tom Counihan, who later went on the same errand of mercy for Jim Larkin and Ernie O'Malley. As he waited to be let in to Mountjoy, he saw a lorry-load of Auxiliaries arriving. Inside, he could see barbed wire, machine-guns and military everywhere. The British were taking no chances.

He was led into a very large room in the centre of which was a small table with a chair on either side. In each corner was stationed an Auxiliary with revolver pointing at the table. It was not a comfortable position. These men were glib with the revolver, as he had witnessed many times in the Dublin streets.

He had not long to wait when he heard the sound of men marching. The door swung open and Kevin appeared under heavy guard. He came and stood at one side of the small table, gave Tom a military salute and then sat down. He had a slight smile on his face and 'appeared to me to be in perfect health and so calm and self-possessed.'

We were out of earshot of the four Auxiliaries . . . Kevin produced a telegram with a beam of delight. It was from Father John Fahy, S.J., then in Mungret College, Limerick, sending Masses and prayers and blessings. It was Father Fahy who had received him into Belvedere in 1916. He was overjoyed that such a man was with him in spirit . . .

He was perfectly well aware of the fact that there would be no pardon. I go so far as to say he would feel he had been cheated out of something precious if he had been pardoned. He had made up his mind that the sentence of death would be pronounced by the court-martial. He never had any thought save to die for God and for Ireland. I knew that the greatest precautions had been taken by the Chaplains to keep all hints of a rescue from reaching him . . .

He was anxious I should be with him in the morning. That was not possible. I told him I would be with him at Mass and prayer in the college he loved . . .

The command then came for the end of their meeting and the bodyguard approached. Kevin clasped Tom's hand firmly and warmly whispered a last word. He stood to attention with a smile, saluted and marched out of the room.

In the Rector's archives[8] in Belvedere lies a report on Tom Counihan's visits to Kevin Barry. The report concerns itself more with the spiritual state of the condemned man's soul than with any more dramatic aspects of their meetings. 'When a chap is young', Kevin is quoted as saying in the report, 'it is hard to die and it takes more than love of country to keep one up'. And of his general confession, the report quotes him as saying:

> I have a clean slate now, and am glad to offer my life in atonement for my sins. I have seen a good deal of the shady side of life since I came to Dublin, and I fully re-alise how merciful God has shown himself to me, in saving me from all this danger.

Tom Counihan was the last friend Kevin saw. His words and Kevin's find an eerie echo in a manuscript found in Roger Casement's cell after Ellis had hanged him:[9]

> It's a strange, strange fate, and now, as I stand face to face with death, I feel just as if they were going to kill a boy. For I feel like a boy — and my hands are so free from blood and my heart always so compassionate and pitiful that I cannot comprehend that anyone wants to hang me.

Michael Collins did not share the hope of many that a last-minute reprieve was possible. Forester in her book, *Michael Collins*, says:

> His intense, painful ability to enter into the victim's mind placed him under intolerable strain. Little habits in his friends, scarcely noticed at other times, assumed enormous proportions. Diarmuid O'Hegarty, for instance, would work, a cigarette drooping from his mouth, the ash falling where it would. Without warning, Michael struck the cigarette away with an oath. The gentle O'Hegarty protested in amazement. Later, Michael would apologise. Now he was all but unbalanced with worry.

Months later he was able to voice something of what then obsessed him. In the old Fenian days, men had gone to prison, and frequently death, unsupported by a word from those who directed the national movement. 'I determined it would not be so in our day', he said. 'I determined that we would accept responsibility for what we believed was necessary. No more lonely scaffolds in our time.'

A block away from Belvedere, where Tom Counihan was composing his prayers for the morning, stood Vaughan's Hotel in 29 Parnell Square. It was Michael Collins's alternative headquarters, the place where one could see 'the real Mick, not the plaster saint he was made out to be'.[10]

When Collins entered Vaughan's on that Sunday night, he was 'in a state of the greatest dejection. He remained brooding the whole night, taking no part in the conversation, the only words he uttered being: "Poor Kevin Barry!" '[11]

His mood was to remain low for some time. It was difficult to see an end to it all. For Collins, as for Kevin, there was to be no peace until the ultimate peace.

18 To Suffer Death

I t was dark, chilly, damp, and muddy underfoot when
Canon John Waters and Father Matthew MacMahon
arrived at Mountjoy from Clonliffe College. Canon Waters, 'a
lovely little man with glasses and the purple things', as Mag
Leonard[1] remembers him, was administrator of Holy Cross
Parish, Clonliffe, and president of the Holy Cross College.
Father MacMahon* was a curate in the parish and dean of the
college.

An hour earlier, long before dawn, a crowd had begun to
collect outside. John McCann has described the gathering of
people from the little streets and the big squares, women with
shawls drawn closely about them, women well-clad and ill-
clad. Men and boys well-attired and some tattered, feeling
the pinch of winter. 'The flickering sickly yellow gas lamps
of alley and avenue; the sizzling great arc-lamps of the main
thoroughfares served only to accentuate the gloom . . .'[2]

By seven thirty, about 2,000 people, including the night-
workers, had gathered.[3] At seven forty-five the party of about
one hundred Cumann na mBan, of whom Kevin had been
told by his sister, marched four deep up North Circular Road
from Dorset Street to the scene. They had come from St.
Stephen's Green. At a prominent position before the jail gate
was Maud Gonne MacBride. The soldiers began to whistle
derisively at the women in uniform, but their jeers were still-
born.

---

*There is some evidence, not conclusive, that Father Matthew MacMahon
was a son of Sir James MacMahon, Joint Under Secretary for Ireland
and a Privy Councillor. Another son was the Rev. J.R. MacMahon, SJ.

In the Dublin newspaper offices, the telephones had not stopped ringing until midnight. People called in search of news of a reprieve. All they could learn was what Lord Mayor O'Neill had said to the reporters: the Prime Minister had told him that the law must take its course.

The chaplains had to wait outside the main gate until seven o'clock when the warders opened the small side door and allowed them inside.

Kevin had spent the night in the company of one of his selected warders and two Auxiliaries. He had not been idle. In the condemned cell he and the warder built a small altar for his last Mass. He wrote a couple of letters. He went to bed early and had a few hours of sound sleep. He was called at six o'clock.

The Republican prisoners in the jail usually sang at night in their cells, but that night, in order to give Kevin a little peace, they kept quiet. At seven fifteen they recited the Rosary. Later after the hangman had cut down the body they sang *Faith of our Fathers*, *Wrap the Green Flag Round Me* and *God Save Ireland*. At ten o'clock they went to Mass in the prison chapel where the celebrant, Dr. Patrick Dargan, spoke of Kevin's courage.

In the hanghouse, John Ellis was up betimes. He and Welles removed the sandbag from the noose, checked the rope and made sure the white cap was ready. The cap was a fairly capacious white cotton bag which was used partly for the sake of the official witnesses, since the varying drop, according to Albert Pierrepoint, 'did not always take a man's head below the scaffold floor', and partly as some mercy to the prisoner – and some aid to the executioner – so that the condemned man could not judge the 'exact moment at which the lever was to be pulled'.[4]

When the chaplains entered the condemned cell, Kevin greeted them calmly and cheerfully. Canon Waters heard his confession and then celebrated Mass at the little altar. He gave Kevin the Holy Viaticum. Ned Proctor his warder-companion also received Communion. The only light in the cell came from the altar candles.

Father MacMahon then said a Mass of Thanksgiving while

Canon Waters knelt beside Kevin. 'At the end of this Mass', Waters wrote later that morning to Mrs. Barry:

> I put him in a chair to rest as he had been kneeling nearly an hour. I stood by him and whispered prayers into his ear, which he repeated with the greatest docility and fortitude. He made Acts of Faith, Hope, Contrition, Charity, Resignation, Forgiveness and also said prayers to the Sacred Heart, Holy Mary, St. Joseph, Angel Guardian, St. Patrick, St. Oliver Plunkett (*sic*) with the greatest fervour.

Outside the prison, the crowd swelled to an estimated 5,000. In a lane at the side of Mountjoy police station, a party of soldiers was stationed. A double-turreted armoured car, with its guns always trained on the people, moved slowly about the road. Prayers could be heard everywhere, some in Irish.

As the prison bell began to toll, the people knelt on the soggy ground. 'A silence, awe-inspiring and almost painful in its intensity, fell upon the gathering . . .', wrote the *Evening Herald* reporter. Honoria Aughney, who was accompanied by Anne Stafford of Wexford, says: 'It was a bad minute'.[6]

A few minutes before that, the hangman had come into the condemned cell. They pinioned Kevin's arms with leather straps. He told them he did not want pinions because he was a soldier and was not afraid to die. Canon Waters continued to pray and Kevin responded firmly.

'Are you quite done, Father?' asked Ellis and Canon Waters said yes. Walking between Waters and MacMahon — it was a tradition in Ireland to have two priests at an execution — Kevin moved through the door to the hanghouse thirty yards away. There the Governor, C.A. Munro,* and his discipline officers awaited him. Downstairs, under the trapdoors, the Medical Officer and the trades officers stood.

The execution chamber was neat and workmanlike. The two hinged trapdoors in the upper room were now level with the floor. The rope hung from the chain attached to the ceil-

---

*C.A. Munro, late of the Burma Police, lived at Cowley Place, North Circular Road, part of the Mountjoy Prison complex.

ing beam. The operative part of the noose was covered with soft wash-leather. The lever, like a signalman's points lever, pointed towards the drop.[7]

Kevin's legs were pinioned. He repeated his prayers. The hangman drew on the white cap, adjusted the noose, whipped out the safety pin and pulled the lever. All was over.

Father MacMahon moved quickly down the steps while the trades officers pushed a portable staircase from the wall to where the body was hanging. There they steadied the body and watched Father MacMahon climb the steps to anoint Kevin. It was the priest's first execution.

As the death bell sounded outside the gates, the thousands fell quiet. When the prison gate opened, Canon Waters emerged, tears in his eyes. They crowded around him, asking how Kevin had died. 'Bravely', he said. 'I never saw one meet his death with such courage. He died with prayers on his lips for friends and enemies'.

Then a warder came out and pinned the typewritten notice on the wall: 'The sentence of the law passed on Kevin Barry, found guilty of murder, was carried into execution at 8 a.m. this morning. By Order'.

The police told the crowd to go home, but a student began the Sorrowful Mysteries of the Rosary in Irish and once again the people knelt down on the muddy roadway. It was announced that Mass would be said at University Church at nine o'clock for the repose of Kevin's soul.

At eight forty the City Coroner, Dr. Louis Byrne, received a message from the Lord Lieutenant instructing him to hold no inquest.

Dr. Hackett wrote in the Medical Officer's Book: 'I was present at the execution of Kevin Barry at 8 a.m. and attended a court of inquiry at 10 a.m. and gave evidence that death was instantaneous and due to fracture of the cervical vertebrae'.[8]

The court of inquiry found that the sentence had been carried out in accordance with law. In the prison's Register of Deaths, begun in 1846 and still in use, the column headed: 'Whether inquest was held' is marked 'Yes'.

A plain deal coffin without breastplate or ornament was used to enclose the body. It was substantially made and roughly painted in the prison workshop.

The chaplains were summoned to bury Kevin at half past one that afternoon. They found the grave already dug near the gate separating the male and female prisoners, beside a little clump of laurel bushes. Only prison officials attended, and Canon Waters told Mrs. Barry that the coffin was already closed and fastened down when he got there.

The Requiem Service began in a large workshop near the grave, and then four warders bore the coffin to the graveside, described by the chaplain as 'a quiet spot not likely to be desecrated or walked on and still near enough to the highway to remind [us] of him and say a prayer as we pass.' Canon Waters continued with his description of the scene in his letter to Mrs. Barry.

> The grave appeared to me to be about 3½ feet deep. There we laid all that was mortal of poor Kevin in blessed clay and with all Catholic prayers and rites. The warders covered in the grave and we said the De Profundis.
>
> Some half dozen soldiers who came to the door of the barracks close by, and some matrons who were looking on from a neighbouring window, were the only spectators. It was a sad funeral indeed but I hope to live to see him removed from this and to receive from his Countrymen the honours due to his heroic virtues.
>
> ... The Governor of the prison told me that his face was in no way changed except for a very slight discolouration and that beyond this there was no sign of violence.

Quicklime was deposited in the grave with the coffin.

19 Beyond Reach of Sorrow

The Barry family went to the seven thirty Mass in the Carmelite Church in Clarendon Street and stayed for the eight o'clock Mass. As they left the church, they saw the University branch of Cumann na mBan marching back up Grafton Street. Led by Captain Eileen McGrane* and Lieutenant Kathleen Murphy, the company recognised Mrs. Barry and, as a mark of respect, gave the 'eyes-right' salute.

Once home, the family met Tom Counihan, who had arranged to be telephoned by one of the chaplains. He was asked to tell Mrs. Barry of Kevin's calm and prayerful ending. The multitude of duties that attends a death in the family kept them busy until the telegrams, letters and callers arrived. They sent wires to the family in Carlow. Joe Doyle of Tuckmill was at the door when his mother got the wire: 'Kevin executed this morning'.[1]

Canon Waters wrote the first of his two letters to Mrs. Barry and proved to be a warm and loving man.

> Poor Kevin, your dear boy, is gone. Deep as is my own grief, I know it is as nothing to that which must fill your heart and I pray that God, who alone can do it, will comfort and console you. . . .
>
> You are the mother, my dear Mrs. Barry, of one of the bravest and best boys I have ever known. His death was

---

*Later, as the wife of Dr. Paddy McCarvill, Dr. Eileen was a well-loved lecturer in English and Joyce scholar at UCD. Paddy McCarvill, who like Eileen took the anti-Treaty side in the Civil War, was elected to the Third Dáil for Monaghan. He was jailed and went on hunger-strike for forty-one days.

one of the most holy, and your dear boy is waiting for you now beyond the reach of sorrow . . . The little book and picture which I am sending he used in his last minutes and I told him I would give them to you.[2]

The picture may be a small card, still extant, depicting the Sacred Heart and an inscription on the back: 'To mother from Kev, on eve of his death'.

Seán Ó hUadhaigh straightaway sent a letter to Dublin Castle asking the authorities to hand over the remains of Mrs. Barry's son for burial. 'Please let me know where and at what time an undertaker on her behalf is to attend for that purpose', he wrote.

James MacMahon, the Joint Under Secretary, replied at once: 'I am directed by His Excellency to . . . say that it is regretted your request cannot be complied with'. And indeed the law directed that burial in such cases must be within the prison precincts. As a tribute of respect to Kevin's memory, Dublin Corporation adjourned its Monday meeting on the proposal of Alderman W.T. Cosgrave, TD.* Mrs. Jennie Wyse Power said there was a time in the early 1880s when the scaffolds were almost worn out with their number of victims. But during all that period, no child had ever trod upon the fatal stair.

Her sentiment was echoed in Cork that day when an old woman saw the poster: 'Kevin Barry Hanged'. 'Oh Christ!' she said, 'so they have hanged that child'.[4] More formal tributes were paid to his memory by institutions, councils, local authorities and societies all over the country. But the woman's words hardened the belief felt by ordinary people that, as a pro-British shopkeeper in Rathgar said to Robert Brennan**:

---

*William T. Cosgrave (1880-1965) was born in Dublin and educated at CBS Synge Street. He fought in the GPO, was sentenced to death and had his sentence commuted to life imprisonment. He was the first President of the Executive Council of the Irish Free State (1922-1932) and in 1935 became President of Fine Gael. He retired in 1944. His son, Liam, a senior counsel, became Taoiseach (1973-1977).

**Robert Brennan (1881-1964) was a Volunteer and IRB member from Wexford, and acted as Director of Elections for Sinn Féin in 1918. General

'When people have to hang young boys like that, their cause is lost, their day is over'.[5]

The impressive new front of UCD was the scene of a small protest led by Seán MacBride* and involving about a dozen students. There was a basement room where the young men played cards and there MacBride, who at sixteen was so young that his mother, Maud Gonne, was not yet aware that he had graduated from the Fianna to the IRA, gathered such fellow law-students as had Republican sympathies.[6]

The group included, MacBride recalls, Kevin Haugh and Dick McLoughlin. Kevin Haugh later became a High Court judge and was on the bench of the Supreme Court when he died in 1969. Richard McLoughlin had a similarly distinguished career and died in 1972.

Forcing their way through a door to where the college's stock of flags was stored, they climbed the steps to the roof and raised the Tricolour at half-mast. Seán MacBride, who does not recall whether they first removed the Union Jack, had brought the National Flag from his home at 73 St. Stephen's Green nearby. They were all hauled up before the President, Denis Coffey, a few days later, and threatened with expulsion. Nothing came of it.

In Cork, Father Augustine re-arranged the timetable of the

---

manager of the *Irish Press* in 1931, he served as Minister in the Washington Legation from 1934 to 1947, when he was made Director of Broadcasting, Radio Éireann.

*Seán MacBride (1904-1988) was the son of Maud Gonne and Major John MacBride, who was executed in 1916. Born and reared in Paris, he later went to Mount St. Benedict and UCD. He fought in the War of Independence and, on the Republican side, in the Civil War. He became a journalist, engaged in a number of radical political movements and was Chief of Staff of the IRA (1936-1938). He was called to the Bar in 1937 and took silk in 1943, defending Republicans and others. He founded Clann na Poblachta in 1946, became Minister for External Affairs in 1948 and was a leading influence on the Inter-Party Government until it fell in 1951. His party rapidly declined and he became involved in international human rights causes. He was a founder-member of Amnesty International, established by Peter Benenson, and with the late Karin O'Donovan, set up the Irish section. He was awarded the Nobel Peace Prize in 1976 and the Lenin Peace Prize a year later.

Bon Secours Hospital. He had been to see Kevin's aunt, Sister Cecilia, the day before, and promised her that he would say Mass for Kevin at the hospital on the morning of his execution. Sister Cecilia (née Margaret Dowling) was by then matron of the hospital. She felt 'greatly consoled' by Augustine's assurance of Kevin's peace and happiness. That morning, 'of set purpose', he began Mass about ten minutes to eight o'clock in one of the wards upstairs, which was then being used as a temporary chapel. By a happy coincidence that he never forgot, the clock struck eight, the time of Kevin's execution, as he was turning around to say *Orate Fratres*. 'I felt then and feel now that the devout congregation *did* pray, and that my sacrifice and their sacrifices mingled with his sacrifice and were acceptable to God the Father Almighty'.[7]

Nowhere in Ireland was Kevin Barry's execution more keenly felt than in the countryside around Tombeagh. About half past seven that morning, Pierce Butler of Coolmana was passing the roadgate of the Barry farmstead when he saw a sizeable group of people gathered in silence. Butler, who was a justice of the peace and a county councillor, was with his daughter Bride.[8]

Both joined the anxious crowd and Pierce Butler led them in saying the Rosary. Everybody had heard, and no one believed, the rumours of reprieve. Pierce Butler, who had worked with Kevin when he was organising a concert in Hacketstown, then took his daughter to the town to hear eight o'clock Mass. There was still no word from Dublin.

'Second Mass' was at eleven, and Bride Butler's sister May (now Deering) was there. Father Thomas Monahan, the parish priest, was conducting the service when Pat Gorman walked up the aisle and handed the celebrant a note saying that Kevin was dead.

'Father Monahan – imagine – cried. He asked the people to pray for the repose of the soul of Kevin Barry, "whose soul is just departing" ', May recalls. 'Nearly everyone in the church cried. I knew him to see. Indeed I had my eye on him – he was a grand fellow.'

Peg Scully, Pat Gorman's kinswoman, was also in the congregation on All Saints Day. She says that Father Monahan 'stood out from the altar and declared that the Mass was being said for Kevin Barry. "I know", he said, "that a child of Tom Barry's could only die in a state of grace and go straight to heaven" '.[9]

Father Monahan had been in Hacketstown parish since 1906. He and Pierce Butler had known Tom Barry well and were at his funeral. Mrs. Barry was a regular attender at second Mass whenever she was in residence at Tombeagh. She went in her pony and trap, and was always in church for the First Friday devotions as well.

Acting President of the Irish Republic, Arthur Griffith had just returned from Cork having attended the funeral of Mac-Swiney the day before. He wrote to Archbishop Walsh from 122 St. Laurence Road:

> Dear Lord Archbishop . . . The most brutal act yet perpetrated was the hanging of this poor boy Barry. It is a great consolation today to his mother and sister to know how holily and bravely he died. I am, your Grace most faithfully yours, Arthur Griffith.

His letter is dated 1 November, 1920.

20 The Balanced View

Almost everybody in the country who had a platform used it to express sympathy with the Barry family and to praise Kevin's courage in the face of death. Almost all the baby boys baptised in the Catholic churches on Tuesday and Wednesday were given the name Kevin. Or so the *Irish Independent* declared on Thursday, 4 November.

Le Matin and other Paris newspapers published photographs and carried headlines such as: 'Implacable Repression'. Shemus, the irrepressible cartoonist of the *Freeman's Journal*, drew a submarine of the Reprisal Class lying under the Irish Sea. Below the heading 'Puzzle — Find a Man', the submarine's picture window showed a group of men and the caption announced: 'Shemus has given us this morning a puzzle-picture. We have found Lloyd George, Greenwood, Macready, Sir Henry Wilson and Carson. We dare our readers to find A MAN'. The cartoon was cut out and kept in the War Office files.[1]

General Macready reported to the Irish Situation Committee of the Cabinet that the execution of the man Barry was being extensively exploited by the press for propaganda purposes. It would be a good thing if some person in authority in England would explain publicly that the man was conclusively proved to have 'shot a soldier with an expanding bullet'.

A curious flashback to the court-martial now occurs. On 2 November, Captain Barrett wrote from the Lower Castle Yard to GHQ Ireland:

It will be remembered that at the trial of [Kevin Barry]

172

a solicitor appeared (Mr. Seán Ó hUadhaigh) on behalf of the accused, and after 15 minutes' adjournment to enable him to consult his client, he returned into Court. The Court and the Prosecution then understood that he was still representing the accused whereas such was not the case, as the accused, during the 15 minutes interval, had declined his further assistance. However, although representing no client, he made a statement to the court before the case was opened, in which he alleged that after arrest the accused had been subjected to improper treatment, and desired the President, Brig.-Gen. Onslow, to cause inquiries to be made and to let him know the result. This the President agreed to do and the solicitor withdrew from the Court.

The President, having carried out his undertaking, has addressed a letter to my Courts-Martial Officer, of which the enclosed is a copy and speaks for itself.

I have directed my Courts-Martial Officer to quote this letter verbatim to the solicitors in question and not to send them a copy; this was done today. I have done this because from the same channel attempts have been made to learn the names of the President and Members of the Court.[2]

The letter, signed by Captain Barrett (though not in his capacity as Courts-Martial Officer) is initialled 'H.W.', that is, Colonel Warburton.

Brigadier-General Onslow had asked Barrett to tell Ó hUadhaigh that there was 'no foundation' for his allegations. Ó hUadhaigh replied that Kevin's subsequent affidavit verified the allegations that he had made in Court.

The point is puzzling. The British authorities are distinctly annoyed with Ó hUadhaigh for making a statement when the Court thought he was still acting for Kevin and only some time later discovered that he was not. Yet the President knew, and the *Freeman's Journal* reported, exactly what took place at the time.

What lay at the base of Captain Barrett's anger? Certainly the treatment that Kevin had been given in the defaulters' room of the North Dublin Union, immediately after the Monks' Bakery raid, remained a potential flashpoint. But there was more to it than that.

More than a week prior to the court-martial on 20 October the Judge Advocate General's staff in London had got wind of the interrogation that Kevin had undergone. They wanted to know more, for the purpose of seeing justice done at the court-martial. However, the military authorities in Dublin were determined to cover up what had happened and made a rather clever reply to London's inquiries. The *dramatis personae* in this little sub-plot were Colonel Foster MacGeagh and our friend Captain Barrett.

On 12 October, Foster MacGeagh wrote to GHQ Ireland:

It is observed that the accused seems to have had some conversation at the North Dublin Union with an officer of the Lancashire Fusiliers. If he said to this officer anything of importance, in addition to what was overheard by Lance/Sergeant Banks, the officer should be called to give evidence of the statements made and notice thereof given to the accused . . .

Writing to GHQ Ireland two days later, on 14 October, Captain Barrett says:

. . . Regarding the possible conversation between an officer of the Lancashire Fusiliers and the accused at the North Dublin Union, my Courts Martial Officer [himself] is doing his best to trace this, but up to the present he and the adjutant of the Lancashire Fusiliers have been unable to locate the officer in question.

Nobody pressed the point and Captain Barrett got away with his whitewash. It may be relevant that Captain Cross, the adjutant of the Lancashires on the day of the action at Monks' Bakery, was replaced within a few days, so that Barrett was being economical with the truth when he referred simply to 'the adjutant of the Lancashire Fusiliers'. He was in fact dealing with Lt. H.C. Lonsdale, a man who was not posted to the North Dublin Union until four days after Kevin was interrogated there. Barrett's anxiety to hush up the incident in the defaulters' room obviously left him in an uneasy frame of mind with regard to Seán Ó hUadhaigh.

The protests continued. In the House of Commons on 5 November, T.P. O'Connor said the Chief Secretary was adopting an entirely wrong and disastrous attitude in blatantly defending every act of frightfulness. Joe Devlin said it was the Government's hands that were reeking with the blood of policemen and civilians.[3]

The leader of the Labour Party, J.H. Thomas, said of Kevin: 'He was a studious boy, loved by everyone who knew him, brave and educated... he walked to the scaffold as a man, saying: "I believe I die for the good of my country" '. Having affirmed his belief in its contents, Thomas then read Kevin's affidavit and this gave the Chief Secretary an opportunity to say:

'It is a question of veracity as to whether that man swore the truth or whether the officers of the regiment, who deny it, told the truth. I accept the word of the officers'.

'I accept the man's word', said Mr. Jack Jones, 'a Catholic going to his death. I am not going to stand quietly and hear my faith insulted'.

Commander Kenworthy asked if the officers had made a sworn statement.

'No', replied Sir Hamar Greenwood, 'but I am sure they are prepared to do so'.

And there was laughter in most parts of the House.

John Mowbray, a medical student at UCD, remembers the wave of intense anti-English feeling generated in the College the day after the execution.

As we stood around, numbed with the shock of it, the Castle authorities gave further proof of their complete failure to understand the Irish mind by sending their Auxiliaries to the College to institute a gigantic search for arms and incriminating documents.

As my class of first-year medicals was lined up in the dining hall to await searching, I was amazed to see boys, whom I regarded as harmless callow youths, produce massive revolvers and sheafs of papers and hand them to even less guileful waitresses who were, of course, members of the College Cumann na mBan.

A large part of my hereditary attachment to parliamentary methods drained away from me and completely forsook many others, on that morning. . . .[4]

The *Evening Herald* said more simply that armoured cars and 150 soldiers raided UCD at eleven a.m. on 2 November and took the register of students and some correspondence. The male students were searched. The register was at Dr. Coffey's house, so he went with the soldiers to get it.

In London, the *Freeman's Journal* correspondent reported that comments on the execution were, on the whole, very unfavourable to the Government. The man in the street was deeply impressed by the fact that no appeal for British clemency came from the friends of the doomed man and impressed also by the folly of the Government, when it had an opportunity to show mercy, in throwing it away. 'The Englishman does not like it. It jars upon his feeling of confidence in the magnanimity of the Empire.'

And the correspondent finds the belief in well-informed circles that Dublin Castle and not the Prime Minister had the deciding voice. It was a belief which, as we now know, was well founded.

Also in London, the Registrar of the General Medical Council, Norman C. Kelly, asked the Government for information on Kevin Barry, a registered medical student. 'By arrangement with the Chief Secretary, the council is notified of the convictions of all registered medical and dental practitioners and also of students. . . . I desire to report the matter to a meeting of this Council which will take place very shortly', he explained.[5]

On 3 November, a very angry Ernest Aston wrote a stinging letter to the *Irish Independent*. He indicted Field-Marshal Sir Henry Wilson — 'a member of a distinguished Irish family of Ulster reactionaries' — for his part in the Ulster gun-running of 1914 and described the CIGS as now 'supreme dictator of the Irish Government'.

Aston, claiming that Kevin Barry had modelled his conduct

'precisely on that of Sir Henry Wilson at Larne', described his own visit to London the week before. Then, and since his return to Dublin, he had come into possession of these 'facts':

1. The Prime Minister clearly stated his personal wish and intention that the sentence should not be carried out.

2. That Sir Hamar Greenwood personally disapproved of the execution.

3. That no single leading official of the Irish Government was opposed to the reprieve.

4. That Sir Nevil Macready and Lord French on Sunday declared that they had no power to alter the sentence.

'Where then', asked Aston bitterly, 'was the power that tied the hands of the Prime Minister, Chief Secretary, Lord Lieutenant and Irish Commander-in-Chief, and forced them to become parties to the blackest crime and the most brutal murder in Anglo-Irish relationships?'

> One word from any member of the Carson-Wilson-Bonar Law gun-running junta would have stopped the execution. Mr. Lloyd George was threatened with the resignation of Sir Henry Wilson if a reprieve was granted.
> To that threat Mr. Lloyd George yielded, and replied to the eleventh-hour appeal of the Lord Mayor of Dublin that 'the law must take its course'. The law! What law?. . . .
> I write not as a Sinn Féin partisan, far otherwise. . . .
>
> E.A. Aston.

It was a courageous letter and must have convinced many people of its veracity, for the perception went widely abroad that Wilson ensured that Kevin would hang.

But it was not so. Unless Wilson was the world's best liar, it simply was not so. On 23 October, the Chief of the Imperial General Staff, Field-Marshal Sir Henry Wilson, wrote to the General Officer Commanding-in-Chief the Forces in Ireland, General Sir Nevil Macready: 'I care not for age, name or sentiment. Law is law and terrorists come under jurisdiction of the law. What does worry me is your unenviable position in Dublin. If this fellow hangs we are in for a spate of real trouble over there.'

Again on 29 October, Wilson wrote to Macready: 'As much as I detest thuggery and sneaking terrorists, the balanced view, in my opinion, is to hold our hand in Dublin. It means that we shall have weakened our right there because of one man. But to execute is to invite the pot to boil over and we couldn't control it.'

Thus with hindsight is the bouleversement of a persistent theory accomplished. The facts reflect no greater credit on Wilson, who clearly saw that by losing Ireland now, Britain would eventually lose the whole Empire. But they do show that Macready, who readily admitted that he had had nothing but unfailing support from Wilson in his Irish command, was either unable or unwilling to reciprocate at the crucial meeting with the Viceroy in the Phoenix Park the morning before the execution.

More controversy arose in Tuesday's newspapers when the High Sheriff of Dublin, Dr. J.C. McWalter, told reporters that neither he nor the Sub-Sheriff had been consulted about or notified of Kevin Barry's execution, and neither officer nor anyone representing the High Sheriff was present.

'If there is a writ of Habeas Corpus, as in the Wolfe Tone case, I do not know what answer the Governor of the jail can make', said Dr. McWalter. 'He is bound to produce the body unless there was a legal execution, which cannot take place if the Sheriff was not there.' The legal position was further elucidated by Dr. McWalter to his audience of reporters.

In the Wolfe Tone case, the court held that the military law could not overrule the civil law . . . if the military themselves chose to execute him, it would be a different thing, but it seems that they passed him over to the civil authorities with the request to them to execute him . . .

In this present case it might be argued that it comes

under DORA* but court lawyers hold that you cannot quote that against the Habeas Corpus Act.

Albert Pierrepoint[7] tells us that it was the function of the sheriff of the county to choose the executioner and of the governor of the prison to appoint his assistant. We do not know who appointed either Ellis or Welles. The point was an academic one in the week of Kevin's death, and the controversy soon died down. The Barry family took no part.

Dr. McWalter, who was a retired British Army captain, was President of the Dublin branch of the Discharged and Demobilised Soldiers' and Sailors' Federation, and was one of the band of honourable men who, sharing nothing of Kevin's ideology, nevertheless sent an urgent appeal on his behalf to the Lord Lieutenant to exercise the prerogative of mercy.

---

*The Defence of the Realm Act (DORA) was the first in a series of emergency Acts, passed in November, 1914, partly to prevent collaboration between Irish separatists and Germany during the Great War. It ceased to be in force on 31 August, 1921.

21 Old Fogeys

In Hacketstown, the Tricolour flew for two days until the military removed it. The execution was the talk of the whole district. Ned Toole, the headmaster of Rathvilly School, had, as we have seen, sent a telegram to Joseph Devlin, MP, in London on 28 October and next day had got a reply in which Devlin said:[1] 'I am sanguine we shall get a reprieve, though not yet certain'.

In a further letter dated 1 November, a devastated Devlin sent his apologies:

> I did everything humanly possible for Kevin Barry. On Thursday, I went to the Prime Minister to whom I had not spoken for two years, and I made what I thought was an effective appeal. . . . In order that the matter would not be forgotten, I then wrote him a letter on the next day further emphasising the matter. . . . I had a letter on Saturday morning to say that the matter had been before the Cabinet. . . . Mr. T.P. O'Connor and I subsequently drafted a telegram to the King. . . . I cannot tell what sinister or evil influence is at work because I was convinced that I had succeeded, and I felt tremendously disappointed, apart altogether from my feelings of pity for the poor boy whom I have just learned was executed this morning.
>
> I hope you will realise that I did all I could. . . .

There were no votes for Devlin in Rathvilly or Hacketstown, so one has to accept his explanation at its face value. He must have written the same letter to many others who had called on him to interest himself on Kevin's behalf. There is at any rate a familiar ring about his letter to Hanna Sheehy-Skeffington, widow of Francis Sheehy-Skeffington, executed in 1916 at the order of a captain judged guilty of murder but insane: 'I did everything humanly possible for Kevin Barry . . .' and so forth.[2]

A man much troubled in spirit wrote to Michael Barry[3] in Tombeagh a few days after Kevin's death. Father Paddy Kearney,* then working in St. Patrick's College, Maynooth, had been refused a visit to Kevin in Mountjoy by Kathy Barry, and he was distressed, lonely and anxious to make amends for what he felt were his shortcomings as a friend of the family. 'Dear old Mick', he wrote on 4 November.

> Were you ever by yourself of a cold rainy night when outside the leaves are off the trees and inside the fire is out and the lamp is low and you are alone. And every time you think, it's to ask the question: What in the world is the good of living? And you can never find the answer. Well, that's how I feel and all because of Kev. And if I feel that way, how must you feel? Poor old Mick. . . .
>
> Kev is infinitely happy and we are infinitely miserable and after all that's a bit of a paradox, isn't it now? Kev, I believe firmly, is now at home . . .
>
> My associations with old Kev — so terribly clear now — are centred round Tuckmill and the little room there and the fire and the songs. . . . Lord, imagine . . . old

---

*Father Kearney, a native of Dublin, was educated at Belvedere. Kevin Maher recalls him as 'always a friend of my mother's. He gave me a shilling one day when there was no one else at home.' Kevin Maher's sister Triona 'used to hate Father Kearney; he brought presents to Kevin and not to me. I suppose he didn't know what to buy for a girl, but Kevin would get cricket bats and things.' He visited Michael and Mrs. Barry in Tombeagh on his motor-cycle. He was a curate in Kilcullen and Ballymore Eustace, then served as parish priest in Whitehall, Dublin; Dalkey and Blanchardstown. His library in Whitehall covered two rooms, most of the books being about travel. He always sent Shel a present and a cheque at Christmas and he was fond of golf. He had a private income, and would take Kevin Barry's nieces to tea when they were boarding in Loreto Convent, Dalkey.

Kev walking about with a halo on the side of his head. . . .
Mick — I want you to be a pal of mine for the sake of
old Kev, and that is why I asked you to write to me. . . .
Kev was purest gold, through and through, and I am in-
clined to think that you are of the same metal. . . .
I could have been a pal of Kev's, I think, if I hadn't
been a damn fool. I didn't understand him until it was
too late, and I don't think he understood me. . . .

When I was up in town, I felt so helpless to say anything or do anything which would help you. I knew you
were suffering intensely, and especially so because you
seemed to be keeping it to yourself. I was tempted that
last morning outside Mountjoy to put my arm round you
and say things to you, but I feared your manliness and
didn't know what things to say. I wasn't sympathetic
— I don't like that word. You can be sympathetic when
you are sitting in an armchair, but not when you feel
like him with whom you should sympathise. Had you
sympathy for Kev? Neither had I. It was something else,
and neither had I sympathy for you. Do you understand
me? . . . .

Give my remembrance to all at home and Sheila —
and Joe Farrell if you see him. Tell your mother that I
am sorry that my Roman collar didn't carry with it this
time the consolations which are usually associated with
it, and that I'm ashamed of having appeared so much
more like a Press reporter than a lover of Kev's. But —
well, I won't give any excuses.

This emotional missive is signed 'Paddy', and there is no way
of discovering Michael's feelings about it.

Tombeagh has a secret attic in which Michael once hid during a raid by the British. But when he was finally captured,
on 31 December, 1920, it was in a motor-car. 'They found the
whole back of the car full of hand-grenades', says Pat Gorman.[4] Within two months, the Barry family had lost both of
their men. Michael was taken first to the Baltinglass Union —
the workhouse, where the hospital he eventually died in is
now — and then to Lincoln Jail in England. There he was

lodged for over a year until the Anglo-Irish Treaty was signed.

In Baltinglass, the British garrison was commanded by a very decent officer, according to Pat Gorman. Captain Bridges, remarking that 'we don't want to see Paddy cold', ordered the soldiers to break up the furniture for firewood.

Michael's sister Elgin recalls: 'When Mick and I went to Tombeagh after Kevin's death, Mick was soon arrested, and suddenly all the men in the district went underground.'[5] She had nobody to help her and did not know where the British had taken Mick. Eventually she harnessed the pony and trap and went to Baltinglass, where she found him.

When Michael was a prisoner in Lincoln, the Truce was declared, but he was not released for nearly eight more months. Kathy and Elgin went to see him. 'We had tea in the town', Elgin says, 'but of our visit to the jail I remember nothing. It's extraordinary how things really do leave your memory.'

In the meanwhile, the family solicitor, Seán Ó hUadhaigh, was attempting to put some order on the trusts left by Thomas Barry.[6] The confusion arose from Kevin's premature death and the need to give the other children one-sixth instead of one-seventh of the estate. He wrote to the Governor of Lincoln Jail on 3 August, 1921, enclosing four transfer deeds 'for execution by Michael Barry'. Ó hUadhaigh also helped the Barrys over the years to assign their interests in Tombeagh to Michael.

The farm was necessarily being neglected, but as Pat Gorman remembers, 'a lot of people, farmers around, used to help. Jack Keeffe of Ballysallagh, who was also a Volunteer, was one of them'. Jack recalls that Kevin was 'a bit wild', when he was down from Dublin and on IRA operations with Michael.[7]

Mrs. Barry, in one of her rare letters, displays a nice sense of humour. Writing to Michael from Fleet Street on 18 July, 1921, she tells the prisoner that everything is going on well at home. 'The Coolmanagh boys came on Wednesday last and worked at hay, mangels and some turnips and did a lot. That's the first time; the others came while you were in Baltinglass.'[8]

Then she tells him the big news. Gerry McAleer and Charlie O'Neill had gone down to Tombeagh to help out after Charlie's

exams. They were caught in 'a general round-up from Rathvilly for several miles at our side of the road', relates Mrs. Barry.

> Every old fogey in the country was taken for a few hours,
> even your uncles. . . . Gerry and Charlie was (*sic*) taken
> before 5 in the morning. . . . We motored to the Curragh
> on Monday and after a lot of fuss saw them and gave them
> clothes, food, etc. Jim Murphy went there on this Mon-
> day. He says they are fine and do not expect to be kept
> too long. . . . I hope Gerry does not lose his exam through
> it. Charlie's is over.

Gerry McAleer and Charlie O'Neill were, in fact, first taken
to Carlow Barracks, where Gerry wrote a sarcastic letter to
Honoria Aughney, his classmate from Tullow: 'Thanks for the
hospitality we're getting in Co. Carlow. We came down to
help Mrs. Barry with the hay and this is what we get.'[9]

A few days later Gerry and Charlie were moved to the Curragh internment camp, where Gerry asked a British officer to
lend him his field-glasses so that he could watch the races
across the plain. Soon he was relaying the results to half the
camp.

Other members of the family add their tuppence-worth to
their mother's letter, Elgin telling the prisoner that Paddy
Foley was arrested in the round-up and is in the Curragh. So
is Joe Deering. And Gerry and Charlie — mostly Charlie —
were trying to fish in Tombeagh. 'If they were at it still I
don't think they'd catch one. They knew all about it alright
but the fish were too sly for them.'

Monty says: 'You heard all the men in Co. Carlow were
rounded up. They (the Carlow men) thought Jerry and Charlie
were spies. Joe F [Farrell] has been tried for ammunition. I
think he got four years. But he hasn't left Mountjoy. His leg
got better but bad again: he is only getting better now. Luke
McD [Donnell]* is in some English prison, I believe. Slán leat.'

Kathy adds a short note to say she is too busy to write and
wants to be forgiven, and Shel tells her brother that Eileen is

---

*Miley, Luke and Dan McDonnell of Baltinglass were cousins, one of
whom became a priest. Their sister was a nun, Sister Benignus.

Dr. Dixon now. This part of the letter is badly worn, but it is possible to see that Michael himself has overwritten his name and the date, 22 December, 1921. It looks as if it took some months for a four-page letter to get to him, the delay, if there was one, having been caused by the necessity to get all the sisters (except the youngest) to write to their brother.

Mrs. Barry's letter to her son was begun, and all the excitement she described happened, a week *after* the Truce came into effect.

Gerry and Charlie were released after three weeks' internment.

22 The Long Fellow Calls

Michael Barry was released from Lincoln Jail in February 1922, just fourteen months after his arrest. He at once resumed his duties as adjutant of the 3rd Battalion, Carlow Brigade, and set about getting Tombeagh back into cultivation. The Anglo-Irish Treaty had just been signed on 6 December, 1921. Eight months of his sentence had been served while there were no hostilities between the two sides, although trials of Irish prisoners for political offences continued.

The Treaty was ratified by the Dáil on 7 January, the vote being 64 to 57, and five days later 400 political prisoners sentenced in Ireland before the Truce were released under an amnesty. Why Michael's case was delayed a few more weeks is not explained.

Éamon de Valera led those who rejected the Treaty and saw themselves as the legitimate Second Dáil. Open internecine warfare broke out on 28 June, 1922, when Government troops bombarded the Four Courts in Dublin, occupied by Republican forces. The subsequent Civil War dragged on through the death of Arthur Griffith (12 August) and the killing of Michael Collins (22 August), after which military courts and summary executions began.

Tradition in the Barry family had it that de Valera was a frequent visitor to Tombeagh, which he used as a 'safe house'. Pat Gorman says: 'Dev often stayed in Tombeagh. My father [James O'Gorman, a garage and hackney owner in Hacketstown] drove him several times and one time another man, Todd Andrews. Mick [Barry] used to talk of himself and Dev going over the mountains to where the Bartons live, Glendalough House in Annamoe. They stopped at Tommy Fallon's near Aughavanagh. Going down the hill to Fallon's they saw some nags and ould Dev got the wind up and wouldn't go any further.'

Pat Gorman's recollections are confirmed by pencilled notes in Michael Barry's handwriting.[2] The notes refer to 'convoy of G.H.Q. officers and members of Republican POW [?] through Battalion and Brigade area' and 'Safe conduct of President de Valera, General Aiken,* Comdt. Dowling,** Austin Stack*** and others through Brigade and Battalion area going to and returning from the South'.

Evidence of contact with 'the long Fellow' is there, but it was left to Professor T.P. O'Neill,[3] de Valera's biographer, to supply the author with details of two occasions on which de Valera stayed overnight.

'De Valera was', says Tom O'Neill, 'in Gougane Barra quite near to Collins on the day Collins was shot. He was within twenty minutes of meeting him. When he arrived at Newces-

---

*Frank Aiken (1898-1983) was born in Co. Armagh and educated at CBS Newry. He joined the Irish Volunteers in 1913, was commandant of the 4th Northern Division during the War of Independence, and tried to stay neutral in the Civil War, concentrating on the fight against the new Northern Ireland. Eventually he became Chief-of-Staff of the Republican forces in 1923. He was a founder member of Fianna Fáil and a Minister in every Fianna Fáil Government until his retirement to the back benches in 1969.

**Seán Dowling (1896-1988), a Dubliner educated at Synge Street, St. Enda's and UCD, where he studied English and then dentistry. A polymath, he played a distinguished part in the Easter Rising, the War of Independence and the Civil War. He spoke Irish, played the piano, painted and sang. He was art critic of *Ireland Today* (1936-38) and spoke to the author's inaugural address to the English Literature Society in UCD (1949). He had two plays produced in the Abbey.

***Austin Stack (1880-1929) was born in Tralee. An income tax inspector, he was a founder member of the Irish Volunteers in 1913, a commandant during the Easter Rising, and Minister of Home Affairs in the First Dáil. He led the hunger-strike in Kilmainham in 1923 and was greatly weakened by it. Stack established the Dáil Relief Bureau in May 1921. Gaughan says: 'However, it was not until the beginning of August, when Miss Kathleen Barry, sister of Kevin Barry took charge of it, that it began to function effectively'. Its purpose was to alleviate distress among the prisoners' dependants.[4]

town, near Béalnabláth, about eleven o'clock in the morning, Collins had just passed, going out west. Next day, he heard from Siobhán Langfort, who came on her bicycle, that Collins had been shot. That was the first he had heard of it.'

During the course of his journey back to Dublin he stayed in several houses, eventually being driven to Tombeagh by Jim Byrne, who lived opposite Tom O'Neill in his native Ballon. Jim was an engine-driver for Fenelons and used to drive for them. From Tombeagh, Pat Gorman and Michael Barry drove de Valera to Bartons of Annamoe in the Model T Ford.

Elgin Barry recalls that while he stayed in Tombeagh, de Valera would sleep in 'the New Room'[5], now occupied by Michael Barry's two schoolboy grandsons, Kevin and Michael. His faithful sentry, Tom Molloy of Ticknock, would keep watch all night at the roadgate, crawling down the muddy drive if he had anything to report.[6]

Time was running out for the Republicans when de Valera made his next journey north. He had gone on foot and on horseback from Dublin to Bliantasour, on the western slopes of the Monavullagh Mountains in Co. Waterford. There on 23 March, 1923, a crucial meeting of the Army Executive was held. But Free State troops forced the meeting to move onward, to the Nire Valley, where the session was resumed in John Wall's house in Knockanaffrin. It lasted until 26 March.

De Valera's diary for his first day's journey home indicates what he endured: 'March 27th. Left before daylight for Rathgormack. Got drenched to the skin through overcoat, leather jerkin etc. Wildest night I ever experienced. Falling at every step. Misled by the guide. Ignored stepping stones and walked through the streams. Stuck my left leg into a bog hole up to the groin. Arrived in the morning, clothes and leather jacket all ruined.'[7]

Coming through Carlow, Father Kelly of Rathoe gave him shelter and his next stop, it seems, was Tombeagh. Certainly Elgin Barry (now Madame O'Rahilly) remembers that his boots, which by then must have been in an appalling condition, were polished in the kitchen and left outside the door of the New Room until he awoke.

When de Valera stayed at Tombeagh, Michael Barry told a member of the family,[8] it was not as a friend dropping in for the night. His arrival was signalled ahead; his bodyguards came first; the family was shepherded into the kitchen, and the Presidential visitor, keeping himself to himself, said neither hello nor goodbye to anybody. Michael Barry recounted this pattern of behaviour with some bitterness later, long after the diehard Barrys had parted political company with the more pragmatic de Valera.

When Mrs. Barry died in 1953, de Valera was Taoiseach. He and his aide-de-camp, Colonel Seán Brennan, who had connections with Rathbawn near Rathvilly, attended the funeral Mass at St. Teresa's Church, Clarendon Street. The celebrant was Father Laurence, ODC. The Barrys ignored de Valera.[9]

Church Street, immediately after the arrest of Kevin. Courtesy RTE, Cashman Collection

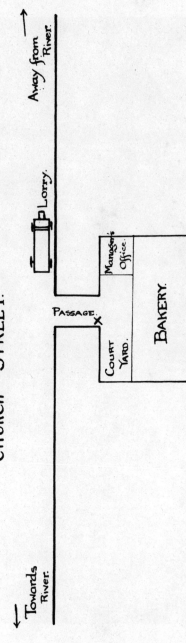

CHURCH STREET.

Towards River.

Away from River.

Lorry.

Passage.

Manager's Office.

Court Yard.

BAKERY.

✗ Man seen standing

Army sketch of bakery raid

Mountjoy. The shed in the foreground attached to the lower end of the main buildings, immediately right of recreation ground (white lines) is the hanghouse

REGISTRY OF DEATHS.

DATE of Death	No.	NAMES ~ Reg No.	Age	Sentence	Medical Opinion of the Cause of Death	Date	Whether Inquest was held	Verdict of Jury	OBSERVATION
1914 Nov 2nd	1	Peter Brown 3266	60	14 days 94		11 1914	Yes	Died from acute peritonitis following a fractured growth which caused perforation of the intestine	
1920 Nov 1st	1	Kevin Barry 930/20	18½	Death +		10 20	Yes	-	Hanged at 8am 1 11 1920

Mountjoy. Registry of Deaths

23 Endings

Sometime in the winter of 1920-21, the author of the ballad *Kevin Barry* called to No. 8 Fleet Street. He was, says Kathy Barry, 'an Irish worker on the Clydeside, home on holiday. I do not remember his name. He showed us the verses. We were polite.'[1] Then later they heard it being sung on all sides. 'These days were so full that we may be excused for forgetting the name of the writer of that particular song.'

What may without disrespect be called the Kevin Barry industry had begun with poems published in the newspapers on the day of his execution. The unknown visitor to Fleet Street was the subject of a letter many years later to the *Irish Press* on 5 August, 1951, by Séamus de Burca, one of the theatrical Bourkes who are related to the Barrys on the Dowling side. He protests against the melody being used for other songs. 'The melody, like the words, belongs to the man who wrote it, who gave both to the Irish nation without any reward. Let us preserve this song about a gallant soldier inviolate.'*

The immediate and universal success of this ballad continues seventy years later. It has been recorded — though in truncated form — by Paul Robeson, and played by Eddie Calvert on his silver trumpet. By the oppressed everywhere, it has been adopted as a protest song, and for folk and ballad groups in Ireland it is still a popular part of the repertoire. In World War II, both British and American troops sang it.

The story of how Paul Robeson, the great American black

---

*De Burca is almost certainly wrong about the melody, which before *Kevin Barry* was written was the air of *Rolling Home to Dear Old Blighty*[2], and probably of other songs. It is, of course, quite usual for balladmakers to use established tunes.

singer and socialist, came to sing *Kevin Barry* was outlined in a letter written by Columba O'Hagan, a London-based architect, to the *Irish Post* in 1985:[3]

Peadar O'Donnell* and a friend were travelling in America by car when a tyre burst. A limousine stopped and offered help. The passenger asked Peadar and his friend to join him while the two drivers fixed the puncture. The passenger was Paul Robeson, then at the height of his career. He did not know O'Donnell, who knew all about *him*, but he was well informed about Ireland and said he would like to record an Irish song.

Peadar suggested *Kevin Barry*, which he said conveyed the spirit of Ireland. Robeson wrote down the words while Peadar went over the melody a few times. Then Robeson sang the air with corrections from Peadar and his friend.

The recording was made on the English label TOPIC, which has made a remarkable contribution to building a worthwhile and permanent folk music catalogue. Alan Booth is the accompanist on the 78 record, which was first made in the early 1950s. The version contains none of the ballad's anti-British sentiments, probably because in the McCarthy era Robeson received massive support from British Labour MPs in his struggle to have his passport returned by the US State Department.

The B side of the Robeson song carries *Joe Hill*, an appropriate choice. This record, TRC 96, is now rare.

Republicans in successive generations sang *Kevin Barry* to keep up their spirits in adversity. In the 1940s campaign, Harry Whyte the veteran IRA man, held in a basement cell in Mountjoy, gave a new twist to the tradition. 'The only lift I

---

*Peadar O'Donnell (1893-1986) was from Meenmore, Dungloe, Co. Donegal. A socialist, a Republican and a writer, he began his career as a teacher. He went to Scotland to help migrant workers from Donegal to strike for better conditions. In the IRA, he took the anti-Treaty side in the Civil War and fought in the Four Courts garrison. He and Frank Ryan were expelled from the IRA in 1934 for their socialist activities. He was a founder of Saor Éire, edited the *Republican Congress*, and supported the Spanish Republic against Franco. He succeeded Seán Ó Faoláin as editor of *The Bell* and wrote many books including *Islanders* (1929) and *The Gates Flew Open* (1932).

got was hearing a warder humming outside, of all things, *Kevin Barry*.'[4]

Songs, poems and ballads abound. The number of people to whom Kevin Barry's death was an inspiration to write was legion. Quantity is not lacking; the poems and ballads possessing any intrinsic merit were few enough. Perhaps the finest tribute was paid in Pádraic O'Halpin's *For Kevin Barry* which ends:

He gave not to you or I, we do not own him
Yet do you think the streets fail to see him
Or the tree roots in vain feel for his bones?[5]

A play by Gerard Westby was published by P.J. Bourke of Dublin, a kinsman of the Barrys. It is best forgotten.

Two *in memoriam* cards were printed, one by the Barry family; the other by the Students' Representative Council of UCD. Both used similar phrases in Irish — '*d'Airm an tSaor Stáit*' (family) and: '*n-arm Saorstáit na hÉireann* (UCD). The pedantic point is worth pursuing — *Saorstát* (two years later to be institutionalised as the Irish Free State) was then the word for republic. *Poblacht*, now used, was invented only in 1913 by Liam Gogan, then *reachtaire* (auditor) of An Cumann Gaelach in UCD.[6]

When the joint secretaries of the SRC, G.P. Sarsfield Hogan[7] and Richard Johnson, conceived the idea of printing their own card, they sought the advice of Dr. Douglas Hyde*, Professor of Modern Irish at UCD, about the wording. 'He', says Sarsfield Hogan, 'insisted that *poblacht* was a bastard word, unknown to Irish, and that *saorstát* was the only word properly used as equivalent to republic. Foolishly, I accepted this amendment, which afterwards caused annoyance to the Barry family and other republicans'. The Barrys had no case: their

---

*Douglas Hyde (1863-1947) was a Gaelic scholar and first President of Ireland (1938-45). Reared in Frenchpark, Co. Roscommon, he was educated at Trinity College, Dublin. He was co-founder of the Gaelic League and under the name *An Craoibhín Aoibhinn* (*The Sweet Little Branch*) he published poetry and drama in Irish. While he was President, he published three volumes of verse for private circulation.

own card contained the same term, which only later became odious to them.

The students sold 500 copies of the card, which was printed by Paddy Mahon of Yarnhall Street in the week after Kevin's death. At a shilling (5p) a time, the council netted £25, which formed the nucleus of the Kevin Barry Memorial Fund. Fourteen years and many more subscriptions later, the fund paid for the very fine stained glass window which was erected in the Council Chamber of the College.

The O'Rahilly[8], who seems to have been auditor of the Commerce Society, treasurer of the Literary and Historical Society and a member, if not the chairman, of the Kevin Barry Memorial Committee while he was a student in 1923-24 at University College, Dublin, drafted a significant letter during the year: 'Funds are urgently needed in order to build the memorial to Kevin B [Barry] and F.F. [Frank Flood]. £100 was collected in the College for this purpose in 1921. . . . The above-mentioned amount is inadequate for the purpose and the Committee proposes to collect another £400.'

O'Rahilly describes the two students as having been 'murdered in Mountjoy Gaol by the British Army of Occupation'. But the importance of his letter lies in the joining of Frank Flood's name with Kevin's. Where, one wonders, in the next ten years, did the meritorious suggestion disappear to?

Impatient with the delay in erecting the memorial, the students in 1931 elected The O'Rahilly as their representative on the Governing Body of the College. In only three years more, the choice of memorial and a suitable site had been decided on. The window is by Richard King, the Castlebar artist who joined the Harry Clarke studios in 1928 and stayed until 1940.

The Kevin Barry window lies undisturbed and forgotten. The College has moved to Belfield and the old Council Chamber in Earlsfort Terrace has been renamed the Kevin Barry Room. At present the room is full of engineering students and their drawing boards. Below and behind it is the National Concert Hall. The window was unveiled in 1934 by The O'Rahilly, who subsequently married Elgin Barry. The President of UCD, Dr. Denis Coffey, officiated and gave the veteran Republican,

Frank Ryan, an opportunity to write in *Republican Congress:*

> At last, a Kevin Barry Memorial has been unveiled at University College, Dublin. The present committee were people who had no connection with the War for Independence nor with the organisations which participated in it. It is understandable, therefore — though inexcusable — that few of Kevin Barry's comrades were invited by the committee and that, instead, a Blueshirt* presided and the anti-Republican President of U.C.D. was given an opportunity to shed tears for the Boy-Martyr of 1920. We are glad that Frank Flood, the University student who also gave his life in the war of 1920-21, was remembered by one speaker. . . .[9]

In the 1920s, when Father Peter Hayes was parish priest of St. Catherine's church in Meath Street, and Father John Costello**, a man of strong Republican leanings, was curate, a strange thing happened.[10] Mr. Wall, a salt merchant of 117 Thomas Street, decided to pay for the redecoration of the church and Leo Broe, later to found the well-known firm of monumental stonemasons, was commissioned to cast the heads of the Irish saints in plaster, including St. Kevin of Glendalough.

They were erected at the top of the pillars that run up the aisle. On the second pillar on the left, opposite (then) Blessed Oliver Plunkett, Broe placed a fine head of Kevin Barry. It could be argued that, since no likeness of the seventh-century

---

*Blueshirts was the common name given to members of the Army Comrades' Association, who wore blue shirts from April 1933. Their basic philosophy came from the Papal encyclical *Quadragesimo Anno* and from Mussolini's Corporate State. Led by General Eoin O'Duffy, the sacked Commissioner of the Garda Síochána, they attacked both de Valera's Government and the IRA, and held fascist-style marches complete with flags and salutes (e.g. 'Hail O'Duffy'). The Blueshirts were banned in August 1933, and by 1937 the movement had died.

**The Rev. John Costello was in the Hammam Hotel in July 1922. He was then a curate in SS. Michael and John church and tried to stop the bombardment of the Four Courts. He was parish priest of Roundwood, Co. Wicklow, when he died.

saint exists, the sculptor was within his rights in choosing to model his work on a man recently dead. Certainly Kevin Barry, who had such fond memories of Glendalough, must have enjoyed the joke.

Leo Broe's son Desmond was the sculptor of a second likeness of Kevin. Without knowing that Gerard O Donovan[11] was a nephew of Kevin's, Broe asked him to sit for a monument to be erected in Rathvilly. The pillar, topped by a head of Kevin, was unveiled in 1958 by Mrs. Kathleen Clarke, widow of the 1916 leader Thomas Clarke. This memorial, for which the site was donated by Lord Rathdonnell, was the scene of a fiftieth anniversary ceremony in 1970. President de Valera attended. This time two of the Barry family went to talk to him, at his request, in his Rolls-Royce landaulet.

On the site of the Church Street raid, a plaque was unveiled by Éamon de Valera in 1938. It was the work of Albert Power, RHA. It disappeared after that side of Church Street was demolished. A new plaque, on the wall of The Tap public house nearby, replaced the original.

Joseph O'Hanrahan executed a handsome bust which was shown at the Royal Hibernian Academy's exhibition, but its present whereabouts are unknown. Other smaller busts were produced in 1922 and can be found in scattered places around the country. One is in the National Museum; another in the possession of Michael Barry's widow, Rita.

In Co. Carlow, Matt Cullen[12] records, funds were collected throughout the county and transferred from the county committee to a Hacketstown committee, of which Father Dunne, the parish priest, was chairman, and Father Broe the vice-chairman. They bought the town hall cum cinema and renamed it the Kevin Barry Hall. Surplus funds were later devoted to the purchase of new pews for the Catholic church, a gift which the parish priest, Father Boylan, 'kindly accepted', says Matt Cullen. A plaque in the porch of the church marks the donation.

About three weeks after Kevin's death, Mrs. Barry received a courteous letter from the Governor of Mountjoy inviting her to name a time at which it would be convenient for her, and any of the family who wished, to visit the grave. She did so. It was another twenty-six years before she got another invitation. General Seán MacEoin*, Minister for Justice in the first Inter-Party Government, wrote in July 1948, saying that it had come to his notice that she had never been invited to visit her son's grave and asking if he might have the honour of taking her there. He also said that he was sending her a permanent pass for herself and her friends. She expressed her appreciation and said she would like to go quietly by herself. She never got the opportunity. Kathy went once without a permit from the Minister. She was told by prisoners who were there in the British era that soldiers on guard planted flowers on the grave and kept it spotless.

In Mountjoy Jail, Kevin's remains still lie. In 1922, 1932 and again in 1948, native Governments suggested that re-internment would be appropriate. 'We', says Kathy Barry, 'said he died for the Republic and should stay where he lay until the Republic was established'.[13] In spite of that declaration of principle, her son Paddy Moloney recalls, the Tricolour flew over her house to celebrate the Republic of Ireland's formal inception on Easter Monday, 1949.

Kathy wrote of her family in 1920:

> We were all Republicans. Mick was active in the Carlow Brigade and therefore had to keep out of the public eye. Shel was active in the Carlow area too. Elgin, Monty and Peggy were at school. I was the eldest. Mother was a staunch supporter but busy minding two homes, and diffident, protected. Our uncles were friendly but not active Republicans. I was therefore forced by circumstances to take a prominent part.[14]

---

*General Seán MacEoin (1894-1973) was born in Bunlahy, Co. Longford and went to school in Kilshrule before becoming a blacksmith. He joined the Volunteers and rose swiftly through the ranks. Two days after Kevin Barry's death, he led the IRA in a famous ambush on the Black and Tans which earned him the nickname 'the Blacksmith of Ballinalee'. Captured and sentenced to death in Mountjoy, he was the object of a gallant but unsuccessful rescue attempt. He supported the Treaty and became Chief of Staff of the Free State Army in 1923. He was TD for Sligo and Longford (1929-65) and was unsuccessful in two presidential elections, 1945 and 1959. He was Minister for Justice (1948-51) and Defence (1951 and 1954-57).

After Kevin's death, she worked tirelessly for independence. She joined the University Branch of Cumann na mBan late in 1920, when Captain Eileen McGrane was still the officer commanding. When Eileen McGrane was arrested, Lieutenant Kathleen Murphy (later a doctor who married Dr. Paul Farrell) was promoted captain. Kathy, who says she 'attended parades and carried out the usual routine duties', remained a plain member, in close touch with every battalion of the Dublin Brigade, especially the Fifth, the Engineers' Battalion.

She left Ernest Aston's employment and showed herself to be capable of organising much more than an engineer's office. She was close to Collins, to Stack, to Mulcahy and to de Valera. Inevitably, given the depth of her commitment, she opposed the Treaty. Inevitably too, given the strength of her personality, she swept the family along with her. Her high regard for Collins never left her, however, and she noted in the 1950s: 'I personally wept buckets when I heard Mick was dead. And so far from loathing his memory, I have often since his death called on his spirit to fulfil the promise he made me that last time I saw him. . . .[15]

Early in 1922 de Valera asked Kathy to become one of the Republican delegation to the United States. A Provisional Government delegation had gone to seek American support for the new State, and de Valera, who knew the importance of obtaining the good opinion of the United States, asked Austin Stack, Father Michael O'Flanagan*, J.J. O'Kelly**, Countess Markievicz and Kathy Barry to speak for the Republican cause.

*Father Michael O'Flanagan (1876-1942) was born near Castlerea, Co. Roscommon. Ordained for the Elphin diocese, he toured America in 1907 in search of funds. He was deeply involved in land agitation, became Vice-President of Sinn Féin in 1917 and was a judge of the Dáil Courts. He visited America again (1921-26) as a Sinn Féin propagandist. He was silenced in 1932, supported the IRA under Frank Ryan, and went to Spain to fight Franco. He edited fifty volumes of the *Letters* of John O'Donovan (1924-32).

**John J. O'Kelly (1872-1957) was from Valentia, Co. Kerry. President of the Gaelic League (1919-23), he was Deputy Speaker of the First Dáil. He opposed the Treaty and succeeded de Valera as president of Sinn Féin in 1926. He wrote in Irish under the pen-name *Sceilg*.

To Kathy, de Valera entrusted the special care of the way-
ward Markievicz. 'Keep Madame on the rails. Make her act
every inch the Countess',[16] he advised. And indeed the Countess was seen by Americans everywhere as, in Diana Norman's
words, 'some sort of amalgam of Joan of Arc and Grace
O'Malley'.[17]

The two women sailed on the *Aquitania* on 1 April, 1922,
and were met in New York by fifty reporters and photo-
graphers. One of them, a woman, wrote of Markievicz in the
New York Evening World: 'Despite her martial achievements,
she is not a martial looking person — frail, rather, and almost
deprecatory except when she is talking about the Irish Republic. . . .' Kathy's smile was described by another journalist
as slow and sweet; her accent captivating. The two, an unlikely
pair anyway, did not immediately become fast friends: Kathy
found, her son Paddy says, that Markievicz's initial attitude
towards her was somewhat condescending.

On Easter Sunday, they were in Philadelphia. Kathy and
the Countess went to church in great style, escorted by 500
Irish Volunteers and a brass band. In Detroit they went to a
banquet given by the Kevin Barry Club and the Gaelic Club.

It was a two-month punishing tour right across the United
States. In Butte, Montana, Kathy was found to be 'a winsome
Irish lassie, with dark blue eyes, the matchless skin of her soft
climate, white teeth well set behind a mobile mouth and a
wealth of brown hair that her black sailor hat did not half
conceal'.

Wherever they went, the two women made a point of asking to see the local jail and of inspecting the condemned cell.
Constance had become a connoisseur of prisons.

They were just home when the Civil War proper began.
Kathy, Mary MacSwiney and Linda Kearns* were the only

---

*Linda Kearns of Sligo, a trained nurse, is one of those people who was
in everything during the War of Independence and the Civil War, but
has not yet got her due meed of praise. She escaped from Mountjoy during
the Truce, while she was serving a ten-year sentence. She already had
served time in Walton Jail, Liverpool. Tony Woods tells a hair-raising
story about Frank Thornton shooting him, then telephoning 'Dr.'
Linda Kearns at Baggot Street Hospital and saying: 'Look, I am in a bit

women left in the ruins of O'Connell Street after the week-long siege that ended with Cathal Brugha's single-minded plan to die a martyr's death. They were an indomitable trio and epitomised the spirit of Cumann na mBan.

At the height of the Civil War, there were about 400 women in prison. Among them was Elgin Barry,[18] who was moved to the North Dublin Union — where two years earlier her brother had been 'interrogated' by the British. The Union had been converted into a jail to take the overflow from Kilmainham, and the women went on hunger-strike in sympathy with those in Kilmainham. Elgin was eighteen, and taking her place with veterans such as Maud Gonne, Dorothy Macardle, Grace Plunkett, Nora Connolly, Mary MacSwiney, Lily O'Brennan, Kate O'Callaghan, Máire Comerford and Eithne Coyle.

Between June and October 1922, Kathy[19] had organised and maintained a line of communication between Dublin and General Liam Lynch* in the South. In October, moving north-ward slowly, mostly on foot, Lynch got to Dublin via Carlow and Wicklow, probably staying in Tombeagh and certainly spending a night in Bartons' of Annamoe. He set up GHQ at Tower House, Santry, where Michael Fitzgerald and his family lived. In September, Kathy met Lynch in Kilavullen and went with him to Rossadrehid in the Glen of Aherlow.

As the Civil War drew to a close, Kathy had a long discus-

---

of a jam. I'm after shooting Tony Woods. The old lady (Tony's mother) will have my life. Come over and do something'. She did. She later married Charlie McWhinney of Derry. In 1925, Linda Kearns and Kathy Barry (by then married to Jim Moloney) went to Australia as delegates of the Irish Relief Mission and were very well received by the Australian Irish, still generous with help for Irish people in distress. Two years earlier, Cardinal Mannix informed a monster meeting that £3,400 had been sent from Victoria to Kathleen A. Barry, Secretary of the prisoners' relief fund'. So Colm Kiernan tells us in his life of Mannix.

*Liam Lynch (1890-1923) was from Anglesborough, Ballylanders, Co. Limerick. He played a prominent part in the opposition to conscription, commanded the Cork No. 2 Brigade in the War of Independence, and was a leading member of the IRB. He opposed the Treaty and was appointed Chief of Staff of the IRA. He tried to prevent the spread of civil strife, but eventually was shot by Free State troops in the Knockmealdown Mountains.

sion with Lynch in Kilcash near Drimoleague, on Good Friday, 30 March, 1923.[20] He told her that there were three courses open to the Republican forces — to fight on, to surrender, or a third that he would not name. It was, in fact, to dump arms, the course that was followed after Lynch's death ten days later.

Kathy and Shel, Michael and Elgin — all the older Barrys played their part in passing on the torch lit by Kevin. But the mainstream of Irish politics moved on and left them lying in the bitter backwaters of uncompromising Republicanism. Kathy at least, with her style, leadership and experience, could have gone on to add lustre and weight to any Cabinet; panache and persuasion to any embassy.

In 1924 she married Jim Moloney, not long before she embarked with Linda Kearns on the tour of Australia to raise funds and create publicity for Sinn Féin. Jim Moloney, having fought in the War of Independence, became Intelligence Officer in the Southern Command during the Civil War. Before he was captured, he was Director of Communications and during his internment was OC of Newbridge Camp. His brother Paddy was killed in action by the Black and Tans and his brother Con was Adjutant-General of the Republican forces during the Civil War until he was captured and wounded. The brothers were sons of P.J. Moloney, TD, a chemist in Tipperary town. Jim and Kathy had five children: Mary and Helen, twins; Paddy, Katherine and Judith, who carried on the Republican tradition until her tragic death in California in 1972. Mary married the late Pádraic O'Halpin. Helen is a distinguished stained-glass artist. Paddy, who was an executive with an American oil company in London, died in July, 1989. Katherine, the widow of Patrick Kavanagh the poet, died in August, 1989. Kathy Barry Moloney died in 1969, Jim in 1981.

A fine new set of gravestones, unveiled by President de Valera in 1961, marks the spot in Mountjoy where Kevin Barry lies with Thomas Whelan, Patrick Moran, Thomas Bryan, Patrick Doyle, Frank Flood, Bernard Ryan, Thomas Traynor, Edward Foley and Patrick Maher, all ten of them hanged in Dublin between November 1920 and June 1921.

As for Kevin himself, one of the many good-hearted people who had petitioned the Viceroy on his behalf should have the last word. Father Frank Brown of the Society of Jesus wrote editorially in *The Belvederian* of 1921:

> It was to be expected that within the calm harbour of our College walls some ripple would be raised by the great storm that is surging around and over our land, but we little thought that through our boyish lives would come so great a wave as that which swept across the land when Kevin Barry died.

'We loved him here, we saw him go, we watched him die. May God rest his soul'.

Notes

CHAPTER 1
1   Family tree in the possession of Triona Maher
2   Rent receipt in Kevin Barry's private papers (KB)
3   Will in Kevin Barry's private papers (KB)
4   Assignment in Kevin Barry's private papers (KB)
5   Letter in possession of Kevin Barry (KB)

CHAPTER 2
1   Information from Triona Maher
2   Information from Elgin Barry (Madame O'Rahilly)

CHAPTER 3
1   Information from Shel Barry to James O'Donovan (GOD)

CHAPTER 4
1   Proceedings of the RSAI, 1939
2   Curran, *Dublin Decorative Plasterwork* (London) pp 86-87
3   Bowman and O'Donoghue (Ed.), *Portraits: Belvedere College 1832-1982* (Dublin, 1982) p 21
4   Information from Bruce Bradley, SJ
5   Notebook in possession of Kevin Maher
6   Cronin, *Kevin Barry* (Cork, 1965)
7   Information from Dr. Gerard Ward McAleer
8   Letter in possession of Patrick Barry Moloney
9   Letter in possession of Triona Maher
10 The Belvederian, 1970
11 Ibid
12 Information from Thomas Counihan, SJ, to James O'Donovan (GOD)
13 Essay quoted in Cronin, *Kevin Barry* (Cork, 1965)
14 MacEoin, *Survivors* (Dublin, 1987) pp 314ff

CHAPTER 5
1   Information from Bob O'Flanagan to James O'Donovan (GOD)
2   *Liberty*, April, 1960
3   Seán Cronin, *Capuchin Annual*, 1970, p 534
4   Letters in possession of Triona Maher and Patrick Barry Moloney
5   Patrick Barry Moloney, *The Belvederian*, 1945

NOTES

CHAPTER 6

1. Information from Dr. Gerard Ward McAleer
2. Information from Dr. Honoria Aughney
3. Information from Dr. Gerard Ward McAleer
4. *Irish Independent* 1 November, 1961
5. Letter in possession of Triona Maher
6. Letter in possession of Triona Maher
7. Letter in possession of Triona Maher
8. Information from Peggy Barry to James O'Donovan (GOD)
9. Information from Helen Moloney
10. Erskine Childers, *Daily News*, 29 March, 1920
11. Martin (Ed.), *1916 and UCD* (Dublin, 1966) p 112
12. Andrews, *Dublin Made Me* (Dublin and Cork, 1979) p 148
13. Meenan, F.O.C., *Cecilia Street* (Dublin, 1987) p 95
14. Information from Peggy Barry to James O'Donovan (GOD)

CHAPTER 7

1. Denis Holmes, *Dublin's Fighting Story, 1913-1921* (Tralee, 1948) pp 131-2
2. Information from Patrick Gorman and Peg Scully
3. Letter in possession of John Maher
4. Letter in possession of Mrs. Cecil Van Cauwelaert (sister)
5. Information from Matt Cullen to James O'Donovan (GOD)
6. Information from Bridget and Joe Doyle

CHAPTER 8

1. PRO WO 32 4815
2. Dangerfield, *The Damnable Question* (London, 1977) p 320
3. Greaves, *Liam Mellows* (London, 1971) p 194
4. Bennett, *The Black and Tans* (London, 1959) pp 69-70
5. Sir Henry Wilson's diary, 23 September, 1920

CHAPTER 9

1. *Liberty*, April, 1960
2. Cronin, *Kevin Barry* (Cork, 1965) pp 13-14
3. Ms 8043 NLI R/O 2609
4. Information from O'Flanagan, O'Neill and Young given to James O'Donovan (GOD)
5. Names, ranks, actions and quotations of soldiers of the Duke of Wellington's Regiment from Ms. 8043 NLI
6. Information from O'Flanagan, O'Neill and Young given to James O'Donovan
7. Cronin, *Kevin Barry* (Cork, 1965) p 14
8. *Liberty*, April, 1960
9. Cronin, *Kevin Barry* (Cork, 1965) p 15

CHAPTER 10

1 Information from John Doyle, Ballywaltrim, Bray
2 Affidavit sent to world press for publication, 30 October, 1920
3 Townshend, *The British Campaign in Ireland* (Oxford, 1975) p 116
4 *Sunday Press* article, 3 November, 1963
5 Letter in possession of Evanna McAleer Kennedy

CHAPTER 11

1 Information from Kathy Barry to James O'Donovan (GOD)
2 Cronin, *Kevin Barry* (Cork, 1965) p 18
3 Information from Kathy Barry to James O'Donovan (GOD)
4 Ms. 8043 NLI R/O 2609
5 Ms. 31658 NLI LOB
6 Information from Kathy Barry to James O'Donovan (GOD)
7 Ms. 8043 NLI R/O 2609

CHAPTER 12

1 Information from Kathy Barry to James O'Donovan (GOD). Contemporary newspaper reports; Ms. 8043 in the National Library of Ireland, and Sean Cronin's *Kevin Barry* (Cork, 1965) have also been used in this account of the general court-marial
2 *Freeman's Journal*, 21 October, 1920
3 Information from Father Augustine, OFM Cap, to James O'Donovan (GOD)

CHAPTER 13

1 Information from Kathy Barry to James O'Donovan (GOD)
2 Information from Chief Officer James Petherbridge, Mountjoy Prison
3 Information from Mrs. Mag Leonard and John Comerford
4 Mountjoy Prison records
5 Sir Mark Sturgis' diary, PRO 30/59
6 Information from Kathy Barry to James O'Donovan (GOD)
7 Information from Dr. Honoria Aughney

CHAPTER 14

1 Information from Kathy Barry to James O'Donovan (GOD)
2 CAB 23 NLI
3 Information from Kathy Barry to James O'Donovan (GOD)
4 Field Marshal Sir John French's diary for 31 October, 1920. IWM
5 Sir Mark Sturgis' dairy, PRO 30/59
6 Information from Bruce Bradley, SJ
7 Information from Kathy Barry to James O'Donovan (GOD)
8 Macready, *Annals of an Active Life* (London, 1924)
9 MacEoin, *Survivors* (Dublin, 1987) p 428
10 Sir Mark Sturgis' diary, PRO 30/59
11 Meenan, *Cecilia Street* (Dublin, 1987) pp 70, 95
12 Ms. 31658 NLI LOB

CHAPTER 15

1 Information from Kathy Barry to James O'Donovan (GOD)
2 *Liberty*, April, 1960
3 Information from Kathy Barry to James O'Donovan

CHAPTER 16

1 Dr. Gerard Ward McAleer, anonymous obituary, newspapers and *The Belvederian* 1921 p 35
2 Letter in possession of Evanna McAleer Kennedy
3 Information from Father Augustine, OFM Cap, to James O'Donovan (GOD) and *Irish Press* 17 January, 1964
4 Pierrepoint, *Executioner: Pierrepoint* (London, 1974)

CHAPTER 17

1 Photograph NMI
2 *Irish Press* 30 April, 1949
3 Information from Kathy Barry to James O'Donovan (GOD)
4 *Irish Independent* 2 November, 1920
5 Cronin, *Kevin Barry* (Cork, 1965) p 27
6 *Irish Press* 30 April, 1949
7 *The Belvederian* 1970
8 Rector's archives, Belvedere College, undated
9 McMahon, *A Book of Irish Quotations* (Dublin, 1984) p 40
10 MacEoin, *Survivors* (Dublin, 1987) p 427
11 O'Connor, *With Michael Collins in the Fight for Irish Independence* (London, 1929)

CHAPTER 18

1 Information from Mrs. Mag Leonard
2 *Irish Press* 1 November, 1967
3 Unless otherwise stated, this account has drawn on contemporary newspaper reports
4 Pierrepoint, *Executioner: Pierrepoint* (London, 1974)
5 Letter in possession of Triona Maher
6 Information from Dr. Honoria Aughney
7 Visit to Mountjoy Prison
8 Mountjoy Prison records

CHAPTER 19

1 Information from Joe Doyle
2 Letters in possession of Triona Maher. These letters were published by James O'Donovan in an article in the *Irish Press* on 17 January, 1964
3 Card in possession of Sheila Hanna
4 Cronin, *Kevin Barry* (Cork, 1965) p 32
5 Brennan, *Allegiance* (Dublin, 1950) p 285

6 Information from Seán MacBride, December 1987
7 Information from Father Augustine, OFM Cap, to James O'Donovan (GOD)
8 Information from Mrs. May Deering and Ms. Bride Butler
9 Information from Peg Scully
10 Letter in Dublin Diocesan Archives

CHAPTER 20
1 PRO WO 35 187. The collected cartoons of Shemus for 1920-21 were published in book form by the *Freeman's Journal* under the title: *The Reign of Terror*
2 Ms. 8043 NLI R/O 2609
3 Hansard No. 134 (1-19 November, 1920)
4 Meenan (Ed.), Centenary History of the *Literary and Historical Society 1855-1955* (Tralee, 1955)
5 Ms. 8043 NLI R/O 2609
6 Taylor, *Assassination* (London, 1961) pp 55-56
7 Pierrepoint, *Executioner: Pierrepoint* (London, 1974)

CHAPTER 21
1 Copy letters in possession of Triona Maher
2 Levenson and Natterstad, *Hanna Sheehy-Skeffington* (Syracuse, 1986) p 136
3 Letter in possession of Triona Maher
4 Information from Patrick O'Gorman
5 Information from Elgin Barry (Madame O'Rahilly)
6 Papers in possession of Kevin Barry (KB)
7 Information from Jack O'Keeffe
8 Letter in possession of Kevin Barry (KB)
9 Information from Dr. Honoria Aughney

CHAPTER 22
1 Information from Patrick O'Gorman
2 Papers in possession of Kevin Barry (KB)
3 Information from Thomas P. O'Neill
4 Gaughan, *Austin Stack*, Dublin, 1977
5 Information from Elgin Barry (Madame O'Rahilly)
6 Information from Kevin Barry of Tombeagh
7 Longford and O'Neill, *Éamon de Valera* (Dublin and London, 1970), p 218
8 Information from Michael Barry to Michael (The) O'Rahilly
9 Author's observation

CHAPTER 23
1 Kathy Barry's written comments on James O'Donovan's, 'Ms. No. 1' (GOD)

NOTES

2   Information from Johnny Morrissey
3   Frank Dolan's column, *Irish Post*, 20 April, 1985
4   MacEoin, *Harry* (Dublin, 1985)
5   *The National Student*, March 1948
6   Information from Diarmuid Breathnach
7   Letter from G.P. Sarsfield Hogan to Leo Flanagan, 24 November, 1986. Copy from Dr G.W. McAleer
8   Information from notebook in the possession of Michael (The) O'Rahilly
9   *Republican Congress*, 10 November, 1934
10 Information from Father John Meagher
11 Information from Gerard O Donovan
12 Information from Matt Cullen to James O'Donovan (GOD)
13 Information from Kathy Barry to James O'Donovan (GOD)
14 Kathy Barry's written comments on James O'Donovan's 'Ms. No. 1' (GOD)
15 Ibid
16 Coxhead, *Daughters of Erin* (London, 1965) p 114
17 Norman, *Terrible Beauty* (Dublin, 1988)
18 Information from Elgin Barry (Madame O'Rahilly)
19 O'Donoghue, *No Other Law* (Dublin, 1986), p 277
20 Ibid, p 301

Bibliography

Books

Andrews, C.S. Dublin Made Me. Mercier, Dublin and Cork, 1979.

―――― Man of No Property. Mercier, Dublin and Cork, 1982.

Bell, J. Bowyer. The Secret Army. Sphere, London, 1972.

Bennett, Richard. The Black and Tans. Four Square, London, 1959.

Bourke, Marcus. The O'Rahilly. Anvil Books, Tralee, 1967.

Bowman, John, and O'Donoghue, Ronan (Ed.). Portraits: Belvedere College 1832-1982. Gill and Macmillan, Dublin, 1982.

Brennan, Robert. Allegiance. Brown and Nolan, Dublin, 1950.

Byrne, Liam. History of Aviation in Ireland. Blackwater, Dublin, 1980.

Callwell, C.E. Field-Marshal Sir Henry Wilson. Cassell, London.

City of Dublin Electricity Department 1892-1928. 1928.

Conlon, L. Cumann na mBan and the Women of Ireland 1913-1925. Kilkenny, 1969.

Coogan, Tim Pat. The I.R.A. Pall Mall, London, 1970.

―――― Ireland Since the Rising, Pall Mall, London, 1970.

Coxhead, Elizabeth. Daughters of Erin. New English Library, London, 1965.

Cronin, Seán. Kevin Barry. National Publications Committee, Cork, 1965.

―――― Frank Ryan, Repsol, Dublin, 1980.

―――― Irish Nationalism. Academy Press, Dublin, 1980.

Crozier, F.P. The Men I Killed. Michael Joseph, London, 1937.

Curran, C.P. Dublin Decorative Plasterwork of the 17th and 18th Centuries. Academy Editions, London.

Curran, Joseph M. The Birth of the Irish Free State 1921-23. University of Alabama Press, Alabama, 1980.

Dangerfield, George. The Damnable Question. Constable, London, 1977.

Desmond, Shaw. The Drama of Sinn Féin. Collins, London.

Devoy, John. Recollections of an Irish Rebel. Irish University Press, Shannon, 1969.

Dublin's Fighting Story 1913-21: Told by the Men Who Made It. Kerryman, Tralee, c. 1948.

Fitzgerald, William G. (Ed.). The Voice of Ireland. Virtue, Dublin, c.1925.

Forester, Margery. Michael Collins: The Lost Leader. Sidgwick and Jackson, London, 1971.

Foster, Roy. Charles Stewart Parnell: The Man and His Family. Harvester, Sussex, 1979.

Gaughan, J.A. Austin Stack: Portrait of a Separatist. Kingdom Books, Dublin, 1977.

Gillespie, Elgy (Ed.). The Liberties of Dublin. E. & T. O'Brien, Dublin, 1973.

Greaves, C. Desmond. Liam Mellows. Lawrence and Wishart, London, 1971.

Gwynn, Stephen. John Redmond's Last Years. Edward Arnold, London, 1919.

Hickey, D.J., and Doherty, J.E. A Dictionary of Irish History 1800-1980. Gill and Macmillan, Dublin, 1980.

Inglis, Brian. Roger Casement. Coronet, London, 1974.

"I.O." (Major C.J.C. Street). The Administration of Ireland 1920. Philip Allan, London, 1921.

Johnston, Máirín. Around the Banks of Pimlico. Attic Press, Dublin, 1985.

Jones, Tom. Whitehall Diary:Volume III. Oxford, 1971.

Kee, Robert. The Green Flag: Volume Three: Ourselves Alone. Quartet Books, London, 1976.

——— Ireland: A History. Weidenfeld and Nicholson, London, 1980.

Levenson, Leah and Natterstad, Jerry H. Hanna Sheehy-Skeffington. Syracuse University Press, 1986.

Longford, Earl of, and Thomas P. O'Neill. Éamon de Valera. Gill and Macmillan, Dublin; Hutchinson, London, 1970.

Macardle, Dorothy. The Irish Republic. Gollancz, London, 1937.

McCann, John. War by the Irish. Kerryman, Tralee, 1946.

McCartan, Patrick. With de Valera in America. Fitzpatrick, Dublin, 1932.

MacCiarnáin, Séamus. The Last Post. Cumann na n-Uigheann Náisiúnta, Atha Cliath, 1985.

McGready, C.T. Dublin Street Names Dated and Explained. Reprinted Carraig Books 1974 from original 1892.

MacEoin, Uinseann. Survivors, Argenta, Dublin, 1987.

——— Harry. Argenta, Dublin, 1985.

MacLoughlin, Adrian. Guide to Historic Dublin. Gill and Macmillan, Dublin, 1979.

McMahon, Seán. A Book of Irish Quotations. O'Brien, Dublin, 1984.

Macready, General Sir Nevil. Annals of an Active Life. Hutchinson, London, 1924.

Marreco, Anne. The Rebel Countess. Corgi, London, 1969.

Martin, F.X. (Ed.). 1916 and U.C.D. Browne and Nolan, Dublin, 1966.

Meenan, F.O.C. Cecilia Street: The Catholic University School of Medicine 1855-1931. Gill and Macmillan, Dublin, 1987.

Meenan, James (Ed.). Centenary History of the Literary and Historical Society 1855-1955. Kerryman, Tralee, 1955.

Moynihan, Maurice (Ed.). Speeches and Statements by Eamon de Valera 1917-1973. Gill and Macmillan, Dublin; St. Martin's Press, New York, 1980.

National Association of the Old I.R.A. Dublin Brigade Review, 1939.

Norman, Diana. Terrible Beauty: A Life of Constance Markievicz. Poolbeg, Dublin, 1988.

O'Brien, Conor Cruise (Ed.). The Shaping of Modern Ireland. Routledge and Kegan Paul, London, 1960.

Ó Broin, León. In Great Haste. Gill and Macmillan, Dublin, 1983.

——— No Man's Man. Institute of Public Administration, Dublin, 1982.

O'Callaghan, Seán. The Easter Lily. Allan Wingate, London, 1956.

O'Connor, Batt. With Michael Collins in the Fight for Irish Independence. London, 1929.

O'Connor, Frank. The Big Fellow. Corgi, London, 1969.

O'Connor, Ulick. A Terrible Beauty Is Born. Panther, London, 1985.

——— The Troubles: Ireland 1912-1922. Bobs Merrill, Indianapolis and New York, 1975.

O'Donoghue, Florence. No Other Law. Anvil, Dublin, 1986.

O'Farrell, Patrick. The Irish in Australia. New South Wales University Press, Sydney, 1987.

O'Halpin, Eunan. The Decline of the Union. Gill and Macmillan/Syracuse University Press, 1987.

O'Hegarty, P.S. The Victory of Sinn Féin. Simpkin Marshall, London: Talbot Press, Dublin, 1924.

O'Kelly, Seán T. (Ed. Pádraig Ó Fiannachta). Seán T.: 1916 go 1923. Cló Mórainn, Dublin, 1972.

O'Mahony, Seán. Frongoch: University of Revolution. FDR Teoranta, Dublin, 1987.

O'Malley, Ernie. On Another Man's Wound. Rich and Cowan, London, 1936.

——— The Singing Flame. Anvil, Dublin, 1978.

O'Sullivan, Donal. The Irish Free State and Its Senate. Faber and Faber, London, 1940.

O'Toole, Jimmy. Grange: The Path to the Present. Grange G.A.A. Club, Co. Carlow, 1987.

Pakenham, Frank. Peace by Ordeal. Cape, London, 1935.

Pakenham, Thomas. The Year of Liberty. Hodder and Stoughton, London, 1969.

Pierrepoint, Albert. Executioner: Pierrepoint. Harrap, London, 1974.

Share, Bernard. The Flight of the Iolar. Gill and Macmillan, Dublin, 1986.

Taylor, Rex. Assassination. Hutchinson, London, 1961.

——— Michael Collins. London, 1958.

Téry, Simone. En Irlande: De la guerre d'independence à la guerre civile

(1914-1923). Ernest Flammarion, Paris, 1923.

Tierney, Michael (Ed.). Struggle for Fortune. Browne and Nolan, Dublin, 1954.

Townshend, Charles. The British Campaign in Ireland. Oxford, 1975.

Van Voris, Jacqueline. Constance de Markievicz. University of Massachusetts Press, 1967.

Walsh, Senan. The Irish Capuchins 1885-1985.

Wells, Warre B. John Redmond: A Biography. Nisbet, London, 1919.

Westby, Gerard. Kevin Barry (play). P.J. Bourke, Dublin, 1971.

Winter, Ormonde. Winter's Tale. Richards, London, 1955.

Younger, Calton. Ireland's Civil War. Frederick Muller, London, 1968.

——— A State of Disunion. Fontana, London, 1972.

Papers and Manuscripts

Diary of Sir Mark Sturgis. Public Record Office, London.

Cabinet Papers. Public Record Office, London and National Library of Ireland.

War Office Papers. Public Record Office, London.

Colonial Office Papers. Public Record Office, London.

León Ó Broin Papers. National Library of Ireland.

James O'Donovan Papers. National Library of Ireland.

Mountjoy Prison Records. Department of Justice, Dublin.

Diaries of Sir John French. Imperial War Museum, London.

Periodicals

Capuchin Annual 1970. Article by Seán Cronin.

Belvederian 1917, 1919, 1921, 1935, 1945, 1970.

An Phoblacht 9 November, 1929

Liberty April, 1960.

Songs, Ballads and Poems

KEVIN BARRY

In Mountjoy Jail one Monday morning
High upon the gallows tree,
Kevin Barry gave his young life
For the cause of liberty.
But a lad of eighteen summers,
Yet no one can deny,
As he walked to death that morning
He proudly held his head on high.

'Why not shoot me like a soldier,
Do not hang me like a dog,
For I fought to free old Ireland,
On that bright September morn.
All round that little bakery,
Where we fought them hand to hand.
Why not shoot me like a soldier
For I fought to free Ireland.'

Just before he faced the hangman
In his dreary prison cell,
British soldiers tortured Barry
Just because he would not tell
The names of his brave companions,
And other things they wished to know.
'Turn informer or we'll kill you!'
Kevin Barry answered 'No!'

Calmly standing to attention,
While he bade his last farewell
To his broken-hearted mother,
Whose sad grief no one can tell,
For the cause he proudly cherished
This sad parting had to be;
Then to death walked, softly smiling,
That old Ireland might be free.

Another martyr for old Ireland,
Another murder for the crown,
Whose brutal laws may kill the Irish,
But won't keep their spirit down.
Lads like Barry are no cowards,
From the foe they will not fly;
Lads like Barry will free Ireland,
For her sake they'll live and die.

Kevin Barry you must leave us,
On the scaffold you must die,
Cried his broken-hearted mother,
As she bade her son good-bye.
Kevin turned to her in silence,
And said: 'Mother do not weep,
For it's all for dear old Ireland,
And it's all for Freedom's sake.'

Written by an exile in Glasgow in November, 1920. Many shorter versions
differing in detail have been published, including one in *The American
Songbag*, edited in 1928 by the poet Carl Sandburg. (Harcourt Brace
and Company, New York). This book carries the musical score of the
ballad and may be unique in that way. It was arranged by 'M.N.' (Mollie
Nemovsky — Mrs. Ben Abramson). Sandburg wrote: 'Tongues of love
and hate, breaths of passion and suffering, all mingled with a strange
bitter-sweet, are in this song out of the violent events in Ireland . . . In
Nashville, Tennessee, one may look at the statue of Sam Davis, who died
refusing to turn informer and thus save his life. Davis has a statue in
bronze; Kevin Barry has a song. . . .'

THE PRISON GRAVE OF KEVIN BARRY

You are dead to-day, and the cold, cold clay of a prison graveyard lies
On your body still, though your spirit still lives in the Land beyond the
skies.
With the martyred dead, who for Ireland bled, and who perished at the
tyrant's hand,
And inscribed their name on the roll of fame, of Ireland's patriot band.

Chorus
Oh dear brave Kevin Barry! May your spirit guide us through
The path you tread of the martyred dead, that we shall follow too.

When the savage horde, with fire and sword, sought to crush Dark Ros-
aleen,
And her grand old flag, in the mire to drag, the Orange, White and Green.

You joined the fight, for your Motherland and Right, in the legion of
    your comrades brave,
To strike a blow at the mighty foe, your own dear land to save.

Chorus

The prison cell or the sad death knell no horrors hold for you;
Nor the cruel blows of ruthless foes could your young soul subdue.
You preferred to die, on the gibbet of Mountjoy and to vindicate the
    Nation's cause,
Ere you'd bow your head in fear and dread of the tyrant alien laws.

Chorus

You are dead to-day and your sacred clay in a prison graveyard sleeps,
While out beyond those grim, grey walls, an anguished people weeps,
And kneels to pray that the Great God may a million more imbue
With that courage pure that can endure, that we shall follow too.

Words by Richard Clarke; music by John Stanley. This song appeared in
The Soldiers' Song Book, published by the Irish Book Bureau, Dublin
at 2d. The book, which is undated, ascribes the song to 'Anon'.

BALLAD

I've a sad but true story to relate
Of a brave young Irishman's cruel fate.
It is written down in the roll of fame
And Kevin Barry is the brave lad's name.

When scarcely eighteen years of age
To the Republican Army he was engaged
For Ireland's sake he struck a blow
To free his country from a tyrant foe.

In the fight with the foe against the crown
Young Barry shot a British soldier down,
He appeared and was tried by military
And sentenced to die on the gallows tree.

In the condemned cell awaiting his fate
He was asked to confess before it was too late:
Come tell us where your comrades may be
A pardon will be granted and we'll set you free.

Young Barry gazed with a look of scorn:
An Irish traitor never yet was born!
Carry out your sentence was the proud reply,
For Ireland I fought and for Ireland I'll die!

Outside the jail his comrades fell
On their knees in prayer to the prison bell
For to pray for the soul of a martyr friend
Who would rather die than to foemen bend.

Out from the jail then walked a priest
And the tears rolled down his manly cheeks;
Have they hanged him, Father? his comrades cried.
— He's gone, but a braver lad never died.

Anonymous, quoted in Seán Cronin's *Kevin Barry* (1965)

BITTER THE DEATH
(*Air: 'Emir's Farewell'*)

Bitter the death they gave you soldier lad,
    You of the boyish heart and fair blue eyes;
Hanged like a dog! God mercy, it would be sad
    Did we not know you lived beyond the skies.
There nigh the Throne of Christ Who died to save,
    There shall you plead for the land that claimed your love;
Silent you sleep in your lowly prison grave,
    Many shall plead with you in the realms above.

Mary, beloved Queen of this land of Faith;
    Patrick, who taught the truths for which you died;
Colm, who went into exile worse than death —
    Every Saint of Eirinn stands by your side.
See through the Courts of Heaven what an array
    Muster to second your pleading, Kevin lad;
Heroes of old and martyrs of to-day —
    How do you wonder, boy, that our hearts are glad.

(Rev.) D.A. Casey, from *The Second Song Book*, Brian O'Higgins, Dublin.
This song also appears in *The Soldiers' Song Book*, Irish Book Bureau,
Dublin.

IN MEMORIAM — KEVIN BARRY

The strangled boy lies on a prison bier
Who asked for prayer but not for pity's tear;
Tortured! — reviled! Yet victor to the death.
His spirit lives, 'spite the poor stifled breath;
All that he endured is recorded where
Much is promised to even one brief prayer!

Profane their haste who decreed that this day
Should see his life in anguish ebb away!
Virgins and Martyrs! in your now happy throng
Whose voices raise in never-ending song!
Welcome the dead who walked the path you trod
The brave young heart stilled on your festal day!
Receive him now who first showed him the way —
The thorn strewn way that leads direct to God!

M. Barry O'Delany. From the *Evening Herald*, 1 November, 1920. Mary Barry O'Delany was the daughter of a doctor in charge of the mental home in Kilkenny. She was probably a governess in France when she first met Maud Gonne MacBride in Paris and herself became a revolutionary. Under various pen names or initials such as 'M.B.' or 'M.B.O'D.', she contributed to several Dublin newspapers, including the *United Irishman*. She had independent means and in 1925 she lived in 4 Upper Gardiner Street, Dublin, where she privately published *The Heart of Lorraine*, a long poem about Joan of Arc. She kept up her friendship with Maud Gonne, who offered her a room in Roebuck House. She died there during the harsh winter of 1947.

THE GRAVE OF THE REBEL

Mark the plain grave! 'tis hallowed by a name
That power hath idly sought to link with shame.
Reckless of shame — unaw'd by selfish fear,
Boldly I bless the glorious clay that's here,
Sure that the pure and good shall sympathise
With him who mourns where martyred virtue lies.

Is it the nickname bandied round the land,
The felon's death dealt by the ruffian's hand —
Is it the cry of 'treason' still renewed —
The bugbear of the brainless multitude?
Is it the doom decreed by tyrant laws,
That damns the patriot and defiles his cause?
Nay! slaves, to craft and cruelty allied,
Taking their own base feelings for a guide,
To the frail frame their torture may apply.
Or spread, when life hath passed, the blasting lie;
Still, still, the character this altereth not;
Be praise or blame — be weal or woe his lot.
Truth in her hour asserts her sacred claim,
And virtue stands in every change the same.

Let not the hangman's hand, the headman's blow.

Sink him whose dust is gathered now below;
Let not the horrors of unworthy strife
Mar all the moral beauty of his life:
Let pitying zeal his name from censure save,
And truth be heard in whisper, o'er his grave.
What were his crimes? Come let his torturers tell;
The first — he loved his native land too well;
The next — the darkest, blackest, let us see —
He longed — he hoped — he tried to make her free.

Thomas Furlong. From the *Evening Herald*, 1 November, 1920.

STANDING TO ATTENTION

'There was a most touching and dramatic incident in the prison cell on Sunday, when, between 4 and 5 o'clock, the prisoner's mother and sister saw him for the last time.

He was quite calm and composed. He put on his trench coat with belt, as the nearest semblance to a soldier's uniform in his possession, and when his relatives had bid him good-bye, he stood to attention and gave his mother a military salute.

As she passed, with her daughter, down the corridor and looked back, the last thing she saw was the prisoner standing to attention'.

He was 'standing to attention' when she left him there behind her,
In the shadow of the dreary prison cell.
There he stood so calm and gravely,
And he looked at her so bravely,
As a child looks at its mother when he knows that all is well;
And she thought in silent anguish of the baby boy she cherished,
Of the tiny little nothings mothers never can forget —
The words of childish wonder,
The turns of boyish anger,
For to her he's never grown up — he's but a baby yet.

He was 'standing to attention' when she left him there behind her,
With the dying streaks of sunlight crawling thro' the stifled air,
Shining — ah, so sad and lonely,
For the last — and last time only,
On the splendid boyish figure that was standing sentry there,
He is gone! and still she sees him, as she ever more will see him,
For he still 'stands at attention' where the tyrant dare not come,
And he'll smile again as bravely
And salute his mother gravely
As he takes her to his Master in the Everlasting Home.

KEVIN BARRY AND HIS TIME

Rita Davin-Power. From the *Evening Herald*, 1 November, 1920. Rita Davin-Power (1887-1967) for many years was the principal of Tranquilla National School, Rathmines. She was a close friend of Sinéad de Valera and, in the words of her grandson, David Davin-Power of RTE 'was an inveterate composer of occasional verses and sentimental doggerel'. He possesses the original manuscript of *Standing to Attention*. Her only son Maurice was the well-known playwright.

YOUTH GREETS DEATH

I thought that you would come to me
On leaden feet dragging wearily their trembling weight
And that your face would be ashen grey as a winter sky at close of day
With mantle of sombre lightless shade of the colour of clay
And your breath come hard and slow, Death.
But now I behold you!
All radiant bright
Sweeter than shines the kind moon's light
When she treads as a high-born maiden might
O'er mosaic floor, on cirrhus clouds of a Summer night,
Nay! Sweet as she is sweet you are
But brighter far.
The sun in mid-summer's blue-white sky
Shines not as glorious as you. And I
Go to you gladly, for you are not Death
　　that men tell of
No
You are Glory.

Francis J. Kelly, 16 St. Joseph's Ave., Drumcondra. From the *Evening Herald*, 1 November, 1920.

THE PASSING OF KEVIN

The night is near at hand; in grim Mountjoy
The morrow's victim chats with winning grace,
His Mother's wistful eyes are on her boy;
He bends to press fond kisses on her face

Then suddenly he holds her to his heart
With strange, fierce tenderness of boyish love:
The time is up, his dear ones must depart;
Again they'll meet in God's fair Home above.

Through tears they see him 'at attention' stand
(Traits of his babyhood come back to mind)

218

Kevin salutes them with his strong white hand;
The scene is ever in their hearts enshrined.

He decks the Altar for the morning Mass
Like some bright, splendid Martyr boy of old;
Now Heaven seems near, and as the moments pass
His prayers ascend with faith and love untold.

'The Lord of Hosts is coming as my Guest,
Two Masses I would have,' is his fond plea,
'That in my heart He may find pleasing rest,
And this, my last thanksgiving, best may be.'

* * *

I love to think the Angels vigil keep
And wake him up to greet All Hallows' feast,
At morn, refreshed by youth's untroubled sleen,
With Rosary in hand he greets the Priest

O Saviour Crucified, true Light of Light,
We offer up his sacrifice with Thine.
Adoring Angels see a wondrous sight,
The human Victim fed by the Divine

* * *

Without, 'neath murky skies, the kneeling crowds
Send up their *Aves* to the Virgin sweet;
A brilliant ray of sunlight parts the clouds
When Kevin's soul flies to the Mercy Seat.

Anon. This poem was found in manuscript form among the papers in
the possession of Triona Maher. These papers were owned by her mother,
Shel Barry, and her grandmother, Mrs. Mary Barry. The poem has not
been published before, nor is its author known. It clearly was written
soon after Kevin's execution.

TO KEVIN BARRY, HERO AND MARTYR

In this quiet haunt of peace we stood
   A year ago at eventide,
The sun beams in a glimmering flood
   The hushful fields and valleys died.

And as you gazed on the mountains blue
   I wondered why your face grew pale:
Why you whisper'd the sweet name Roisin Dhu
   To the stars and the silent vale.

KEVIN BARRY AND HIS TIME

To-night I know at last that in that hour
    You saw the cross upon the hilltop lone,
And laid renunciation's flower
    Beside your bleeding sireland's throne.

Maire ní Riain. From the *Freeman's Journal*, 3 November, 1920.

AFTER NEWS OF AN EXECUTION

Was it all folly — yonder, hour by hour,
To choose, not peace, but strife, and there to dare
The lion couched in his unnative lair
The world-feared lion, mighty to devour?
O that some folly as splendid were a flower
Not, on all shores but those, so wondrous rare!
Common as weed in Ireland everywhere
That splendid folly blooms, and hath the power
To make a mere slight boy not only face
Death with no tremblings, with no coward alarms,
But like a lover woo it to his arms,
Clasp with a joyous and a rapt embrace
Death's beauty, Death's dear sweetness, Death's pure grace,
And count all else as nought beside Death's charms.

Sir William Watson. From *Ireland Unfreed: Poems and Verses*, written
in the early months of 1921 (John Lane, 1921). Some of the poems in
this book had been published before, in the *Daily News*, *The Times* and
the *Daily Mail*. Watson published about two dozen books, mainly of
poetry, beginning in 1880. He wrote a series of sonnets called *The Purple
East* on 'England's Desertion of Armenia'. His collected work was edited
by J.A. Spender.

CAOIMHGHÍN DE BARRA

Go moch ar maidin 'sa' carchar dubh
Do crochadh de Barra gan taise gan truagh —
An t-óglach oilte a throid go tréan
'Uaghaidh foirneart foirtil na mbodach gclaon.

Lasmuich bhí mílte ag guidhe go fraoch
Go scaoilfí Caoimhghín as geimheala géar',
Ach b'feárr le Dia é bheith leis féin
Go h-árd 'na ríoghacht i measc na naomh.

Mar mhairtir d'éag sé — an buachaill bocht —
Gan eagl', réir ba dhual dhá shliocht,
Ar son a thírín chéabhta thláith
D'fhulaing pianta ghéara chrádha.

Ar Láimh Dheis Dé go raibh ár laoch
Le Pádraic Naomhtha is treibh na naomh,
Leis an bPiarsach, Aghas, Mac Suibhne séim —
Ag guidhe gan spás ar Chlainne Gaedheal.

Seán Mac Giolla Buidhe. This poem appeared in *The Gael* for 6 February, 1922.

KEVIN

We knelt at Mass with sobbing hearts
    Cold, in the dawn of day.
The dawn for us, for him the night,
    Who was so young and gay.

Then from the Altar spoke the priest,
    His voice rang thin with pain —
Bidding us pray, a boy must die
    At England's hands again.

The cruel English tortured him,
    He never shrank or cried;
Sublime his faith, the gallows tree
    He faced that day with pride.

Proudly he gave his life for her.
    To whom his heart was given;
His dying eyes knew Freedom near,
    Saw death the Gate of Heaven.

Bright flaming dawn of a young life,
    Simple and pure and brave;
One childlike prayerful sacrifice,
    His end — a felon's grave.

His end! No end to lives like his;
    With us he lives alway.
Bright through our night, a shining star,
    He lights for us the way.

And Christ, who died for love of us,
    Tortured and bruised and shamed,
Gives courage to such hero souls,
    Unbending and untamed.

Constance Markievicz, November 1922. From *Wolfe Tone Annual*, 1936.

THOUGHTS AT THE MUSEUM

One would not hope to meet
the concentrated poignancy of
'sixteen'
but it's there in a grey-green coat
of Casement's
a pierced soiled hat,
in the gilt of a solitary button
and the photograph of many a young head held high.
And the soul of it's wove
in the letters there
'We do not fear to die':
'I do not fear to die':
'I shall watch the fight from above' . . .
Then a little boy says
hushedly
'Kevin Barry — see',
and reads aloud the proclamation.
Words, words, words.
So many relics of those dead.
Did they fight for symbols unseen?
And will others again fight for words,
for a veiled Kathleen —
or united for an undivided free land
for soil that the people will care and share
for a land with a home and a life
for the like of the wan little fellow there?

Eileen Brennan. From *Goodbye, Twilight: Songs of the Struggle in Ireland*, compiled by Leslie Daiken, published by Lawrence and Wishart, London, 1936.

LINES ON THE MEMORY OF KEVIN BARRY
Written in Mountjoy Gaol, 1 November, 1922

Two years ago to-day since you are dead,
And men are moved to weep, the while they praise
The glory of your going. Pass the time.
They do not feel the splendour of your deed —
A boy of eighteen summers facing death
For love of country, freedom, honour, truth.
They cannot understand this grand ideal,
This godlike sacrifice of youth — they soon forget.
The terror ends, then tears are quickly dried,

222

A Land of Promise floats before their sight.
What if a youth has died for noble things —
Perish the thoughts that lead but to the skies.
The earth to creep upon for slaves is good,
The poisoned fruit is tempting to the touch;
It will not harm them forsooth, they eat,
They shrivel up — not you, but they, are dead.

Did you e'er think to see the King restored,
The 'old gang' reintrenched as masters here,

The Empire saved; the wound upon her side,
The running ulcer, healed; the Republic underfoot;
And in its stead a state partitioned, nominally free,
A prisoner caged within the Empire's net;
The Free State Irish, tightly bound by Oath
To 'British Brothers' sharing Britain's debt?
You did not die for this, you well were spared
The cruel disappointment and deceit of men,
Who rising, on your suffering and your death,
Seemed glad they had a country fit to sell.
No! when you faced the hangman, heartless, cold,
And felt the cruel cord around your neck,
You did not wince, but proudly meeting death —
A man encouraged, though a boy in years —
You proudly went, that all of us might live
As freely as the birds, bondslaves to none,
Friendly to all, sole masters of our fate.
                    Be at peace.
If others have forgotten, we have not,
And, while we hold the memory of your deed,
Your Day returning shall not bring us shame
Until in Freedom we may speak your name.

S. O'Conner. *Goodbye, Twilight: Songs of the Struggle in Ireland*,
compiled by Leslie Daiken, published by Lawrence and Wishart, London,
1936.

THE GALLOWS GRIM

The gallows grim a group of people kneeling,
The prison grey against a sullen sky,
To Our Lady of Sorrows they are pleading
As a youth of tender years walks out to die.

See, here he comes with footstep slow and steady,
With upward gaze and lips that move in prayer,
To sacrifice his young life he is ready,
God comfort his poor weeping mother there.

Those memories of the past seem left behind us;
What sorrow yet shall be our destiny;
The little wayside crosses still remind us
How brave men died to set their country free.

Such were my thoughts as shades of night surround me,
Living again the past as sad tears flow,
Saying a fervent prayer 'ere morning found me,
For the lad who died for Ireland long ago.

Pádraig Widger

I CANNOT FORGET

I cannot forget
The sight of that straight young neck
In the clasp of the hempen rope
That day in November

And I see always
The minions of the Saxon foe,
And hear the wailing of the women
That day in November.

I think of his youth
And the years that beckoned him on,
And he dying in the grey shadows
That day in November.

Where was our manhood,
O sons of the sorrowful Queen,
To let the brutal foeman triumph undisturbed
That day in November?

Have you sworn deeply
That the day of reckoning is near,
For the evil crew who murdered Kevin Barry
That day in November?

Terry Ward. Terry Ward from Derry was a well-known and much-loved journalist on the *Irish Press*, for which in 1934 he wrote an article on Kevin Barry. He spent from 1946 to his death in 1955 as London Editor of the *Irish Press*. His son Seán is now Editor of the *Evening Press*. This poem first appeared in *An Phoblacht* under the pen of 'F. Mac A.' on 4 November, 1933. It was published again under the title 'Kevin Barry' in *Goodbye, Twilight: Songs of the Struggle in Ireland*, compiled by Leslie Daiken, published by Lawrence and Wishart, London, 1936; and yet again in *1,000 Years of Irish Poetry* (New York, 1947).

KEVIN BARRY

They have taken him — a soldier of the people
　　A boy in years, a man in fearless faith —
They have tried him with a mockery of justice,
　　And the sentence of his enemy is — death.

They have offered him the freedom of the traitor,
　　They have hurt him with the cruelty of hell,
But their tortures and their bribes were unavailing,
　　No tale of black dishonour would he tell.

The hour has come to test a true man's courage,
　　No craven fear he feels, no pang of shame,
For God is with him walking to the scaffold,
　　And faithful Ireland kneels to bless his name.

The deed is done; the tyrant's blow has fallen;
　　The brave young soldier's hard-fought fight is o'er,
The bell is tolled; the prayers are like a chorus —
　　And Kevin Barry lives for evermore.

Brian O'Higgins. From a calendar for 1936.

KEVIN BARRY

An old dream,
Slow-drifting where the Spring-trees bowed;
Pensive as saddened youth, pink-lidded,
Calling good-bye in laughter . . . . Kevin Barry.

A new dream,
Quick-flowing to the end of youth,
By dawn-light, harvest fields, new graves,
Red with garnered blushes . . . Barry.

A dream,
Old, slow, immovable, fresh-eyed,
A lovely sadness where the young seas meet,
Calling 'come on!' in laughter . . . . Ireland.

225

KEVIN BARRY AND HIS TIME

Lochlinn MacGlynn. From the *Wolfe Tone Weekly*, 30 October, 1937.
Lochlinn MacGlynn, a native of the Donegal side of Clady, Co. Tyrone,
was a journalist and writer whose short stories were broadcast on BBC
Northern Ireland. Ned Gallen, Republican friend of Maud Gonne and
Seán MacBride, was a formative influence on Lochlinn, who worked on
the *East Coast Express* (published in Bray) and the *Dun Laoghaire Star*
in the 1930s. During the Emergency, he served in the Army and then
worked in the Irish News Agency. He was sent to Copenhagen by the
Government in 1969 when senior journalists were enlisted in a world-
wide publicity campaign on Northern Ireland. He died in 1987.

KEVIN THE ACOLYTE

Haste, Father, haste, November's dawn is breaking;
The acolyte is kneeling at his post.
'In the Name of the Father', the Sagart's voice is shaking:
But the acolyte, how firm his 'Holy Ghost'.
No worshippers in aisle or nave or chancel,
This edifice is but a felon's cell:
The 'felon' now as acolyte is serving —
The Elevation chimes sound like his knell.

Haste, Father, haste, November's dawn is breaking,
An Empire's thirst lost time can now allow;
Your acolyte — a martyr in the making —
Is kneeling to receive his Master now.
Bend down to where he kneels with face uplifted,
Pale composure in the candle's flickering glow,
That face which God from millions more has sifted,
Haste, Father, haste, it's almost time to go.

Haste, Father, haste, November's dawn has broken,
Lead forth your acolyte to meet his fate.
A prayer . . . Amen . . . the final words are spoken,
And a victim of a frenzied Empire's hate
Embraces death — that Empire's might defying
In prison dark, unsteeled by battle's hum.
A soldier brave your acolyte is dying:
Kneel, Father, kneel, a martyr's hour has come.

Martin O'Brien. From the *Wolfe Tone Weekly*, 30 October, 1937.

SONGS, BALLADS AND POEMS

KEVIN BARRY

Couriers from each hill and glen
Spread the dread news far and wide
A comrade dies at break of day
Speed it o'er the countryside
> Count your beads in every home
> In cloisters let the Mass be said
> A valiant soldier of the Gael
> Will soon be numbered with the dead.

Dip the nation's flag for him
Who dies to right our country's wrong
Trumpeters on every hill
Sound the last post at the dawn
> Army of the rank and file
> Marshal for the bugle calls
> Trumpeters in every glen
> Sound the last post as he falls.

Trumpeters of hill and glen
Sound the call for he has died
Light the candles for the dead
Let his wake be nationwide
> Heroic youth of tender years
> To ambuscade the foe's patrol
> Oh! Let his name be e'er revered
> Pen it on the martyr's scroll.

Desmond Crean. While Desmond Crean was a political prisoner in Northern Ireland in 1922, he wrote a collection of poems called *Songs of an Old I.R.A. Man*. The result was published in pamphlet form in 1939 with an introduction by Carl G. Hardebeck (1869-1945), the musician and collector of Irish traditional music. Hardebeck, who was blind, was born in London of German parents. He invented a type of Gaelic Braille later adopted by the National Institute for the Blind. Desmond Crean's 'Kevin Barry' is not included in the 1939 collection.

KEVIN'S CROSS FOR VALOUR

Not mid the dash and crash of arms
Where martial companies advance
In fight, equipped for war's alarms,
And well prepared for war's mischance;
Not with the aid of heavy gun,
Or barrage fire to clear the way,

Was Kevin's cross for valour won,
That hero-testing day,
But in a lowly prison cell,
All helpless — held by Britons brave.

Seabird (published in the *Irish Press*).

KEVIN BARRY
Hanged in Mountjoy Jail, 1 November, 1920

God bless you, lad with the hurley and you, with the ball,
Skipping along to the field on this clear, cold day;
With your quick, straight limbs answering the young blood's call;
But, listen a minute, and then be on your way.
There once was a boy — oh, not much older than you:
Merry and light on his feet and straight as a staff —
Honest and kind, to God and his country true:
With a ready smile, like you, and a ringing laugh.

It's a good while now — long before you were born —
Ask your fathers, they'll tell you the times were bad.
Poor Ireland's way was set with pitfall and thorn,
And her cry of anguish was heard by a little lad,
Sure, that's all Kevin Barry was; he was just eighteen —
Ah! You've heard the name before — so well you might.
Kevin Barry's name will live while the grass grows green:
He fought and lost and was captured in the fight.

And the snug, sleek men said wisely 'What a shame
'That a misled boy who knows neither right nor wrong
'Should have to die: But only himself's to blame,
'And hang he must, to show we are stern and strong;'
And die he did but, in dying the victory was won:
For any fool can fight, but only the good can die
With a smile and a prayer on their lips, like this widow's son,
Young Kevin Barry. May his soul be with God on high.

No: Don't look sad, boy: Come, it's pride you should feel!
Go and enjoy your game, but think as you play,
That one who was young and strong and true as steel
Gave everything, even life, that you might be happy to-day.

Leo Maguire. In *The Faithful and Few*, published by Walton's, Dublin, 1959. Leo Maguire was a poet and balladeer long associated with Walton's Musical Instrument Galleries in North Frederick Street and Lower Camden Street, Dublin. For many years he produced and presented a sponsored programme for Walton's on Radio Éireann. *The Faithful and the Few* contains songs and recitations by Maguire. It cost 1s. (5p.) in 1959, and was one of several dozen publications containing over 1,000 songs, ballads and poems about Ireland.

A BALLAD OF KEVIN BARRY

At the time when trees of Autumn
    Call to wind and mitching boy,
Soldiers noosed the lad and caught him
    To a tree before Mountjoy.
Calvary and Kilmashogue,
    Both must watch the mercenary
Hang the hero for a rogue
    Knot the rope for Kevin Barry.

Saints were dancing on All Hallows,
    Apples patched on the streets, and nuts,
Soldiers rigged a prison gallows
    With the devil's wiry guts.
Rainbows flowered the cobblestones
    For the roads were wet and tarry,
When they jerked the flesh and bones
    From the soul of Kevin Barry.

Samhain fog and beauty — muddy
    Pavements — hills as fair as God,
Autumn like a queen all bloody,
    Through the streets of Dublin trod,
Deirdre-like, a wounded rose,
    Here where all her sorrows tarry
Through the shadows that she knows
    Autumn keened for Kevin Barry.

Fish on stalls before the Castle
    Stank and silvered in the rain,
Oranges had lost Hy-Brasil
    For the kerb of Golden Lane.
Carts of hay and carts of straw
    Squandered gold they could not carry
On the day the English law
    Choked the fire from Kevin Barry.

Sailors dark with grape stained weather
    Spat out sunlight on the quays,
Old books stirred their skins of leather
    Dreamt of sunburnt centuries.
Down the river Manannan
    Drove his white-maned steeds to harry

KEVIN BARRY AND HIS TIME

Lissom ships, towards a Dawn
   Lit to honour Kevin Barry.

Round the miry Pillar streeling
   Boys as lithe as Plato's Greeks
Laughed and cursed at women wheeling
   Cabbages and ivory leeks.
Sparrows jeered the tolling clocks
   Pigeons flushed and cinerary
Smouldered on the salty rocks
   While they haltered Kevin Barry.

From the Three Rock to the scaffold
   Mountain winds came singing down,
Gay to see how youth had baffled
   Hell-fire in an Irish town,
Gay to see old Satan's thrust
   Fended with a scornful parry
'Dust returns unto star-dust'
   Sang the winds round Kevin Barry.

Red leaves scattered by the breezes
   Blew along grey streets and pale,
You'd have said the feet of Jesus
   Had walked round about the gaol.
And a shining host of youth
   Made the city wild and starry
With their eyes of love and truth
   Comrades these of Kevin Barry.

Sea-gulls, rapiers of light, winged
   Gleaming to the gallows place,
Death came soaring like the white-winged
   Victory of Samothrace.
Sea-gulls sprayed the gallows tree
   From the Liffey's estuary
Crying of the courteous sea
   To the young lad, Kevin Barry.

Dublin Hills and Dublin City
   He'd had eighteen years to tread
High disdain has youth for pity
   Swinging at the gallows' head.
Swinging fairly as a flower
   Hung on shrine or sanctuary
Youth is gay in Passion's hour
   Who will weep for Kevin Barry?

Michael Scot. (Privately circulated). Michael Scot was a pseudonym (she used two) of Kathleen Goodfellow, contributor of a translation of Verlaine to the *Dublin Magazine* and, as Michael Scot, author of a slim volume of stories entitled *Three Tales of the Times*, published by the Talbot Press, Dublin, 1921.

FOR KEVIN BARRY

Is he his own, the tired lover? This one
When in the sheath of clay he put
His body and his rifle, did he for ever
Leave over giving, or is in privacy
No ghost grieving? Is his glory all spun?

He could say of thieving he had none but ill luck,
My bandit brother: time and life piled somewhere
He knew not, where if he had made caution in taking
A way through the lilies he could have raided:
His own executioner, among the lilies he stood: and little he took.

The lilies leave where they lie, bent over glory:
His room is not yours, the sucking sod prized him
Now, in love with his hiding: so shrewdly he mantled
His treasure of skeleton, the good bones well warmed
In quick lime, the roof weaved over the incomparable soldier.

Living is not better or worse: they whistle in the evening

Make a little pile truck driving, look sometimes at the sky:
He gave not to you or I, we do not own him
Yet do you think the streets fail to see him
Or the tree roots in vain feel for his bones?

Pádraic O'Halpin. From the *National Student*, March, 1948. Pádraic O'Halpin (1923-1978) was an engineer, first with the ESB, then in his own company, Quadrant Engineers. He became managing director of Ceimicí Teoranta and later left to take up a research fellowship in Trinity College, Dublin. He was married to Mary Barry Moloney, who survived him. One of their children, Eunan O'Halpin, is the author of *The Decline of the Union.*

A CROWDED YEAR

Are you the nephew of?
Who tried to inveigle the elegant tart
In the train from Rathvilly
Who murdered a gallon of Smithwick's

KEVIN BARRY AND HIS TIME

Lying on a bed with a Belgian bird
In the Glendalough inn by the lake beyond Laragh

Are you the nephew of?
Robbed a Lewis gun laughing
From the King's Inns showing
Dinny Holmes his new toy

Are you the nephew of?
Was caught under a soldiers' lorry
Was tortured, tried and fed apples and grapes
Till he hang-dangled dead from an alien rope

Donal O'Donovan, 1989

Index

INDEX

Calvert, Eddie 190
Campbell, James 91, 134, 138-40
Campbell, Laurence 105
Campbell, Richard 35
Capuchin Order 106
Carey, James 23
Carl Rosa Company 54
Carney, Kathleen (Mrs. Vincent Gogarty) 94, 136
Carrigan, Jimmy 82, 144
Carroll, John Joe 45, 79, 82, 84-5, 142
Carson, Sir Edward 172, 177
Casement, Sir Roger 103, 152, 156, 159
Case, Mrs. 20
Catholic University School of Medicine (CUSM) 51, 56
Cavendish, Lord Frederick 23
Chamberlain, Austen 72
Chaplin, Charlie 148
Chartres, John 80
Chatham, Mrs. 83
Childers, Erskine 55, 80
Childers, Erskine Hamilton 55
Chomley, Capt. R.S. 99, 115
Christian Brothers 32
Churchill, Winston 72-3, 77
Clancy, Peadar 46, 59
Clan na Gael 46, 74
Clann na Poblachta 169
Clarke, Armour Sgt. Edward 114
Clarke, Basil 135
Clarke's dairy 83
Clarke, Mrs. Kathleen 155, 195
Clarke, Percival 109
Clarke, Thomas 46, 195
Cleary, M. 83, 116
Clements, Nathaniel 138
Clonliffe College 162
Clune, Archbishop 46
Clune, Conor 46
Coffey, Dr. Denis 56, 169, 176, 193, 194
Cohalan, Judge 74, 140
College of Science 53, 106
Collins, Michael 12, 43, 49, 59,
142, 144, 160-1, 186-8, 197
Collins, Paddy 95
Columbus, Father OFM Cap 106
Comerford, Mary 199
Commercial Hotel, Dungannon 39
Commerce Society 193
Communist International 73
Congregation of the Holy Ghost 33
Connolly, James 21, 38
Connolly, Lillie 21
Connolly, Nora 199
Connolly, Roddy 73
Connolly College 153, 158
Conroy, Jimmy 144
Cooke, Dr. W.A. 123
Cooney, Andy 56
Cope, A.W. 123, 124
Cork Jail 73
Cosgrave, Liam 168
Cosgrave, W.T. 168
Costello, Father John 194
Cotter, Maj. E.B. 104
Counihan, Tom SJ 35-6, 41, 153, 158-61, 167
County Medical Officer of Health 51
Coyle, Eithne 199
Coyle, Miss 53
Coyle, Patrick 26, 28
Coyne, Bridget and James 21
Crean, Father Charles 64
Crockett, Johnny 151, 152
Cromwell, Oliver 16
Cronin, Seán 143
Cross, Capt. 174
Crozier, General Frank Percy 76, 151, 155
Cullen, Matt 64-5, 67-70, 195
Cullen, Tom 91
Cumann na mBan 155, 156, 162, 167, 175, 197, 199
Cumann Gaedhlach, An 192
Curran, Con 34
Cusack, Michael 103

235